Men, Women and Relationships – A Post-Jungian Approach

This book offers Jungian perspectives on social constructions of gender difference and explores how these feed into adult ways of relating within male–female relationships. Phil Goss places this discussion within an archetypal context drawing on the fairy tale *Jack and the Beanstalk* to consider the deep tension in western culture between the transcendent masculine and the immanent feminine.

Offering both developmental and socio-cultural frameworks, areas of discussion include:

- the use of story and myth to understand gender
- Jungian and post-Jungian approaches: updating *anima/animus*
- working clinically with men and with women
- the developmental pathways of gender difference
- power relations between men and women in the home.

Men, Women and Relationships – A Post-Jungian Approach will be a valuable resource for all those with an interest in analytical psychology, including psychotherapists, psychoanalysts and counsellors, as well as those in the broader fields of social work and education who have an interest in gender difference and identity.

Phil Goss is a Jungian Analyst and a member of the Association of Jungian Analysts and the IAAP. He is also Senior Lecturer for Counselling and Psychotherapy at the University of Central Lancashire.

Men, Women and Relationships
– A Post-Jungian Approach

Gender Electrics and Magic Beans

Phil Goss

Routledge
Taylor & Francis Group

LONDON AND NEW YORK

First published 2011 by Routledge
27 Church Road, Hove, East Sussex BN3 2FA

Simultaneously published in the USA and Canada
by Routledge
270 Madison Avenue, New York, NY 10016

Routledge is an imprint of the Taylor & Francis Group, an Informa business

Typeset in Times by Garfield Morgan, Swansea, West Glamorgan
Printed and bound in Great Britain by TJ International Ltd, Padstow,
Cornwall
Paperback cover design by Andrew Ward

British Library Cataloguing in Publication Data
A catalogue record for this book is available from the British Library

Library of Congress Cataloging in Publication Data
Goss, Phil, 1961–
   Men, women and relationships, a post-Jungian approach : gender electrics
and magic beans / Phil Goss.
       p. cm.
   ISBN 978-0-415-47674-4 (hbk.) – ISBN 978-0-415-47675-1 (pbk.) 1. Sex
differences (Psychology) 2. Man-woman relationships–Psychological aspects.
3. Interpersonal relations–Psychological aspects. 4. Gender identity. 5. Men–
Identity. 6. Women–Identity. I. Title.
   BF692.2.G67 2010
   155.3–dc22
                                                                2010013882

ISBN: 978-0-415-47674-4 (hbk)
ISBN: 978-0-415-47675-1 (pbk)

Dedication

To Claire, Oliver, Jacob and Louisa, for letting me work on this book amidst the hubbub of family life, so helping me locate my writing in the crucible of home. I dedicate this book to them, as well as to my mother and sisters, and to the memory of my father.

They need to remember the gendered, so that they wake from their dreams to reality.

(Jung, 2009: p. 264)

Contents

Tables and figures

Tables

Figures

Acknowledgements

I would like to thank the following people for reading and commenting on chapter drafts: Jack Bierschenk, Ann Casement, Susan Rowland (and for her generous sharing of ideas), Joy Schaverien and Robert Segal. Thank you to Ann Moir for permission to use her 'brain-sex' material, and Andrew Samuels for access to recent material. I also wish to thank Blackwell publishers and the *Journal of Analytical Psychology* for permission to reproduce material in Chapter 4 from my 2006 paper entitled *Discontinuities in the Male Psyche: Waiting, Deadness and Disembodiment. Archetypal and Clinical Approaches*.

I am grateful for the support of colleagues at the University of Central Lancashire – Peter Cardew, Natalie Miles, Richard Davis, Janette Torrance, Bernard Gibbon and the School of Nursing, and in particular Dr Peter Gubi, for helping me find time to write – and to many students for ideas and encouragement. Thanks to Val Vora for help with the title, and to colleagues in the Association of Jungian Analysts (particularly Dale Mathers) and the International Association of Jungian Studies for the many lines of thought which have helped stimulate this project. I wish to thank the following members of the South Lakes Jungian reading group for providing a valuable forum for playing with ideas: Des Brady, Caroline Cattermole, Wendy De Paucer, Peter Entwhistle, Paul Jacques, Wendy Jones, Nancy Morris, Jean Ann Naylor, Abbie Parkes, John Pepper, James Van Lint, Sundar Walker, Michael Ward, Gavin Willshaw and Beth Wood. Thanks too to Liz Mouel. Also, to all pupils and staff I have worked with in special schools, especially Jack Taylor and Ickburgh Schools in London, for bringing questions about gender to life. Finally, I am most grateful to those people who have given their assent for me to draw on disguised clinical material.

Introduction

> The anima/animus relationship is always full of 'animosity', i.e. it is emotional, and hence collective . . . often the relationship runs its course heedless of its human performers, who afterwards do not know what happened to them.
>
> (Jung, 1959: para. 31)

What this book is about

In what ways might being a man be different to being a woman? Is it possible to describe those differences without getting caught in double binds about identity, power, role and relationship? How might these differences unconsciously define what happens in a male–female relationship, as Jung implies in the quote above? He asserted that every man carries a contra-sexual image of woman – *anima* – and every woman carries the image of man – *animus* (Jung, 1953/1966). How might this, and other readings of female–male relations, help us make fresh sense of gender in our post-modern, pluralistic world?

Furthermore, is it credible to make general assertions about how women and men may develop, and experience, life differently? If so, what can be usefully 'done' with these in our thinking about relationships and parent-ing? From an analytic viewpoint how might a framework for describing similarity and difference between men and women inform clinical thinking and practice?

This book aims to scrutinise the nature of relationships between the sexes in original ways which can usefully inform academic, clinical and political debates about gender, which remain central to what it means to be a person in westernised societies in the twenty-first century.

I draw on two frames of reference. First, from my training and practice as a Jungian analyst and my interest in the tensions and possibilities inherent in building on Jung's awkward but vivid portrayal of the male–female polarity manifested in both inner and outer relationships. In my practice I find myself reflecting on whether there are ways in which (generally) a woman experiences analysis differently to a man and how the gender of the analyst impacts on this.

My clinical experience has suggested to me that, as well as fundamental similarities, there *are* differences at work, though these are clinically, not to mention empirically, hard to pin down – and, possibly, politically contentious. I will draw on disguised clinical material, which I have permission from patients to use, to explore these differences constructively.

My second frame of reference is a personal one. I grew up as the only male in a female household, after my father died when I was five. Getting to know the world in the company of three sisters and my mother crystallised the reality of being the 'other', gender-wise. This almost certainly shaped my intuitive and intellectual interest in possible differences in how men and women, girls and boys, experience life – and may develop divergently from birth.

Further consonant experiences come from adult life. Before becoming an analyst I spent fourteen years teaching and managing in special schools in the UK for pupils with severe learning difficulties. These schools are staffed overwhelmingly by women; not just a predominantly female teaching staff, but also many unqualified or partly qualified women who live locally to the schools and perform vital (and low-paid) roles as teaching assistants for often very needy pupils. This is thrown into even starker relief by the trend for boys to predominantly populate such schools (Goss, 2003). So, settings which offered a challenging but fascinating experience of how gendered 'otherness' can operate.

These subjective experiences and observations of 'otherness' between being a man/boy or woman/girl inevitably colour my perspective. I propose this dimension of subjectivity, where used in a critically reflexive way, can be seen as an asset to what is hopefully a worthwhile struggle to scrutinise questions of 'sameness' and 'difference'. I am sure the reader will be able to hold my own subjective influences in mind as well as their own as I develop my argument – this, I suggest, is vital to fostering a healthy mode of enquiry, alongside the upholding of academic and clinical rigour.

My premise is that there are aspects of the masculine–feminine dynamic which remain hidden from view because they are fundamental to sustaining patterns of relating and are core to how we have lived for centuries, so need to be 'taken as read' in order to be preserved. I aim to validate the postmodern emphasis on gender as a flexible and pluralistic notion, while also highlighting these often obscured, embedded aspects of it. I will also offer a developmental framework for understanding these.

This applies particularly to unspoken conditions set up between parent and child – patterns which need to be made conscious in order to help society tackle, for example, the malaise around male identity and capacity for relationship, and the impact of 'absent fathering' on girls. This process could also act as a resource for the recalibration of roles within heterosexual relationships, particularly within the domestic sphere. I also suggest that aggression in the mother/wife role remains relatively unexplored but needs to be aired as an important factor.

Gay and transgendered experience and relationships

There is one aspect of this exploration I have wrestled with in planning and writing this book, which I need to be upfront about from the outset. This relates to the areas of gender, gay identity, transgendered identity and relationships. My dilemma has been whether I can do these areas justice within this book. They would need to be explored substantially alongside my central attempt to make sense of difference and sameness in heterosexual relationships, within a post-Jungian commentary on the developmental, archetypal and constructivist layers of this huge topic.

There is a significant body of writing on these areas. In the Jungian field, examples include McKenzie (2006), with her valuable observations about 'queering gender' (which I explore in Chapter 2); Kavaler-Adler (2006) on the homoerotic transference; and Young-Eisendrath's (1998) clarifications around the nature of desire in heterosexual and homosexual relationships. I will draw on such literature pertaining to sexuality and gender, including Butler's important ideas (1990).

This moves me towards describing the decision I eventually arrived at, after much deliberation and valuable discussion with colleagues. This is, on the one hand, to refer to ideas and clinical insights on gay and transgendered experiencing and relating where they inform discussion on the nature of 'gender' and the living out of whatever 'it' is. This in turn informs the discussion on, and model for, male and female development I offer in Chapter 3, as well as coming into the reflections on clinical matters and wider social links in Chapters 4, 5 and 6.

On the other hand, I have decided *not* to look explicitly at the nature of gay and transgender relationships closely, as I fear this would end up as rather tokenistic, simply because there is not the scope to do them justice within the scale and central frame of reference of the book. These ways of being human, and how they translate in terms of subjectivity, sexuality and relationship, deserve a separate book.

Story, archetype and relationship

I will take as my starting point the traditional English fairy tale *Jack and the Beanstalk*, with its powerful imagery of the son having to prove himself to the initially furious mother, and the access he gets to the world of giants as a resource for 'solving' this problem. I will also utilise clinical experience and theory, making connections between psychoanalytic theory (e.g. on narcissism), Jung's notions of *puer/puella* and *anima/animus*, and the presentations of what I argue may be gender-specific difficulties in the consulting room. These include a specifically male form of *anima* 'discontinuity' which can hamper maturation, and ways in which versions of *animus* can trap women in equally pervasive suffering. I will apply to this reworked versions of *anima* and *animus* as they may present in men and women.

The book aims to arrive at a new model for understanding the powerful forces at work between men and women, be this as lovers, parents, siblings or friends. The electricity in the interactive field that lies between and within genders, like the 'magic beans' which make things happen when everything seems stuck, is explored in all its main forms: familial love and relationship, erotic, sexual and aggressive energies – as they might be expressed differently between men and women – and how these may influence our ways of seeing each other.

The search for love and friendship lies at the heart of gender relations. But so does provocation. The electricity of provocation or stimulation is needed for anything to happen, for the circuits of either aggressive or erotic activity to light up and begin, alter, nourish, consolidate or end relationships. People act in relationships when prompted or provoked – by love, anger, attraction, fear or even boredom. People act in response to such provocation in order to get what they need, protect their territory or show how much they care.

This observation pertains to family, friends or lovers and I begin this book with it to provide a wholehearted challenge to the fuzzy but alluring illusion that relations between the genders are meant to be solely predicated on stability and care. For sure, these two elements are enormously important for the long-term preservation and consolidation of loving and familial relations, but they also have a capacity to deaden them without the complementary presence of relational 'electricity'. Without this, the forces of stability fall prey to a harmful form of *enantiodromia* – they turn into their opposite state: destructive and implosive.

I argue that our familiar ways of thinking about relationships between men and women, brothers and sisters, fathers and daughters, and mothers and sons seem to often conspire to filter out the power, the 'charge' of energy at work in the fields within which these relationships operate. Getting behind this pattern can bring a clearer understanding of the intrapsychic and interpersonal processes which may be at work between women and men. This also aims at serving as a basis for making wider social and political extrapolations about their meaning and how they may get us unhelpfully caught between the ideal and reality of *relationship*.

I suggest that there is a deep well of emotional investment at work in us, men and women alike, in preserving the templates of gender relations which have been around in the west for at least a couple of millennia. However, there is another complementary premise to be factored in, I believe: there is an equally strong wish for things to be different to how they are now – where broken relationships, broken families and layers of mutual incomprehension between women and men are wearily accepted as common features of the social and relational landscape. It is the blocks and incomprehensions we buy into both consciously and unconsciously, I suggest, which make it so difficult to properly see how faulty our perceptions of what it means to be either a man or a woman can be.

This discussion is placed within a framework which attempts to blend the many influences on our thinking about gender. These influences are of course multi-layered; from the messages we have each had from family, school, work and wider society of what it means to be a woman or a man, through to the academic and clinical readings of what we might mean by 'gender'. My loose initial definition of gender is: *our experience of being, and identity as, a man or a woman.*

This definition is deliberately open, and accounts for its subjective (*experience of being*) and socially ascribed (*identity as*) aspects. This allows the foggy mix of biological factors, archetypal dimensions and socially constructed aspects of gender scope to reveal forms or insights not often glimpsed – while recognising that this 'fog' is an important part of the 'gender' picture.

Describing gendered experience

One of my aims in writing this book is to see it as a project in which experiences of being a man or a woman can be more confidently described. This refers to what Samuels highlights as 'Not what being a woman is but what being a woman is *like*' (Samuels, 1989: 297) – which can likewise be applied to men, of course. I will also try to describe what aspects of being human 'free float' between men and women and might be described as archetypally *human* rather than specific to 'being a woman or a man'.

Culturally the context for this discussion is mainly a westernised one, though with increased globalisation it is important to factor in the influence of, and blending with, the multiplicity of 'other' ways of thinking about women, men and how they relate, which we derive from our encounters with different cultures – face to face or through media and online sources.

This book analyses how unconscious processes relating to gender intimately inform the human condition and how, in turn, these processes may feed into 'gendered experiencing'. The burgeoning literature in depth psychology will be an obvious reference point, but so will research arising from the field of neuroscience, and ideas from psychology, sociology, anthropology and feminist and cultural studies.

In Chapter 2 I will draw on these to look at 'gender as problematic', before proposing a working model for describing the dynamics of gendered experiencing. Then, in Chapter 3 I will attempt to construct a viable model for describing the development of boys and of girls, identifying where these may diverge, informed by an application of a reworked formulation of Jung's *anima–animus* archetypal dyad.

Writing as a man, about women

I am aware of a certain trepidation about writing as a man about what a woman, as 'gendered other', might experience. This is not unlike the anxiety I noticed in myself when I wrote previously on *animus* (Goss, 2008). Fears and fantasies about being labelled as stereotyping or even misogynistic are around as I type these words. Nevertheless, this very situation is a source of fascination for me. What is it about writing as a *man* on what it might mean to be a *woman* that is so fraught?

There is a feeling of breaking a taboo in doing this. I can own some of this as a familiar feeling for me from childhood, when I experienced the territory which seemed to 'belong' to my sisters as a foreign land which I had no permission to explore, let alone speculate about the meaning of. But it also seems to be 'out there' in the culture, where the onus on men and male writers (e.g. Clare, 2001) seems to have been to acknowledge the depth of the 'crisis' in male identity, rather than turning their focus onto what (if anything) women may be contributing to this situation.

There has not been quite the same inhibition for women writing about what it means to be a man (e.g. Gilligan, 1993). This may well relate to the upsurge in collective female consciousness about women's gendered predicament, starting with the seeds sown in the industrialised west over the last couple of hundred years, and culminating in the strong feminist voices of more recent years.

Women, one could say, have been more conscious about gender than men, as they have been more oppressed by the rigid formulations dominating patriarchal structures of society and of personal relations, though the lack of 'gender consciousness' on men's behalf seems to have shifted when one notices the burgeoning reflective literature on being a man and being a father (e.g. Tacey, 1997; Lewis, 2009).

I want to suggest too the possibility of there being, in western culture, an unspoken prohibition (at least in liberal, educated circles) on men being critical of the 'positions' taken by women on women and men, however much reflexivity and respect they may bring to this. Fear of being perceived as unreconstructed in their approach to gender, or as wanting to hold onto patriarchal formulations to protect their interests, can be factors. Then there may be a deep-rooted perception that men have no right to be critical on gender relations, as it is women who have been oppressed for so long, not to mention the possible anxiety about being perceived as conveying ignorance, antipathy or even misogyny towards women (mother?) – all this and more may have contributed to this situation.

What interests me is the possibility that men in a collective sense may not have worked out how to be constructively critical about what women are, do and represent. Something unconscious may be at work, along with the conscious anxieties about saying something out of turn. This is something I will return to later. I highlight this backdrop not least to enable me to explore related themes without self-consciously activating my own version of a collective *negative animus* (or '*thanimus*' as I call it) complex.

It can feel as if the legacy of patriarchy, which may come to feel like the fear of being accused as a man of sexism, weighs too heavily for men to be 'allowed' to critique women. On the other hand (applying a term in a transgendered way to myself) I can tell myself to stop being a 'drama queen' and engage with the potential risks and rewards involved, which is what I intend to do!

The role of personal myth

As Rowland (2002) notes, Jung's ideas on gender operate at two levels – 'grand theory and personal myth' (Rowland, 2002: 39). Jung strove to locate key concepts of his, such as *anima* (the image of woman in a man) and *animus* (the image of man in a woman) within the comprehensive and complex theory paradigm he painstakingly constructed over a lifetime. These figures in the psyche will be explored at length in relation to the various arguments presented in this book. It is important, however, to highlight the way they operated for Jung not just theoretically, but as living entities in the psyche and as gatekeepers to the archetypal influences we might need in order to become 'who we truly are', as Jung defined individuation (1921/1971).

In this sense, he saw his most valuable resource as being within himself – i.e. what his unconscious threw up and the degree to which he could notice, wrestle with and utilise what emerged from his conscious encounters with this material. His emphasis on personal myth is pivotal in this regard, as it provides a corrective seasoning to what can come over as a dish he serves up on how women 'are', which is impossible to swallow now we have moved definitively away from many of Jung's essentialist assertions about, for example, the way *negative animus* may leave women prone to 'irrationality'.

The problematic implications of Jung's thinking in this area will be explored in the light of dilemmas thrown up by the presence of essentialist traditions coming into contact with the inevitably deconstructing tendencies of psychological inquiry. However, the notion of 'personal myth' as being something about the way we each make sense of our own existence via experiences, stories and insights into ourselves provides a vital link between ideas about gender and our subjective experience of it. This is particularly valuable as it has both an 'exterior' quality in that there is a search for definition and clarification in the social and political spheres, as well as an 'interior' quality when considering how 'gender' impacts on each of us. I will therefore apply this notion of 'personal myth' to my own explorations.

Encountering sameness and difference in the consulting room

In drawing on my clinical experience I will offer thoughts on relational experiencing between and within gender dyads – i.e. *man*–woman as well as *man*–man – which are familiar to me. The latter will form a focus to Chapter 4's exploration of what I term male '*thanima* discontinuity'.

To complement this, in Chapter 5 I will draw on the work of women analysts on *woman*–man and *woman*–woman clinical experiences, explored in the context of a discussion on the value or otherwise of *animus* as a relevant concept in women's experiencing. Joy Schaverien's (2006) edited collection of papers, for example, will be one point of reference for this. She describes how, in the consulting room, 'the confusing web of gender roles and sexual identities that the transference weaves may transfix and enthral' (Schaverien, 2006: 7).

This capacity of the transference to 'transfix and enthral' seems to reflect an archetypal transfixing presence which likewise can grip our relationships, whether this be falling in or out of love, or our day-to-day need to be needed (or not). In this respect I want to try to keep the air flowing through the space between day-to-day experiencing and what happens in the consulting room. This space, it seems to me, can easily become an *air lock* in depth psychological practice; there is the 'moment-by-moment experiencing' – to borrow a phrase from Carl Rogers (1961) – of the daily life of the patient 'out there', and then they pass through the 'air lock' between that world and the analytic space where, in my experience, the 'moment-by-moment' experiencing is qualitatively different. This has both strengths and pitfalls, and I see this dichotomy as a kind of parallel of the movement between the world 'down here' and the one 'up there' which Jack moves between, up and down the beanstalk.

Suffice it to say at this point that the space between, or even *split* between, a 'big' gendered backdrop to relationships and our daily being in the world (Heidegger, 1962) is a theme in this book's discussion of clinical considerations. In fact, I take a deliberate stance in writing this book to amplify the gendered aspects of life and relationships. I recognise it is possible and maybe more current to 'let go' of possible differences between men and women and let them float to the back of our minds while we all get on with the challenging enough task of being human together. Maybe we do this so as not to get fixated on differences when there is no need to, especially where it can feed tensions, or even ill-treatment.

However, for the purposes of exploring the questions raised in this book, I invite the reader to join me in putting a pair of 'gender spectacles' on and making the most of what really scrutinising this challenging but fascinating area can throw up for us. Feel free to take the specs off when you finish reading . . .

Being postmodern

Another dimension of the multifaceted nature of 'gender' relates to how the twenty-first-century world can be adequately characterised to reflect the question around sameness and difference which this book aims to explore. The term 'postmodern' can become a catch-all phrase to describe responses and reactions to, or discontinuities from, the rationalist emphasis on enlightenment values and 'modern' ways of thinking. However, it is valuable in situating and opening up discussion on gender.

As Hauke (2000) argues, the powerful influence of feminist ideas, combined with the opening up of fluid perspectives on reality and 'truths' which postmodernism affords, provide new ways of perceiving gendered experiencing. The essentialist positions on gender which Jung gets roundly criticised for are highly problematic in this context. And yet one of the possible difficulties set up by reacting to the old ways of thinking – in the way an adolescent might react to parental attitudes – is that something of value might be overlooked.

As Hauke (2000: 114) acknowledges, the 'grand narratives' of modernist thinking have not disappeared; instead they sit there in the background (or like giants in the sky in the *Beanstalk* story) and influence our attempts at being postmodern. This is not unlike the influence of archetypes, which although pluralist and variable in the different ways they manifest in each of us, are just *there* as psychic realities which can constellate in complexes and then inhabit our bodies, minds and souls. They become 'real' psychically at times, like the other reality discovered by Jack when he reached the top of the beanstalk.

In that respect I see modernist, essentialist, ideas on gender – which after all are still hugely influential across the western world, especially among the older generations – as still alive, *still here*, and functioning like the 'up there' to the 'down here' of the complicated, fluid experiencing of gender we may be familiar with.

Hauke also highlights the possibility that the space between the 'up' and the 'down' may have thinned considerably, and there is 'depthlessness . . . [to] . . . the postmodern condition' (Hauke, 2000: 67). So, our sense of self as a man or a woman may have changed, filtered through a gathering ambiguity about what our gender identity might 'mean'. Our feeling, thinking, sensing and intuiting about ourselves, others and the grand narratives we have inherited will be influenced by this 'thinning out' of cultural, political and religious 'truths'.

This 'thinning out' may have had a counterproductive impact on our collective attitudes towards gender roles. While we have come to assume 'all has changed', in fact there are ways in which fixed role assumptions in the domestic/familial sphere are overlooked. Perhaps controversially, I argue a real problematic exists in attitudes towards the place of men in the home, which is reflected in an ongoing 'lack of fit' for boys and men in western societies. The suggestion that this may need some psychological work in relation to the traditional 'territory' of women will be a recurring theme, particularly in Chapter 8.

This will follow two discussions which link developmental (psychosexual and neurological), socio-cultural and clinical observations made in earlier chapters with emerging implications for understanding distinctions between female and male experiencing, and heterosexual relationships. The first of these, in Chapter 6, looks at how young men and women experience themselves in adolescence and how this might inform their gender identity. The second, in Chapter 7, attempts to identify the main characteristics of female and male 'territories' and what may be shared between them.

Gender and development

Finally, this book will attempt to frame what it means to be born, to grow and to develop as a man or a woman through a post-Jungian frame of reference. Starting from ways in which our experiencing of parents – outwardly or internally (or in *Beanstalk* language, as '*humans*' or '*giants*') – impact on us I will develop a framework which might offer fresh perspectives on gender difference and sameness.

This is attempted against a backdrop of some thinking which tends to stress gender as a purely social construct, implying most differences in experiencing and development between men and women are a consequence of this. In Chapter 2, I will explore these ideas alongside more essentialist ones, including Jung's, exploring whether between biological 'sex' and socially constructed 'gender' there may be other (archetypal?) layers of experiencing and development which are, in a general way, more peculiar to men than women, and vice versa.

As well as utilising *anima* and *animus* as tools in this task (Chapter 3) I will draw on thinking from feminist, attachment and psychoanalytic theorising about early development (e.g. Benjamin, 1988), to consider whether fundamental distinctions can be made between the early experience of boys and girls. There will also be a consideration of Jacques Lacan's important ideas for understanding how 'father' can be seen as symbolically crucial for moving through the oedipal phase and into the 'Symbolic Order' of ordinary life (Lemaire, 1977), and how this may inform comparisons between a girl's and a boy's passage through this phase.

The work of Kristeva will also be crucial here, especially her notion of the 'semiotic' as the unstructured 'otherness' which falls outside efforts to structure reality in a patriarchal, 'ordered' way (Smith, 1998) and her valuable insights into how male and female passages through early life may evoke key experiential developmental differences. This will form the basis of a model for gendered development from infancy through to early adulthood.

Home and road

When I draw together the different strands of these discussions (Chapter 8) I will suggest where our conventional and 'post-conventional' notions about heterosexual relationships and 'family' need to be further challenged, especially in the ways the 'territories' of men and women come up against each other in shared home, work and social arenas.

The implications considered will include how the locational symbolism of 'home' can shift territorial power between genders, and I will suggest a symbol of 'road' to juxtapose predominant symbolic identifications between women and men. This will lead into a consideration on how mothers and fathers bring their 'territories' to families and how these could be better calibrated in the formative early years of a child's life. I will also tie together discursive strands which run throughout the book on the relationship between male–female and feminine–masculine.

The book as a whole attempts to make some sense of what it is to be a man or a woman in relation to the gendered *other*. My attitude towards this is as open as I can make it as a male analyst, father and partner. The right place to start feels to be the story of *Jack and the Beanstalk* – one I have been drawn to as a personal mirror of my own development as well as a template for exploring the relationship between the personal and the archetypal, and gender relations.

So, are you sitting comfortably?

Chapter 1

Jack and the Beanstalk: **Magic beans and angry mothers**

'Beans?' said Jack, 'What's so lucky about them?'
'Well, my boy, these are magic beans. If you plant these in your garden they will grow right up to the sky'

Within the folds of the English countryside, contained in turn within the folds of myth and fairy tale, Jack's story is also a story about the liminal space between grounded reality and the archetypal dimension, between chronological time and a pleromatic, acausal space 'outside time', or between the explicit and implicit orders (Bohm, 1981). Like many influential fairy tales it has a revelatory quality, suggesting ways to compensate for aspects of ordinary life which have fallen out of balance (Zipes, 1991).

It also contains the seeds of powerful configurations between the genders. Archetypal feminine and masculine forces (which are *not* synonymous with female and male, a complex relationship of meanings I will explore in later chapters) influence patterns of being and relating, and in the story these patterns are exposed to the possibility of change. This change can come from anywhere – death and loss, challenges made to authority figures, or the appearance of unexpected figures, natural phenomena and so on.

It is a story which has particular resonance to our developing understanding of what we might mean by 'gender', because it exposes the roots of archetypal patterns of male–female ways of relating and asks us to try and tease out what is open to change and what is perhaps immutable. The beanstalk which Jack climbs provides a powerful metaphor – sometimes we have to reach up and beyond measurable reality to get hold of what is actually there beneath our feet (if we could but see it by simply looking down).

The story

In order to establish the terms of this 'looking beyond', I will briefly elucidate the context in which the story seems to have emerged as well as different possible readings of it from depth psychology. This is done in order to make available the full worth of what it may be trying to say. But first, the story:

'Once upon a time there was a widow who lived with her son, Jack. They were so poor they had had to sell the furniture from their little house so they did not starve. Their cow, Milky White, was all they had left and now she had stopped giving milk. Jack's mother told Jack to stop being lazy and to sell Milky White at the market.

As Jack walked with the cow to market he met an old man.

'Where are you off to?' asked the old man.

'To market to sell the cow.'

'It's your lucky day,' the old man said. With that, he pulled out five beans from his pocket.

'Beans?' said Jack. 'What's so lucky about them?'

'Well, my boy, these are magic beans. If you plant these in your garden they will grow right up to the sky. If you let me have the cow the magic beans are yours.'

The deal was done and Jack took the beans home. But his mother was very angry that Milky White had been sold for a handful of beans. She sent Jack to bed and threw the beans out of the window. When Jack awoke the next morning, the room was in shadow. He looked out of the window and saw an enormous beanstalk which stretched right up to the sky!

Jack decided to climb the beanstalk and with that he stepped out of the window onto the beanstalk and began to climb upwards. He climbed through the clouds until he reached the top. There he saw a road which went straight towards a big castle in the distance.

Suddenly a beautiful fairy appeared in front of him. 'Hello Jack,' she said. 'You are here because in that castle there lives a terrible giant who killed your father when you were a baby and took all that belongs to you and your family. Your mother could never tell you this as she had to swear not to so as to save you from the same fate.'

The fairy disappeared and Jack understood the task before him. He walked towards the castle and saw a figure at the door – the giant's wife.

'Good morning', Jack said, 'I am very hungry, could I have some breakfast?'

The giant's wife was kind-hearted and said she would, but warned him her husband would be back soon and would eat him if he found him. While he was eating breakfast there was a terrific bang – the giant was knocking on the door. The giant's wife told him to hide and put him into an empty kettle.

When the giant's wife opened the door her husband shouted:

'Fee, fi, fo, fum,
I smell the blood of an Englishman:
Be he alive, or be he dead,
I'll grind his bones to make my bread!
I smell boy! Where is he?'

His wife distracted him by giving him his breakfast. When he was done he told his wife he wanted to count his money. She brought him two big bags of gold and he started to count it. But he was tired and fell asleep. Jack leapt out of the kettle, grabbed the two bags and ran out of the castle, along the road and down the beanstalk. His mother was very pleased as they now had more than enough money.

Some time later Jack decided he would like to go back up the beanstalk. So while his mother was out, he climbed up to the top of the beanstalk again.

Jack walked to the castle and asked the giant's wife again: 'Can I have some breakfast please?' She told him to run off at first but then felt sorry for him and sat him down with a hearty breakfast. Once again the giant returned as Jack ate, so the giant's wife pushed Jack into the oven. The giant roared:

'Fee, fi, fo, fum,
I smell the blood of an Englishman:
Be he alive, or be he dead,
I'll grind his bones to make my bread!'

His wife persuaded him he was wrong, and after his breakfast he told her to bring him his little brown hen. The giant shouted 'Lay!' The hen laid a golden egg not once but three times! Once again he went to sleep. Jack climbed out of the oven and crept up to the table before grabbing the hen and racing out of the kitchen. The hen started squawking but before the giant awoke Jack was away down the road and then the beanstalk. With all the golden eggs the hen kept on laying Jack and his mother had much more wealth than they could spend, but Jack thought it worth climbing the beanstalk one last time.

He knew the giant's wife would not welcome him this time so he crept into the castle through a back window and hid behind the curtain. Peeking around it he could see the giant sat at the table. He watched him lift his big, ugly head and then roar once more:

'Fee, fi, fo, fum.
I smell the blood of an Englishman:
Be he alive, or be he dead,
I'll grind his bones to make my bread!'

The giant got up and looked in the kettle, and the oven, before sitting down again. He called for his wife to bring him his golden harp. When he told it to sing it sang the most beautiful lullaby Jack had ever heard. The giant fell asleep and so Jack seized the opportunity to creep out from behind the curtain, grab the harp and leap back out of the window with it. But the harp screamed out 'Master!' over and over. The giant woke to see Jack through the window, running away.

He grabbed his club, and chased Jack down the road. He grew closer by the moment, but Jack was on the beanstalk in a flash and climbing down it, nearly falling off he was going so fast. The giant was less nimble than Jack and made his way slowly down, roaring as he took each wobbly step. Jack shouted to his mother to bring out his axe. When he reached the bottom he took the axe from her and chopped away hard at the base of the beanstalk. It came down with an almighty crash and the giant fell to his end, making the earth shudder for miles around. The sky kingdom was never seen again, but Jack and his mother lived happily ever after, Jack having recovered his father's riches at last.

My contextualisation of the story has a historical flavour (in terms of origins of folk tales and so on) but will mainly draw on theoretical and clinical concepts from analytical psychology and psychoanalysis to elucidate potential links to characters and themes. I also want to acknowledge the temptation to read 'gender' into every nook and cranny of the story. Jack's laziness and irresponsibility at the beginning, for example, could be read as a hallmark of youth, irrespective of gender. However, there is still value in contextualising this within the mother–son dyad and the way it fuels the explosion of *anima* (in Jack) and *animus* (in his mother).

Jack the lad

Westwood and Simpson (2005: 97) note that in folk tales from England: 'Jack is by far the commonest man's name.' As a version of the name 'John', Jack seems to have been a nickname which implies something about the 'common person', or at least the 'common man', who is also able to act heroically. This strongly implies the presence of the *trickster* archetype (Jung, 1954/1968) which can appear foolish but be the instigator of significant change. This applies in the *Beanstalk* story when Jack naively trades the cow for some 'magic' beans and his mother is enraged at this. This is a pivotal aspect of the story, as it opens the door to transformation for Jack and his mother.

This combination of *hero* and *trickster* is a hallmark of the appearance of characters named Jack in cousins of the *Beanstalk* story. *Jack of Batsaddle*, for example, 'killed the last wolf' (and/or wild boar) in England (Murray, 1901). and *Jack O'Kent* traded his soul with the devil for magic powers and then outwitted the latter to keep his soul when he died (Leather, 1912). In *Jack the Butter Milk* (Swift, 1954) Jack gets captured by a witch because, unlike in *Beanstalk*, he refuses to enter a transaction with a stranger – though, as in *Beanstalk* he does outwit and escape the figure which threatens his very survival three times. One of the closest 'cousins' to the story is *Jack the Giant Killer*, differing versions of which portray Jack as disposing of between one (Halliwell, 1849) and seven giants, thereby becoming the saviour of the local community – or the 'Kingdom of Cornwall', as portrayed in the film version (Juran, 1962). There are even stories where Jack *is* the giant – e.g. in *Giant's Hedge* (Bett, 1950) – a good illustration of the projective nature of giants.

Jack as the boy *hero* or *trickster* needs further explication in terms of what we might understand from classical theory about the underlying influences and tasks of a boy in his strivings to become a man. In *Jack and the Beanstalk* these strivings inevitably take the form of a *quest*, a kind of all-or-nothing struggle with a giant where a mistake would be fatal – a fall to the ground way below, or into the ravenous jaws of the bone-crushing giant. The ubiquity of Jack as a carrier of this kind of quest is well illustrated by the American *Jack Tales* (Chase, 1971), based on an oral tradition from the Appalachian mountains, passed down from the earliest settlers from Europe, of tale-telling about Jack's exploits: 'Are these giants very big 'uns?' asked Jack' (ibid.: 3).

In Freud's view, all wishes and actions have some otherwise unexpressed desire at their root (Freud, 1920/1991). For Jack, the oedipal drama has taken the form of the death of his father. Classically, this must leave the boy with both unresolved guilt about father being gone ('I must have killed him'), engendering a kind of fear of his own authority, and feelings of *lack* in not being able to take father's place in relation to his mother's practical, relational and erotic needs.

As Adam Phillips (2007: 4) observes: '[A] little boy doesn't have the wherewithal to marry his mother; for Jack this translates as his being unable to earn a living and "support" her'. This is a dilemma the boy can only try to resolve through acts of extraordinary heroism, confronting the great, angry 'father' in the sky, via a magical and disproportionate blossoming of his phallic power in the shape of the beanstalk.

In turn, Jack needs a little help to access these super-heroic powers, and this is where Jung's notion of the archetypes comes into play. Archetypes are a blend of instinct and image (Samuels *et al.*, 1986: 26–8) which haunt every human psyche awaiting constellation, and through them human dilemmas and shortcomings can be usefully reworked. The immanent influence of archetypes comes about via a complex. As Young-Eisendrath elegantly describes them, they are:

> Laden with non-verbal meanings and feelings. When a complex is activated it grips our perceptual awareness.
>
> Each complex has both a subject and an object pole. For instance, a particularly idealized father complex might include both a charming, seductive father and a needy child . . . In adult life either pole can be projected and the other identified with.
>
> (Young-Eisendrath, 2009: 97)

In relation to the story, Jack finds himself trying to identify with an idealised, heroic son in order to satisfy the projected needy mother (representing his neediness). The tragedy which has left Jack as surrogate (and 'less than') man-of-the-house has stirred up archetypal waters. The unconscious (as ever in Jungian thinking) tries to point up ways to *compensate* for the lack Jack undoubtedly feels and his inability to satisfy his need to please mother. He is in the grip of a *mother complex*: a blend of the archetype of the (great) mother, who needs to be pleased and nourished by the 'goodness of the son', and the realities of the situation that the bereaved and impoverished pair find themselves in.

The presence of the benign giant-wife in the sky, the archetypal bountiful and loving great mother, who takes care of him (rather than the other way around), is a form of compensation which gives Jack a fighting chance of resolving his predicament. However, Jack is also in the grip of a *father complex*. The death of his real father activates the presence of the archetypal violent and abusive father, in the form of the giant. His father's death unleashed all the uncontained aggressive energies which can manifest dangerously through male forms of violence and abuse. This giant, intra-psychically, becomes the inner figure of uncontained power, perhaps because the boy cannot bear his out-of-control fury, which has 'destroyed' his own father – a notion which links to Klein's ideas of how we 'destroy' our inner (parental) objects in early phantasies (Klein, 1952: 63–4).

In this sense, Jack's 'cutting down to size' of this monstrous figure brings him closer to reality, or the 'depressive position' (ibid.: 71–80), where splitting between good and bad father, as well as good and bad mother, is brought into a more reparative frame of authentic relating to the real parent(s).

The archetypal 'good father' is also represented in the shape of the old man on the road. He is benevolent, as well as the chthonic unlocker of Jack's potency, supplying the magic beans which then turn into the bean-stalk. He therefore offers a compensation for the bad, mad, father/giant figure.

It is therefore the presence of the archetypal dimension 'up in the sky' which is, in Jungian terms, the compensatory domain needed to enable ego–self balance or 'homeostasis' to return to the narrative, and to the psyche. It is to the psychic 'giants' who inhabit this domain that I now turn.

There might be giants . . .

The presence of giants in the human psyche has a deep and ubiquitous quality – terror mixed with excited awe characterises our fascination with them. I remember being captivated as a boy by them when they cropped up in fairy tales, as well as ancient and new myths, from *Cyclops* (Graves, 1955/1992: 40) through to *Godzilla* (Honda and Koyama, 1954). It is a fascination I can get in touch with now as I sit in front of my computer typing these words – something about giants as liberated human spirit, grown to its full size, perhaps mingled with anxiety about what being so *big* might feel like (uncontained? dangerous?).

Mathew Everitt (2007), who is over seven feet tall, describes himself as a 'giant' and explains what daily nourishment his huge frame requires:

> For as long as I can remember, a typical day has begun with a mixing bowl of cereal and a pint of milk, followed by two rounds of toast. By mid morning, I need three packets of crisps or a couple of pasties to keep me going until my three-course lunch. Next up is the afternoon filler of four crumpets and a tin of beans, before a tea of two-inch-thick pork chops, eight or nine potatoes, carrots and peas. I'll cap the day off with another mixing bowl of cereal, though if I'm doing a lot of exercise, I'll swap that for a mixing bowl of pasta.

When I first read this I half expected him to mention drinking 'the blood of an Englishman' with his breakfast. This capacity to routinely consume, on a daily basis, what most of us might manage across two or three days activates a kind of awe and fascination which is reminiscent of our childlike responses to stories about giants. Klein, Winnicott and Jung have some valuable things to say about our fixation on, and internalising of, the presence of 'that-which-is-bigger-than-us'. Klein's ideas about introjection – or the 'taking in' of versions of mother (and before that *parts* of her) or father into our infantile inner world – is framed as a normal feature of the way we negotiate the beginning of life, and helps to explain the template for the archetypal presence of giants.

We put into these internalised figures, according to Klein, our rage at the *badness* (or failings) of the parent as well as our idealisation of their *goodness*. Then we feel unbearable guilt when we sense we have psychically destroyed them in our monstrous (giant?) rage and wish to restore them or make 'reparation' (Klein and Riviere, 1937/1964).

Winnicott's (1960) portrayal of how the infant experiences the start of life and the profound levels of fear and confusion associated with being thrust into the world with no bearings also reflects how the child seems bound to experience themselves to be in a world of 'giants'. There is, according to Winnicott (ibid.: 46–7), the constant threat of 'primitive agonies' – experiences which terrify and undermine, such as feelings of being abandoned (however briefly) or the fear of falling 'forever' (with no beanstalk to provide a 'ladder' downwards to the safety of solid ground).

In response to such terrors the geography of our inner worlds gets chiselled out as the dust settles from the 'big bang' of our entry into the world – between the huge, scary, though at times surprisingly benevolent world of giants (parents) and the territory the infant occupies as they try to hold themselves together in the face of the giant 'land' they are in.

Finally, Jung brings this relationship between little '*I*' and giant *you or them* into relief via his emphasis on the presence of 'otherness' in the individual psyche, and through his ideas about complexes. The presence of *shadow* in the psyche – i.e. 'the thing a person has no wish to be' (Jung 1954/1966: para. 470) alerts us to how we project outwards what we fear in ourselves. Giants become representative of this in terms of giving form to feelings and ideas about ourselves that are 'too big' or too uncomfortable to cope with in any other way. It is also possible to look at this in terms of the *self* being projected.

The self, in classical Jungian language, is the underlying, prospective, centre (and totality) of who we are, guiding our individuation – the never ending journey of becoming who we are (Jung 1921/1971). Giants could represent this 'fullness' of our potential being; they could also, of course, be a manifestation of grandiosity – when our ego gets identified with the self and loses its sense of humanness, a narcissistic aggrandisement bringing all the psychic and practical dangers associated with a giant running amok.

As indicated, a complex blends powerful archetypal influences and environmental factors from the present and past which 'constellate' together (Jung, 1960/1969: para. 201) to create a significant locus of influence within the psyche. Parental complexes, in particular, can be constellated at almost any time in life, considering how pivotal the role of mother and/or father usually is. When *they* were giants – i.e. when *we* were little and most vulnerable – influence, introjection and impingement occurred through environmental and archetypal frames of reference coming together. In the adult present, when a complex forms, the giants come back to life.

To be a giant is to be superhuman in terms of size, strength and power over others. There is a god-like quality to them, and in the story the giant and his 'giant-wife' live up in the sky, in a version of heaven, or Mount Olympus, which is above and beyond our world. This contrasts with most giant stories, where the colossus wreaks havoc by terrorising our territory, as portrayed famously by Goya (c. 1809–12). This perhaps gives the giant and his wife in *Beanstalk* more of a numinous quality – they are a version of the king and queen of heaven.

In this case, though, the divine couple's power is toxic. They have all the things the sad, poverty-stricken, dyad down below (Jack and his widowed mother) do not have – an abundance of food and riches and a big luxurious house. In fact, according to the fairy in the story, they have *stolen* these from Jack and his family.

The importance of 'giants' and 'giant-ness' in understanding how important *scale* is in the human psyche hopefully comes across, along with how the huge versions of mother and father, woman and man, feminine and masculine which inhabit the space up in the wide open archetypal 'sky' crucially influence us. I propose to hold these figures in the background as we pass through the various discussions on gendered relations, development and experiencing which will feature in this book. I also suggest the reader will get more fully under the skin of the archetypal dynamics of *Jack and the Beanstalk* if they allow awareness of their inner, introjected, 'giant parents' to inhabit the space behind their reading of this book.

The beanstalk

The boundary between the worlds of the two couples is like one between earth and heaven, the present life and the beyond, or the conscious and the unconscious mind. The significance of this boundary brings into play the importance of the beanstalk. In this story the frail humanity of Jack is given access to the archetypal domain of the giants; and here, however difficult the experiences he has, the giants offer the path to salvation. The motif of the beanstalk bears amplification in relation to this connecting role between the day-to-day and the archetypal (or eternal). In this respect the means for this journey reveals its biblical template. Jacob's ladder up to heaven (Genesis 28: 11–19) and Jack's beanstalk up to the giant's kingdom both perform the function of opening up *the route between*. In Jacob's case he envisions the ladder in a dream while he is fleeing from his brother Esau and the ladder can be seen as representative of the exile the Jewish people would later suffer (the seventy years of exile in Babylon as symbolised by the seventy rungs), as well as of the enduring promise of a Holy Land made by Yahweh to his chosen people. Jacob had the dream while resting at Mount Moriah, where the *Beit HaMikdash* (Holy Temple) would be built for offering prayer and sacrifice to God, thereby consolidating the bridge between earth and heaven.

The ladder also offers a means for angels to journey between the domains of *flesh* and *spirit*. They are able to accompany Jacob via the ladder and, later, when he reaches the border of the land of Canaan (Genesis 32: 2–3), which was to be the future land of Israel, he was greeted by angels specifically designated to guard this 'kingdom of God' on Earth.

Ladders, angels, beanstalks are all motifs for this attempt by psyche to connect earth and heaven, the personal and the archetypal. There are other portrayals of this 'going up' into and 'coming down' from the divine realm – such as Mohammed's ascent into heaven in Jerusalem 'from the Sacred Temple to the farther Temple' (Koran 17: 1). Jung includes the imagery associated with Jacob's vision in his discussions on the role and meanings of dreams (Jung 1936/1968). As well as pointing to the alchemical significance of ascent as a kind of initiation rite into 'sublimation' (ibid.: para. 66) which enables a return to the source of our being, he offers a clear connection to what the beanstalk could represent in the story. Here, he refers to a dream brought by a patient in which the dreamer is on a 'dangerous walk with Father and Mother, up and down many ladders' (ibid.: para. 78):

This 'personal unconscious' must always be dealt with first, that is, made conscious, otherwise the gateway to the collective unconscious cannot be opened. The journey with father and mother up and down many ladders represents the making conscious of infantile contents which have not yet been integrated.

(ibid.: para. 81)

For Jack, the three return journeys up and down the beanstalk to recover what is his has this quality of wrestling with issues from the personal unconscious. In analysis we repeatedly travel with mother and father (whether or not they were both living presences in our early experiences) to and from the realm where they still feel like giants – i.e. in regressed childlike states, some of which may still dominate our adult lives. This, in turn, makes it possible to be fully initiated into life, where, as adults, collective patterns can be lived out with our individual stamp on them. Consciousness is embraced through this work of travelling up and down the beanstalk. It also opens up the possibility of getting closer to the self – represented in its numinous form by the kind of images of God/heaven alluded to in the discussion of sacred texts above.

The beanstalk, as a phallic representation of Jack's awakening capacity to try to resolve the predicament he and his mother are in, can also be seen as a bridging of Jack's relative weakness as a boy and his movement through an adolescent initiation into manhood whereby he becomes capable of substituting for father and bringing material wealth into the home.

Arlow (1961: 381) takes the psychoanalytic observation of a child's 'practically universal fantasy wish to acquire the father's phallus by devouring it and using the omnipotent organ' and sees *Jack and the Beanstalk* as a representation of a basic, childlike wish fulfilment where there is no danger of retaliation after stealing the phallus. He then goes on to portray a maturing of the ego into an awareness of the real risk of being punished (as in Prometheus fearing, and then being punished by, Zeus) and, finally, the ego 'becoming' father by serving him and conveying his message, as Moses did in relation to God on Mount Sinai.

This sequence of ego development, from an unconscious, omnipotent belief the phallus can just be 'taken' without fear of retribution, through to a mature, but sublimated, channelling of the desire to steal into the wish to serve, implies how Jack's story is reflective of a search for maturation. Before he goes up the beanstalk his expressions of potency are self-indulgent, but once he is confronted with the beanstalk's presence he begins the long climb into taking a potency which requires risk-taking and service to the 'father' energy of rectifying the tragedy behind his family's predicament.

This taking of one's potency need not be translated exclusively into the realm of the boy. Feminist rewritings of the tale, such as Mary Pope Osbourne's (2005), illustrate the importance of keeping all meanings in this story open for both genders. In her version, Osbourne describes how Kate is confronted with the same problem as Jack in the traditional version, and likewise uses the beanstalk to confront the greedy giant. Here, the beanstalk could be seen to represent the girl's taking of her own potency (sexual and otherwise) from a father who hasn't facilitated this by playfully, but safely, acknowledging his daughter's emerging erotic identity, something which Samuels (1989: 77–85) has highlighted as important for the development of a woman. Or, it could be seen as a reflection of the shift in the social and political place of girls and women in western societies. Either way it reminds us how downgraded the power of the female characters are in the story.

Transcendent sky and immanent ground

The beanstalk connects more than just the archetypal and the personal realms. The epoch-shaping supplanting of pre-Christian earth mother religions, animism and paganism by the Church's insistence on the transcendent *logos* of the father God is reflected in the landscape of the story. Jack has to transcend the ground on which he and his mother are trapped in poverty and despair, and ascend to the land in the sky in order to solve the problem. This feels much like the religious pull 'upwards' within the monotheistic Abrahamic faiths, exemplified in the resurrected Christ's return to his father by 'ascending' to heaven (Mark 16: 14–19) as well as the Jewish and Muslim examples alluded to above. While conventional religious belief in many western societies has faded, the overarching forms rooted in them remain influential in keeping the search for scientific truths, for example, as detached and *logos*-bound rather than rooted in immanent matter and incorporating *eros*.

As Rowland (2007: 10) argues, the problem here is to do with a fundamental split, or 'that founding epistemological division in western consciousness: between form and matter . . . [which is] . . . a deep wound in consciousness.' This split, I suggest, is of profound significance to our thinking and feeling around gender, for example in how we perceive the gendered 'other'.

Who holds the immanence more? Traditionally it would be women, with the associations of keeping the *matter* of home and family ticking over, and being left 'holding the baby'. Likewise, men have been associated within social convention as holding transcendence; being 'out there', creating or sustaining the *form* of professional and public life, and having the scope to come and go from 'home/wife/baby' as they please, in order to climb the beanstalk while the former stay 'on the ground'.

There is a widespread perception this traditional dichotomy has changed, and indeed the opening up of employment opportunities for women, and the growing recognition of the importance of fathering in its *immanent* (i.e.

present) rather than *transcendent* (mainly absent) form reflects an important shift in collective attitudes. However, in a theme I will return to more fully in Chapter 2, there remains a strong influence of the two territories as reflected in the story; and, I suggest, they remain more or less anchored in gender distinctions.

At an unconscious level, 'home/ground' remains more a woman's territory, and the movement away from it – which I characterise as 'road/sky' – is a man's, at least in the habitual patterns we can fall into (whether imprinted through socialisation or archetypal patterns, or both). So, although women are now much more 'out there' and men are coming more into the home space of childcare and familial presence, the magnetic pull of home/female and 'out there'/male remain deeply influential poles of influence.

This may feel like an undesirable state of affairs but underneath deconstructed ways of gendered being it still seems to be so. I am not arguing here for a conservative position on gendered expressions of identity and family relations. I suggest instead that the pulls of long-established ways of being towards what are male and female 'territories' remain, and that we are living in a time of tension between new, freer ways of expressing ourselves as women and men and this level of embedded influences. The *transcendent–immanent* polarity embedded in western culture, gets personified and played out in heterosexual relationships, and this remains a living reality in twenty-first-century postmodern, post-religious societies.

Jung got caught up in the unconscious influence of this deep-rooted tendency in the culture in the breathtaking ways he wrote at times of women, producing remarks such as: 'In women . . . Eros is an expression of their true nature, while their Logos is often only a regrettable accident' (1951/1968: para. 29). Jung's implication here is to distinguish 'logos' in a healthy sense from any incarnation in the form of women. This has a *territorial* quality of the kind I have alluded to. Jung seemed to need to keep the transcendent in the realm of men, and the immanent mainly with women – other than when it might be growthful for a man to take possession of it.

As I develop my argument I will suggest that such defensive positions taken by men really reflect a deep uncertainty about the maternal, pre-oedipal energy that is associated with the *semiotic* mystery of the feminine as expressed by women, and by the territory of *home*. This territoriality I believe is very important, however much we may find ourselves baulking at the inappropriate, even misogynistic frame in which Jung expresses it. I propose that there may be archetypal rather than just historically 'infected' forces at work here. The problem is not that men and women are different in comprehensively fixed ways. But where they *are* in some ways archetypally different (e.g. biologically women can give birth and men cannot) this might be where the 'historical infection' has taken root. *Immanence* thus becomes rigidified in the territory associated historically with women, and *Transcendence* is located in male territory.

Our perceptions and roles are likewise affected and a screen is created between who we *think* we'd like to be as men and women – less rigidly gendered, open to changing ourselves to be what the gendered 'other' needs us to be and so on; and an archetypal territory behind the screen which maintains a hold on us where it has been historically infected by the 'deep wound' (Rowland, op. cit.) described above.

This wound I suggest is at the heart of *Jack and the Beanstalk*, though in Jungian terms wounding is a necessary part of individuation. As an extrapolation, the evolution of collective human consciousness, the counterpointing of masculine–feminine (e.g. sky–earth), female–male (mother–Jack), and *anima* (fairy–Jack) and *animus* (Jack–mother) in the story, all highlight the suffering – and growth – inherent in these gendered polarities.

Mother and the other female characters

Jack's mother, the cow that is traded in, the giant's wife and other minor female characters could be seen as different aspects of Jack's 'mother complex'.

Jack's mother

Jack's mother oscillates between a kind of passive despair at her widowed plight, and rage at her apparently inadequate son – that is, until Jack proves he can bring home the wealth they long for. She is largely a passive watcher of events in the male world that has let her down.

There is a kind of deadness to this which threatens to overwhelm her and Jack until he is provided with a way of overcoming this. So, this aspect of the story might contain what Green terms a 'dead mother' complex (Kohon, 1999), where a deadened version of mother has been internalised and clouds the capacity for a child to engage with life actively, leaving depression in its wake.

Interestingly, this starts to shift when internalised aggression, which is often a hallmark of depression, gets turned outwards and the mother hurls the apparently worthless beans out of the window. One could characterise the beans as Jack's negative, deadened *anima* (which I term *thanima*), but with the active expulsion of his dubious potency from the home he is freed up to find something truly potent away from the stuck mother–son dyad.

Another way of looking at this sequence is to 'home in' on Jack's mother. Her son may represent her less than mature negative animus (*thanimus*) who struggles at first with responsibility, moving into a more judgemental state with the fury at her son, but when she becomes active in dealing with her *animus* she is able to 'throw out' this naive immaturity and then generate a more positive *animus* (*erosimus*) figure who scales the heights and recovers his potency and resources.

'Milky White' the cow

The cow, 'Milky White' (connoting a kind of unblemished fecundity of mother's breast perhaps?), is exchanged for nothing more than a handful of beans. Jung (1911/1968) refers to the cow as a representation of the mother archetype in her reproductive capacities. As Adams (2003: 56) observes: 'Jung situates the maternal body directly between references to "oven" and "cow". Both are objects commonly used as denigratory representations of women's birth-giving capacities.' This observation points towards an unhealthy strand in patriarchal attitudes – where men may be careless about the elemental power and value of mother, family and home, willing to 'trade in' the value of the embodied feminine for some dream of achievement or wealth.

In the story, Jack's trade-in of the cow is for mother an apparently huge betrayal, the loss of all she has left from the legacy of her marriage for a gamble on 'magic beans' (which also carry a hallmark of the gambles her husband took leading to his death). This sense of exchange between the 'protected feminine' and the 'risky masculine' is another link to possible underlying differences between gendered 'territories'.

The Giant's wife, the hen and the harp

As indicated, I am looking at the 'giant couple' as archetypal versions of mother and father, as well as introjected versions of them, in the Kleinian sense. While the giant is for sure a 'bad father' who can only be outwitted and survived through trickery, his wife is a benevolent 'good' mother who may be compensating for what Jack is not getting from his real mother, who remains locked inside her grief, rage and despair. This benevolent maternal presence also seems to be represented by the hen which lays the golden eggs, and the singing harp.

The gold coins seem to suggest (as symbolically money often does) libido, and the erotic connection between mother and son gets healthily restored through Jack bringing the money home in his first sortie up the beanstalk. This 'first treasure' in the story is important as it reflects how vital the 'first' *erotic* bond with mother is for the son, whose positive *anima* – or *erosima* – seeks out this level of connection with her, and this refers back to the pre-oedipal attachment and how it evolves into the intensity of oedipal desire.

The second treasure (the hen) can be seen as compensation for the loss of the reproductive fecundity of the cow, now returning in a more valuable form, while the third treasure (the harp) makes, with its musical voice, further *feminine* creative processes possible, snatching back the muse of Jack and his family from its Giant usurper. Overall, the compensatory maternal/feminine presence 'in the sky' makes itself available in the midst of the threat of a tyrannical, terrifying masculine presence – one extreme inevitably constellating the other.

The fairy

The fairy, who stands at the threshold of the 'kingdom in the sky', is a classic positive *anima* figure who points the way for Jack's redemption. She can see into his predicament and shed light on what he needs to do to recover the legacy of his father. As Hillman (1979) characterises *anima* in the man, she can provide access to his 'soul' process, where this refers to someone's embodied struggle to become themselves. In a sense Jack has 'lost' his soul through his family's tragedy as well as through his indolence and unwillingness to take responsibility for the problem he has inherited.

Father and the other male characters

In parallel with the treatment of mother in the story, I will be taking Jack's father, the old man and the giant as features of Jack's father complex. I have already highlighted how, in having killed Jack's father, taken his wealth, and then threatened to eat Jack, the giant represents a tyrannical and abusively uncontained version of the aggressive father. This is a key element of the father complex suggested by the story.

Jack's father

Jack's father has a powerful presence in the sense that his death makes the story possible – Jack has to find a way to redeem his family and avenge what has happened. As the good father has gone Jack also has to find a way of replacing this aspect of father before he and mother are destroyed by their desperate circumstances. He is the son who is about his father's business, and the Christ-like dimension of this lends both an unhealthy hero/victim polarity quality to his quest as well as a more numinous quality.

The old man

The man who pays Jack the magic beans for the cow has a pivotal, transformative quality in providing the means for Jack to overcome the enormous challenge he is faced with. This seems to be part of the legacy of father which can still be used to make something happen. He turns out to be a 'wise old man', though he appears to be cheating Jack out of the family cow initially. Jack's capacity to trust his intuition and accept the offer of the beans suggests he has caught a glimmer of his lost father in the eye of the old man, and this awakens his potency.

To conclude

I have made an initial foray into the themes arising from *Jack and the Beanstalk*: the relationship between the archetypal and the personal, and the way Jack is able to bridge the two; the powerful presence of the numinous 'up in the sky' in offering a route to redemption; and, most importantly for our purposes, the way that parental complexes come to be played out in the story.

To sum up the central dynamic of this story from a psychological perspective I would characterize it thus: *a boy loses his father, then uses the giant's realm to grow up and prove himself to his lost father, and to save and improve his relationship with his mother*.

I will interrogate the possibilities thrown up by this tale as this book progresses to better understand the themes set out in the introduction:

- how we experience our sense of self in relation to gender identity
- the *territorial* relationship between 'male/transcendent/road' and 'female/immanent/home'
- the relationship (in both consonant and conflicting ways) between feminine–masculine, male–female and shared and/or distinctive territories
- the place of contrasexual influence (*anima–animus*) in understanding the impact of developmental and other factors on gendered experiencing and relating.

This initial consideration of the 'Jack' story highlights the huge piece of work involved in seeing the 'whole picture' of gender. The challenge can feel like trying to join earth and sky, but the story – at least symbolically – suggests there are valuable ways of playing with this possibility.

Chapter 2

Gender illusion, gendered reality

> While he was eating breakfast there was a terrific bang – the giant was knocking on the door. The giant's wife told Jack to hide and put him into an empty kettle.

The dramas of our lives, as in *Jack and the Beanstalk*, are haunted by gender, where 'gender' refers to our attitudinal, behavioural and possibly archetypal responses to socially embedded frames of reference for being male or female. Jack's drama involves him redefining himself as a boy who is capable of being a man, taking the mantle of father before perhaps he is ready.

We can also find ourselves trying to define ourselves in relation to the templates for being male or female we encounter early in life, as a way of compensating for how small and vulnerable we can feel as children in an apparently huge world peopled by giants (our parents and the other adults who lumber around our homes and beyond it).

Our response to this situation usually takes one of two paths – or more usually a muddled combination of the two. We may attempt to replicate the ways of being a man or woman modelled by father or mother, or reject these and try to create our own versions of being male or female in the shadow of embedded social and psychological messages about how to 'be'. As we build up our repertoire of ways of being a girl or a boy it is hard to discern what arises from something rooted in us as individual persons and what reflects our struggle to adapt to the world we find we have landed in.

This chapter teases out the tensions in understanding what gender 'is' – including how real or not 'it' might be. This will lay the ground for a proposed framework for understanding differences between being a man or being a woman. This project, as it unfolds throughout the book, also acknowledges the fundamental commonalities between women and men, areas of human 'being' which have a more or less archetypal prevalence (and an archetypal capacity for *variation*).

These include: our common need for individual and relational fulfilment; shared potential for, and aspiration towards, personal, professional, intellectual and practical achievement; common values around mutual respect, support and challenge (and a ubiquitous capacity to default on these); and a shared capacity for establishing and maintaining long-term relationships and family responsibilities (with again the rider that we can all reject or mess up these).

I aim to open up new vistas on the possibilities for both women and men, out of a sense that gender can trap the potential of both because of an unconsciousness about what makes us fully who and what we are. 'Gender', I would suggest, works best for us when we allow our assignation as male or female to free-float between the *what* and the *who* of our identity; between acknowledging the presence of gender (a 'what' of my identity – such as my national and cultural 'whats') and how that gets filtered through all other aspects of me – the 'who' which defines my separateness, even uniqueness, as a human being.

I also want to look at gender as it might inform personality structure and development. This is the province of Chapter 3, where how early, archetypal and developmental influences might help form gendered aspects of self is explored. In this chapter, I will explore some of the powerful ideas and debates around gender which have emerged in the last hundred years or so. These include critiques of gender essentialism (e.g. Stoller, 1968; Butler, 1990: 10–17); developments on from Freud which are pivotal to depth readings of gender (e.g. Lacan, 1966/1977) or to understanding how gendered patterns may get reproduced (e.g. Chodorow, 1978); research on gender difference or concordance (e.g. Kohlberg, 1966; Thorne, 1993); recent contributions from neuropsychology and psychiatry which suggest there are endemic physiological and psychological differences between how men and women function and relate (e.g. Brizendine, 2007; Baron-Cohen, 2004); and Jungian and post-Jungian perspectives on gender relations (e.g. Steinberg, 1993; Rowland, 2002; Young-Eisendrath, 2004).

I will then apply Jung's principle of the 'transcendent function' (Jung, 1916/1969: paras 131–93) to these themes. He proposed that this psychic function draws out something new from oppositional influences and thus 'transcends' the impasse. In terms of gender the polarities are: 'gender as a fixed given' (essentialist) versus 'gender as fluid and socially constructed' (constructivist). I also argue for the presence in the psyche of a counterbalancing 'immanent function' which has a compensatory role in maintaining *homeostasis* and *grounding* change.

The emerging working definition of gender will then inform a proposed post-Jungian working model of personality structure which has an explicitly relational dimension. Relational patterns in *Jack and the Beanstalk* will be alluded to where relevant. Also, elements of 'emergent' and dialectical processes (e.g. Solomon, 2007) and collective behaviours (e.g. Mathers, 2001) from an analytical psychology perspective will be highlighted and applied to the proposed model where relevant.

What is 'gender'?

Robert Stoller's seminal thinking in this area offers a starting point in trying to characterise an authentic perspective on gender – one which is not locked into more essentialist ideas of gender as fundamentally determined by biological differences. He suggests 'gender' refers to 'areas of behaviour, feelings, thoughts, and fantasies that are related to the sexes and yet do not have primarily biological connotations' (Stoller, 1968: ix).

When we explore neurobiological arguments about difference, the value of keeping 'gender' free-floating as a counterweight will, I hope, become clearer. This relates particularly to the point about valuing the space between the *what* of our maleness or femaleness, and the *who* of how we live out our lives within gendered assignations arising from social norms.

One of the main arguments I make in this chapter is that while there are huge areas of commonality between them, there are clear differences between the *experience* of being a man and being a woman. But it is a complex and fraught task to attempt to identify with confidence where these differences arise *from*. I will suggest a way of thinking about this within a post-Jungian framework, arguing for the presence of two 'territories', based mainly in the unconscious, which provide the ground from which women and men derive a sense of what makes them different from each other. These territories are not mutually exclusive; there is a burgeoning liminal space between them which enables different ways of articulating identity (in respect to gender, sex, desire, role etc.) – e.g. transgendered and gay expressions of sexuality – to be lived out.

These 'territories' can only be partially 'seen' as they lie, in the main, behind a 'screen' which has protective, and at times regressive, purposes. The illusions which can spring up about gender arise from this 'through a glass darkly' quality of the relationship between our lived experiences and these more archetypally based, though evolving, 'territories'. Susan Rowland (in press) points out that one of Jung's most valuable, but often overlooked, legacies is his way of writing, which, however awkwardly (even unacceptably) expressed at times, experiments with, and thereby allows, the mysteries of the unconscious to become more available to our awareness.

His writing on women and men, with its uncomfortable but extraordinary mix of unreconstructed generalisation (e.g. on women's *animus*) and liberating symbolism (e.g. his prizing of the archetypal feminine [Jung 1958/1969]), thus invests the whole area of gender with enormous potential. As Rowland (2005: 173) puts it, Jung's project to identify and work with contrasexual presences (*anima* in man and *animus* in woman) meant: 'Gender became the means of positioning a dialectics out of a multiplicity, and hence the construction of the very territory of psychological theorizing.' The gendered 'territories' I work with arise in this hazy space between the inevitably incomplete rational attempts to *define* gender and the lived experiences of being a man or a woman. Although they escape reliable delimiting, they derive their core from something collective. I mean this in the sense that our individualised 'being' a man or a woman may come to be more fully felt when we are with other women (if 'I' am a woman) or men (if 'I' am a man). This links to ways that little children identify with their same-sex parent, something I will explicate in Chapter 3, but it also raises the possibility of there being some archetypal roots to whatever gender 'is'.

These roots are as elusively deep in the earth as the source of the beans' magic power in the *Beanstalk* story, but the metaphor of the beanstalk putting in deep roots in order to stabilise its trajectory to the sky is a good one. The archetypal power underlying Jack's identification with father – his (previously dormant) positive father complex – enabled this. Likewise, it is possible that what we struggle to get hold of in our use of the term 'gender' has its own laws, which are constellated when we least expect them – laws of the unconscious which we cannot pretend to grasp with our minds but can feel the power of in mythological dramas, in upsurges of feeling (erotic, aggressive and so on) in our relationships, or in strong reactions to stereo-typing about men or women.

Other working definitions of the term 'gender' help tease out the problems and potential inherent in its usage. Connell (2002: 8) starts from the straightforward assertion that 'in its most common usage . . . the term "gender" means the cultural difference of women from men, based on the biological division between male and female.' He then critiques that position for its binary over-simplification, arguing that human life is not so simply divided up – an argument which lends credence to the notion that we have a tendency to project and seek out such 'basic splits' in life, a tendency arising from a psychological and relational wish for certainty and safety in an unpredictable universe.

As Connell (op. cit.: 8) argues, the risk with equating gender with this difference is obvious: '[W]here we cannot see difference, we cannot see gender.' Gendered gay or lesbian desire would be overlooked here as would the power of collective gender identification (e.g. armed men together). This latter point relates to my earlier argument about how gender may become more powerful and influential as a signifier of identity when *collective* rather than individual.

Connell stresses the importance of seeing gender in terms of its operation as a social structure, generating patterns of relating which have become embedded in how we function and make sense of the world. Connell's point receives its echo at a deeper psychological layer in the work of Jacques Lacan (1966/1977). Although he does not refer to gender in these terms, his notions of 'signifier' and 'signified' (Lemaire, 1977: 6) offer us a vital clue to how gender comes to be so important to how we see ourselves. Our 'maleness' or 'femaleness' exists for us through the signifiers of what we *imagine* we see and experience of it rather than what 'it' is.

Via the oedipal struggle which brings us into the triangulation of 'mother–father–I' (rather than just 'mother–I') we are subjected to the 'law of the Father' (Lacan, 1957) and enter the 'Symbolic Order', wherein language acquires greater power than the thing or feeling it represents. The child has to accept how society (as symbolised by father) ascribes meaning to objects and experiences in order to be accepted by *it*. So, the symbolic power of being named *boy* or *girl* and identifying with the familial and social implications this conveys, sets up a dilemma around knowing the difference between 'gender reality' and 'gender illusion'.

The value of Lacan's observations here need to be weighed in the light of his adherence to the phallocentric emphasis of Freud on the supposedly more powerful and desirable 'position' of the male in the early psycho-sexual dramas of the infant (Freud, 1920/1991). As Lacan implies, behind the 'socially structured' quality of 'gender' are unconscious processes around desire and acceptance, as well as an archetypal tendency to imagine – and idealise – who we are. This stems from the 'mirror stage', which comes prior to the oedipal conflict, when we internalise an image of self as we first notice, identify with, and idealise our reflection in the mirror (Lacan, 1912).

There is, I suggest, a splitting tendency in the psyche which deeply influences our difficulties with gender. In this case the split is between who we imagine ourselves to be and who we are, a useful notion to set alongside my idea of 'territories', because the fuzzy, shifting boundaries between being a man and being a woman may be significantly impacted by this splitting tendency. We cannot see 'who we really are' much of the time because the unconscious is constantly generating a tension between a craving for certitude and a chaotic mingling of psychic and somatic influences from past and present.

So, the unconscious (or something in it) may block access to something which is key to understanding our difficulties with *relationship, sex* and *gender*. I speculate that there is a fundamentally disruptive opposition (due to the very nature of the unconscious) to our attempts to get hold of 'gender'. For example, facilitating understanding of the male/female 'territories' I have alluded to in individual and collective narratives about gender can be inhibited by fears of assigning certitude and stereotype to human identity and activity (or others' perceptions that this is what we are doing). Perhaps there is also a counter-fear. If there are *no* principles relating to gender which we can apply with any confidence, if all bets are off about whether there is anything to gender other than outdated ways of constructing social realities, then the fear of a formless void of identity behind the illusion of gender can also hang around this question. This might feel more of a threat if our own sense of identity has been closely wrapped up in being a man or being a woman, whereby we have become dependent on a sense of 'gender certainty' (Samuels, 1989).

As suggested, the problem of how comfortable we are with exploring the possibilities around the 'reality or illusion' of gender difference appears to be tied up with a kind of archetypal tendency in the human psyche to split experiencing of inner and outer realities. From the good versus the bad breast (Segal, 1979) to the earth versus the sky of our story, we can slip into 'either/or' in our reactions to people or events we encounter in our daily lives. This splitting tendency in the human psyche has a powerful impact on our engagement with gender, and merits further examination.

The basic split

Post-Jungian literature recognises the tension between seeing gender as archetypally/biologically based and viewing it as socially constructed. Steinberg (1993) offers a valuable contribution with his term 'The Basic Split', by which he identifies a *naturally* splitting tendency of the human psyche. He links this to Kohlberg's (1966) research into children's cognitive development and suggests that this splitting tendency gets translated into a cognitive habit of categorising things (e.g. big/small) and experiences (e.g. good/bad) in a split, oppositional way.

So, when it comes to being told *she* is a girl, or *he* is a boy, a child's tendency may be to identify with this in a 'full on' way and look for 'evidence' to reinforce this rigid assignation, e.g. by identifying how they are 'the same as mum' or 'different to dad' (for a girl – and vice versa for a boy), so as to confirm to themselves that they really do belong to the gender assigned to them. As Steinberg (1993: 13) puts it, this means: 'Gender identity precedes and determines gender role.'

The archetypal tendency for us to put things into opposites and create binaries is deeply influential, and, I suggest, has generated the legacy of many generations of splitting into male and female 'territories'. This tendency creates a double bind as it means a child's self-concept gets wrapped up in their socially assigned and self-reinforced gender identity. Whatever distinctions might then be made between constitutionally or archetypally based 'givens' in determining what makes a girl a girl or a boy a boy, and what is imposed by social and familial conventions, are then very difficult to identify.

The outcome of this early process of gender determination tends to lead to what Levinson and Levinson (1996) described as four common, traditional manifestations of what, from their researches into the adult life cycle, they named as 'gender splitting' (Levinson and Levinson, 1996: 38):

1   Splitting of 'spheres', with the domestic 'belonging' to women, and the public to men.

2   The 'Traditional Marriage Enterprise' which acts as the framework in which woman is more the homemaker and man more the provider.
3   The splitting of 'men's work' and 'women's work'.
4   The splitting of feminine and masculine in the individual psyche.

Although social changes and progressive legislation have eaten away at these manifestations, the underlying 'basic split' fades slowly, if at all. As I will argue in the following chapters, rigidified male and female roles and self-concepts may be seen as a version of how negative *anima* and negative *animus* can work to block self-awareness in personal *and* collective ways. This is what Hill (1992: 5) describes as the 'static negative masculine or feminine', where people live by unhealthy essentialist generalisations (e.g. men as rigid and unfeeling, women as submissive and smothering). At the other end of the scale, perhaps to try to compensate for this problem, we can find self-conscious attempts to live as *androgynously* as possible (Steinberg, op. cit.: 4).

Instead of this kind of polarisation of the problem of gender there is somewhere a clearer view hovering on the edge of consciousness which could allow a fuller recognition of what is different between men and women and what is shared. This might become available via the gradual lifting of the fog of unconsciousness, which is charged at times with hostile, fearful energies arising from a history of mutual incomprehension, disappointment and anger.

Gender difference and the brain

One possible tool for lifting this fog is psychological and neurobiological research into where the biological 'brain-sex' of male and female may generate differences that can be reasonably generalised to apply to most, if not all, of us. These distinctions emerge from less than one per cent of our shared genetic coding (Brizendine, 2007: 23) and yet, the literature in this area asserts, they are far reaching. The smallest areas of difference within the 'making' of us, from this viewpoint, generates its opposite – patterns of neuropsychological functioning which strongly influence how we think, feel and relate; the little matter of an additional 'Y' chromosome sending male human beings off on a differing trajectory through life than females.

So, while female brain circuits – supposedly 'designed' to generate more feeling-based, attuned, communication skills – develop unconstrained in a girl in the womb, the male foetus is impacted by the testosterone fuel which will generate the boy's (and man's) aggressive and sexual hardwiring while killing off some of the 'communication' cells. Brizendine (ibid.: 36–7) describes this change, beginning around the eighth week of pregnancy, as a 'foetal fork in the road . . . which defines our innate biological destiny, colouring the lens through which each of us views and engages the world.'

Baron-Cohen (2004: 1) takes this principle of inherent difference between female and male further by asserting that the female brain is: 'predominantly hard-wired for empathy. The male brain is predominantly hard-wired for understanding and building systems.' He emphasises the 'predominant' in his theorising, recognising that it is possible for a man to have a more 'female' empathically wired brain, and for a woman to be in possession of a more systematising one. He describes a continuum where most men and boys are at the understanding/systematising end, and most women and girls are found towards the empathic end. He also asserts that the ends of this continuum can manifest in problematic ways – the 'extreme male mind', for example, resulting in autism, where the drive to systematise and categorise supersedes all others, at the obvious cost of empathy and human relating (Baron-Cohen, ibid.: Ch. 12).

There are two possible criticisms of Baron-Cohen's conclusions. First, he falls (as a man) into the patriarchal trap of making a 'basic split' between man as possessor of *logos*, master of the realm of thoughts which lead to productive actions, and woman as keeper of *eros*, cultivator and sustainer of relationships. There are negative *anima* and *animus* connotations to the flip sides of these strengths for men and women which might find accord with some of Jung's less sophisticated ideas on the subject.

The second criticism of Baron-Cohen might be that he does not factor in the growing evidence on the plasticity of the brain in the early years of life, and the degree to which infant experiences of environment, attachment, and sometimes trauma, can impact on the development of mind and patterns of behaviour and relationship (Wilkinson, 2001: 1–12). The tipping point of slight chromosomal variation, generating deeply influential difference, is one factor; another is surely the possibility of subtle but significant change through the individualised life experience of the young child, where a blend of felt relationship, developing understanding and action is needed to navigate through the first years of life.

Nevertheless, the developing school of research and thinking on constitutional difference cannot be overlooked. It is striking that in the so-called 'hard sciences' of neurobiology and neuropsychology, fundamental differences between being male and being female – which govern how and who we are – are being proposed, while in the realms of depth psychology and cultural, social, political and feminist studies, the dangers of essentialism and the value of a more androgynous attitude are asserted. Another 'basic split', perhaps.

Gender illusion and socialisation

There is also a well established body of writing which deconstructs the 'facade' of gender difference in social and interpersonal discourse. The critiques involved query whether 'gender difference' is based on anything more than socially constructed notions of what a woman is or a man is, and argue that these have become historically embedded and translated into conventions about how to be.

Research into how children may 'grow' into these constructed versions of gender identity provides a strong basis for this assertion. The work of Thorne (1993) is one example: through observations of primary school children and their social interactions, she came to view gender difference as *situational*, so boys and girls were more likely to fall into conventional gender behaviours and use of language when differences were accentuated – say by a teacher dividing them thus for a particular activity. As Thorne puts it, in such situations: 'categories of identity that on other occasions have minimal relevance for interaction become the basis of separate collectivities' (Thorne, 1993: 65).

Thorne writes about 'borderwork' (ibid.: 67), the work we do (largely unconsciously) to reinforce the boundaries between male and female – e.g. in conventionally differing ways of dressing. As Connell (2002: 14) observes, in this sense, 'gender difference is not something that simply exists . . . it . . . must be made to happen.' I am left, though, with the question of *what* makes this 'happen' – is it simply a socially constructed and patriarchal pressure to sustain an illusion of difference? I suggest that *nothing* about gender is simple – and therefore there is always more to any answer anyone might attempt.

Gender illusion and feminist critique

Such studies and observations appear to back up the underlying position of many critiques of essentialist views on gender. These posit that widely held assumptions about gender identity are outdated, illusory and often oppressive, particularly for women. Feminist and other writers have proposed a series of challenges to what are perceived as 'patriarchal' modes of categorising the behaviours, attitudes, roles and status of women and men in westernised societies.

This extends to the argument that the upholding of heterosexuality as the desirable norm in human sexuality reinforces this position. Gay, transsexual and other forms of 'non-normative' ways of expressing gender or sexuality become symbolic of what is 'outside' that norm, and in this sense serve to reinforce it. Butler suggests that gender norms, reinforced through the ascribing of heterosexuality as their flag-bearer, become central to our idea of identity and self. In this respect 'the very notion of the person is called into question by the cultural emergence of those "incoherent" or "discontinuous" gendered beings who appear to be persons but who fail to conform to the gendered norms of cultural intelligibility by which persons are defined' (Butler, 1990: 23). For Butler, challenging normative gender relations can seem fearful because this challenges our sense of self as well as the collective social norms which dominate western societies.

Butler powerfully demonstrates how open to question any normative idea of gender may be, particularly when the ways heterosexual power relations may try to determine these 'norms' are exposed. For example, when she refers to the argument of Irigaray's (1977/1985) that masculine, closed, phallocentric ways of describing the feminine leads to its 'linguistic *absence*' (Butler, 1990: 14), Butler highlights the unspoken ways assumptions about gender get reified linguistically so that the frame of reference becomes exclusive to the dominating 'voice' – i.e. the masculine.

Butler argues that it is this legacy of patriarchy which powerfully blocks our recognition of the illusion which has been spun around us. This legacy promotes an idea of 'male' as present, subject, universal, transcendent; and female as absent, object (e.g. of desire), corporeal – highlighted by De Beauvoir (1973: 301) – as the problem of a woman's body being what defines and limits her, rather than what can enable her to be fully herself – and immanent.

These cultural antimonies are, as Butler notes, well established in general philosophical and feminist literature. I tentatively suggest a loose parallel here with the archetypal polarities arising from Jung's way of thinking. There is some consonance in how feminist writers sometimes write about underlying processes which lead to heterosexual power relations and their impacts on women, and the splitting tendencies in the human psyche highlighted above by Steinberg (1993) and Levinson (1996).

For feminist writers these processes can be predicated on the idea of acquiring power through splitting and consolidating it by reifying that split. Looking at it from a Jungian perspective, the impact of archetypal polarities on the human psyche is bound to have implications relating to power, especially where those polarities are out of balance. Where the energy which constellates the archetype of 'family' is split so the 'masculine' end of the spectrum holds the bulk of the power and authority while the 'feminine' end is disempowered and subservient to it, an unhealthy one-sidedness arises.

I will pursue this in later chapters, suffice it to say here that a by-product of this splitting may have been the polarisation of power bases for men and women in heterosexual partnerships – men's 'out there' in the world and women's 'in here' at home. What was perceived under patriarchy as 'the way God made it' now leaves us with an uncomfortable legacy in which the 'territories' of women and men create endless thorns in the sides of relationships.

Rowland's (2007) consideration of the split relationship between the transcendent masculine and immanent feminine is helpful here. I have already suggested the presence of this split remains powerfully influential despite the social and legislative shifts made in the past forty or so years towards more overt gender equality, and there may be more to this than just social conditioning. If one takes the area of homemaking and care-giving for example, women are *less* identified primarily with this than forty years ago and men are associated with a more active role at home. However, in both cases, I would argue that the basis of social attitudes towards gender *role* remains largely predicated on these binary associations: 'women-home', and 'men-adjacent-to-home'. In relation to work and management, to take another example, things *have* changed but the binary associations remain predominantly 'man-as-manager' and 'women-as-supporting-team-member-or-careworker'.

These base associations reflect, as Rowland highlights, a patriarchal emphasis arising from 'centuries of Christian culture . . . [which] . . . left a rigid scheme of gender dichotomy in which feminine always signalled inferiority' (Rowland, in press: 4). This is reflected in the helplessness of Jack's mother and her reliance on her son's nascent capacity for masculine activity and strength to save her. Rowland (ibid.: 5) also makes the valuable point that although the legacy of this cultural one-sidedness is a strong emphasis on patriarchal symbolism, the *individual* psyche retains the capacity to produce, in a more balanced and dialogic way, imagery of both the masculine and the feminine. Somehow, this archetypal function of the unconscious to generate *anima* and *animus* imagery remains alive and well, despite our forefathers' best efforts. This is of profound importance, I believe, as it illustrates the possibility that differences in gendered identifi-cation and experience draw their power more from a collective than an individual level.

This informs our understanding of how cultures become more 'feminine' or 'masculine' at different stages in their development, imprinting powerful role expectations, and collective symbols and motifs as they come into the fullness of their influence, before dying away again. The pre-Christian earth goddess-based religions (Baring and Cashford, 1991), followed by the sway held by the father god of Christianity reflect this possibility, with at times painful switches involved in moving from sky to earth, earth to sky etc.

This is really about shifting between two whole dimensions of human experiencing and possibility, though it is important not to be simplistic and make the mistake of asserting that this means these are the only two possible psychological 'places' from which cultures may find their roots, or that such shifts are at any time whole or 'clean'; the conflict and muddle of individual life experience in every era of human history suggests otherwise.

However, the metaphor of a struggle between earth and sky has value in illuminating the dynamics of what I am arguing can be a *territorial* struggle between men and women. One application of this metaphor is to observe that in the natural world the earth and sky in a way *communicate* at a distance, such as when the rain comes down from 'up there' and then precipitation gathers to return it (with best wishes) from the ground.

Likewise, there seems to have been a historical to and fro between mother–feminine and father–masculine, in the western collective at least. The precipitation this has caused – the way the masculine (as represented by patriarchy) has made it rain on the feminine (as represented by women), and in a sense the way women have returned the rain back to men (with not such kind regards) through rejecting this oppression – is one way of describing where we seem to be now, in the early twenty-first century.

There is a less fanciful level to this imagery – in terms of power, and sex. 'Man on top', raining (pissing?) down from the sky onto women on the ground holds an obvious parallel with what patriarchal societies could be said to have done to women over the centuries: oppressed them in numerous ways, through denying them opportunity, categorising them as belonging in the home only, and at times inflicting all sorts of crimes and humiliations upon them. Likewise, 'man on top' refers to the classic position of the man in the heterosexual sexual act, implying the subjugation of the woman and in a way reflecting Freud's understanding of the unconscious aim of the boy or man in fulfilling their sexual desires (Freud, 1920/1991).

This earth–sky imagery has a rigidifying potential – i.e. it keeps men in all their oppressive unrelatedness 'up there' and keeps women holding the reins of reality and care 'down here'. I believe that the ground-to-air equation has such lasting resonance that there is little point in trying to dismiss it or supersede it through some stupendous act of will. These are territories which are deeply rooted and it is only through making these more conscious that the equation can be loosened, particularly at a collective level.

The individual human psyche, meanwhile, holds both gendered forms of archetypal instinct and image in the unconscious. The 'basic split' then becomes lived out in our *personal* engagement with *collective* influence, where the 'problem' of gender has not only been projected, but its evolving journey is in some ways also determined. A key way this has influence is in the translating of the transcendence–immanence split into divergent attitudes and 'languages'. Gilligan (1993: xxvi) describes this as a powerful split, more or less approximating to how women and men perceive and speak, 'an endless counterpoint between two ways of speaking about human life and relationships, one grounded in connection and one in separation.' Here, masculine transcendence drives human life towards priorities of autonomy and heroism, while feminine immanence impels us in the other direction, towards relationship and the day-to-day. We live out this collectively generated struggle inside – and between – each of us.

Helene Cixous argues that these distinctions are really about the relationship between differing categories of thought, and these can privilege certain concepts above others in the service of perpetuating patriarchal power – e.g. intellect as 'above' emotion or culture as 'above' nature (Cixous,

1975). The implication for Cixous is that the feminine gets associated with the 'lower' categories, and women become a kind of cultural product which serves the privileging of 'norms' associated with men and the masculine.

The parallel with archetypal polarities is worth noting here, if only to acknowledge Cixous's point that it is in splitting and comparing qualities such as intelligibility and sensibility, where the struggle for more balanced and satisfactory ways of relating, and sharing power (particularly between men and women), can get unhelpfully bogged down. This struggle can be said to impact deeply when it extends to how women might have unconsciously learned to deny aspects of themselves in order to 'fit in' with the gender illusion of the presumed masculine order, and what Gilligan (1993: x) describes as 'the trouble selfless behaviour can cause.' More than this, she describes how women dissociate – split off what they really feel or want to express – in order to maintain the patriarchal status quo and how men appear to talk about themselves and life generally 'as if they were not living in connection with women' (ibid.: xiii).

There are important possible consequences of the cultural and social phenomena described by feminist writers for the inner lives of women and men. There is a clear implication that women's lives have been blighted by a long-standing and invidious frame of reference for male–female relations which depersonalises them collectively and individually. The selflessness and dissociation observed by Gilligan are often unnoticed, but vital, elements which sustain the deep structures of patriarchal western culture.

Julia Kristeva (1980) suggests that rather than trying to reject Lacan's 'Symbolic Order' (1957) and argue femininity is somehow 'better', the wise approach is to acknowledge the metaphysical elusiveness of gender, and understand how this gets symbolised in the cultural construction of 'women' and 'men'. In Kristeva's terminology this refers to the organisation arising out of the 'semiotic' pre-oedipal drives and primary processes. This offers a valuable line of thinking which in Jungian language transcends the sometimes conflicting and confusing symbolic and linguistic interplay between 'the feminine' and 'the masculine'.

Chodorow (1978) provided an influential application of psychoanalytic theory to interrogate a question related to where women find themselves located in the 'Symbolic Order'; why is it mothers who provide the main, or sometimes exclusive, caregiver role in the family, especially for younger children? Her fundamental proposition is women: 'develop capacities for mothering from their object-relational stance. This stance grows out of the special nature and length of their pre-oedipal relationship to their mother' (Chodorow, 1978: 204).

Chodorow argues that it is this defining formation of the early mother–daughter relationship which gears women up to reproduce mother's capacities for nurturing and care, while a boy is not inducted in this way. She argues that this pattern is socially perpetuated, but it stems from the

object relations process rather than being the main influence on the reproduction of mothering. However, she also expresses the view that men have a
tendency to be emotionally unavailable, women have a stronger draw to
relationships with children, and both factors help perpetuate this pattern
(ibid.: 208).

In psychodynamic terms the psychosexual and object-relational aspects
of Chodorow's arguments belong more fully in the developmental
discussion in Chapter 3 where they will be considered with other theories
about differences in the psychic development of boys and girls, such as
Benjamin's (1988). These arguments furnish the perpetuated designation of
mother and father roles with a more psychologically deterministic flavour.

Young-Eisendrath (2004: 105) argues that it is the pervasive influence of
an 'androcentric social system' which continues to result in women coming
into adulthood 'with feelings and significant beliefs about their own
inferiority.' She also points out that the analytic community has helped to
perpetuate this situation, citing, for example, how comments about 'animus
possession' (ibid.: 43) in women members of that community have been
lazily attributed to those asserting their views or personal authority.

A further important consideration is ethics. Noddings (2003) argues
persuasively that not only has patriarchy frozen out the authentic voice of
women, but it has left us in a moral quagmire. She argues that the down-
playing of *caring* as a lodestone for our values – beneath, say, *achievement*
or *autonomy* – has created pervasive confusion about the place of relationship and responsibility in the ethical choices we make (ibid.: Ch. 1).
Noddings makes a strong argument for an urgent re-evaluation of our
ethical norms, concluding that 'one must meet the other in caring. From
this requirement there is no escape for one who would be moral' (ibid.:
201). Noddings thus echoes the 'I–thou' (Buber, 1923/2004) nature of full
human relating – really 'seeing' one another – and highlights the ethical
essence of caring relationships.

Our responsibilities to those we care for, or have some kind of relation
to, are *immanent*: they are right in front of us. Noddings implies that we
cannot avoid them if we are to hold, and act out of, an ethical attitude. Her
approach – arising from women's territory more than men's – has, she
argues, been marginalised; but it is clear ethics cannot be overlooked in
considering gendered experiences and attitudes.

Giants and gendered territory

The disconnection to women that Gilligan (1993) alludes to in how men
supposedly talk about their lives and relationships is fascinating for the
narrative themes I have selected for this book. Gilligan is drawn to the
place of 'giants' in the psyches of men, as I have been. Her reference to
'giants' in relation to men and how they might think and feel, and my

independently sensed importance of this, reinforces the possibility of the presence of an intuitive layer in the human psyche which distinguishes between female and male 'territories'.

Gilligan (1993: 5) quotes from Chekhov's 1904 play *The Cherry Orchard*, where the character Lopahin has a vision of fulfilment:

> "At times when I can't go to sleep, I think: Lord, thou gavest us immense forests, unbounded fields and the widest horizons, and living in the midst of them we should indeed be giants" – At which point, Madame Ranevskaya interrupts him, saying, "You feel the need for giants – they are good only in fairy tales, anywhere else they only frighten us."

In my view, Chekhov and Gilligan are describing the two 'territories' – 'being a man' and 'being a woman' – which occupy an often unseen layer between the socially constructed and the archetypally informed strata of gendered 'being'. For men, the 'giant up in the sky' identifications, and the transcendence and disconnectedness associated with it, suggests psychic phenomena which merit consideration as occupying *generally* distinctive 'territory' compared with women. I stress the 'generally' to guard against the risk of making assertions which prohibit variation in individual experiencing.

Also, all suggestions I make about these 'territories' acknowledge the importance of the enlarging, shared space in the middle of the 'Venn diagram' where the territories overlap. In some circumstances any combination of attributes, attitudes and experiencing from across the range of possibilities can get constellated in a woman or a man. However, like magnetic polarities, I suggest, some identifications (and possibly even *complexes*) arise more commonly in men than in women, and vice versa.

Likewise, the woman's immanent response in pointing out the danger and lack of realism inherent to the wish to be 'giant' could be seen in this 'territorial' way. For her there seems to be an intuitive need to caution the man against this pull. Here, a kind of 'masculine inflation' provokes a reaction which implies a compensatory need for a 'feminine deflation' that will bring him back to earth.

A more contentious reading of this is that the woman feels envious of the man's intuition of his capacity to 'be a giant' and so subtly attacks his fantasy, to keep at bay the possibility of something greater happening. I will explore possible differences in how women and men may emasculate each other's power in Chapter 7.

In the Chekhov quote, the man, Lopahin, starts in the sky as the male giant (like a god-the-father or *puer aeternus*); the woman, Ranevskaya, responds from the ground – or maybe, in the light of how she responds, from the archetype of *wise woman*. The story of *Jack* implies the male *needs* to (metaphorically) go up into the sky and engage with father-power at some point – either in the oedipal conflict or later in life when this has not been resolved. The trick seems to lie in finding the authentic route 'up there'; if it turns out to be an illusory one the wise woman will see through it straight away.

These distinct positions have arisen from the accumulated impact of long-standing Christian patriarchy: archetype and human construction somehow coming together to provide the *positioning* of 'man' and 'woman'. The split is basic in terms of the tendency for binary creation in the human psyche, but also because these differing positions reflect the depth of the wrestling between feminine and masculine at work in human consciousness and unconsciousness over time. The mystery is why men have become associated with the transcendent (vertical) and women with the immanent (horizontal) and whether a cultural, constructivist explanation for this is sufficient.

Men, the dying phallus and the feminine

It is a well-worn observation that men have long been wrestling with the personal, social and ethical challenges arising from the cultural and political shifts in western society. The responses are many and varied: ranging from the embrace of a so-called 'feminine' principle, whereby men adapt to new realities by taking on the sometimes caricatured features of womanhood like 'caring' or 'nurturing', through to Robert Bly's call for men to embrace their wilder, grittier natures (Bly, 1990).

The successful arguments of feminism have carved open professional and other areas of society and exposed the rigidity and vulnerability of the structures and principles which have underpinned traditional social institutions and frameworks for decision making and relating. Men, especially heterosexual men, have had to rethink their ways of relating to women, other than where it has been possible to perpetuate traditional power relations across generations, or where they have chosen to stand Canute-like against the tide of change. The nature and role of fathering (Samuels, 1985) has inevitably come into these considerations.

Suffice it to mention here, though, that father as *transcendent* (head of the household, adjacent to home but being the breadwinner for it) has in many ways gone literally 'up in the sky' in the sense of the *absent* father. The number of fathers in the UK who do not live with their children has risen significantly. Ninety per cent of fathers who divorce leave the family home, for example (Clare, 2001: 135). There has been a sense of crisis around the nature of fathering, reflecting the overturning of key assumptions about the social, professional and familial ascendancy of men. David Tacey (1997) has argued persuasively that men need to work hard on fashioning a relevant, effective and supportive stance for themselves in the postmodern world. He warns against lapsing into 'the dangerous senti-mentalisation of "men's feelings"' (ibid.: 11), as well as arguing for a reinvigoration of the nature of being a man (as opposed to seeing men as little more than a construct arising from a patriarchal legacy).

Tacey advocates a focus on engagement with shifting patterns in society and relationships, rather than becoming either defensively entrenched or fanciful about dealing with the feminine in an outdated 'heroic' way and running the risk of a primitive, macho approach which denigrates women (ibid.: 70–1). Instead, the split between 'men's pain and men's power' (ibid.: 15) can help address the question of what meanings we might derive from the gender splitting referred to earlier in this chapter.

In trying to understand 'how things are changing' in gender relations, the place of 'phallus' as a signifier of masculine ascendency and identification is important (a beanstalk linking boy–man, and son–father). For Clare (2001: 1) 'the dying phallus' is exposed as the increasingly redundant archetype of male power behind a heterosexual man's fixation on his manhood (the size of his penis and his sexual prowess), where the woman he is with becomes the (sometimes abused) object which allows him to experience his power.

The 'phallus' has of course a key role in psychoanalytic theory. Its place in the framing of psychosexual development is pivotal to Freud's analysis of what makes the paths of boys and girls distinctive. The boy 'has' the phallus power, as represented by his penis – but also the fear of losing it (castration anxiety). The girl does not have the phallus and develops envy of its possession by the boy via his penis (Freud, 1920/1991). Lacan took on Freud's model and reworked the place of *phallus* as the signifier of the desire emanating from the Other, so that the woman finds herself having to deny the fullness of her femininity in order to provide a 'version' which will meet the desire of the man. In this way, she becomes phallus for the man. 'It is for what she is not that she expects to be desired as well as loved' (Lacan, 1966/1977: 24)

This links to some of the clinical material I will draw on in Chapters 4 and 5, where women and men realise they offer versions of themselves in order to try to meet the desires or expectations of the other. However, Lacan is obviously referring to unconscious patterns here, when he asserts that 'phallus' symbolises not just penis but also clitoris and that in essence phallus represents *lack*: desire, by the very nature of relationship, cannot be fully met, because: 'The demands of each make the satisfaction both seek impossible' (Sarup, 1992).

Lacan's clear implication that men and women do *not* complement one another at a fundamental level is a healthy counterbalance to the dreamy notion that women represent the 'other half' of men and vice versa, an illusion Jungians can be drawn towards. While the alchemy of heterosexual relationships may enable some features to fulfil a sense of complementarity for the other, the underlying differences between the two create rough edges and conflicts. The phallus could be seen in this sense as an image of unfulfillable desire (unconscious), and demand (conscious), for *full complementarity*.

Clare's reference to the decline of the import of phallic representations of power has, he argues, profound implications for the place of men in western societies. As he puts it, 'The very traits which once went to make us the men we think we are and would like to be – logical, disciplined, controlled, rational, aggressive – are now seen as the stigmata of deviance' (Clare, 2001: 68).

Clare's discussion stems from two main critiques. The first scrutinises arguments that how men 'are' can be simplified as arising purely from the presence of testosterone as a neurobiological driver for aggression, sexual domination, violence and competitive or warlike behaviours (ibid.: Ch. 2). Clare argues that research in this area, and on differences in the female and the male brain is inconclusive. Instead he argues that 'the interaction of man and society' (ibid.: 37) plays a key role in perpetuating the myth that men are biologically primed to be violent. Socialisation is suggested as a generally unhelpful influence on the formation and living out of a man's identity.

Second, he argues that the identity, role and place of men in westernised society is in a kind of freefall with serious impacts on the health and self-esteem of men, the duration and quality of their relationships with women, and the well-being of children. His argument is not one-sided though: he recognises the wearisome ways in which outmoded patriarchal structures and attitudes perpetuate the ways men conduct their lives, often struggling to relate to family life and express feeling, while investing their sense of self in work or competitive (e.g. sporting) activity away from home – not to mention the prevalence of violent and sexual crime among the male population. As with Madame Raveskaya, Clare recognises how the male 'problem' gets reflected in women: 'What men hate in women is that they represent an embodied reproach to man's idealisation of dead, impersonal things – the revolution, the corporation, the organisation – and abandonment of the personal and the life-giving' (Clare, 2001: 57).

Fundamentally, Clare asserts that the crisis which men as social, relational beings are experiencing needs to be made more conscious so that both genders can renegotiate around the domestic sphere and men can redefine their place in society. This is real 'territorial stuff', and applies in particular to what I argue is the matriarchal power relation in home life. However, although Lacan theorises that the demands men and women make on each other may mean we can never arrive at a perfect meeting of need and desire, the hard work involved in reworking such territorial dynamics can bear fruit and allow for the greater likelihood of relationships flourishing rather than imploding.

The gendered collective

As argued already, at the level of *collective* consciousness and unconscious-ness there is a process by which gender identification acquires real power, in turn influencing gendered experiencing of difference. Individually, though, when we get up close to it, 'gender' can seem like illusion. It can then slip through our fingers when we try to grasp it, or become a set of debilitating myths we want to angrily consign to the dustbin of history.

So, I propose there is a layer of collective reality to gender difference which becomes less tangible the closer we get to it in our personal rumina-tions and relations. I will consider the implications of this for two of Jung's key original formulations: the *transcendent function* and *anima–animus*, and then propose a model for visualising how the gender dichotomies arising may play out in relation to a Jungian 'model of the psyche'.

Immanence and transcendence

My deliberations on the archetypal influence of gendered 'basic splits' on inner process leads me to the view that Jung's formulation of the *tran-scendent function* does not take the influence of the *immanent* fully enough into account to describe how change occurs. The location of the transcen-dent in collective patriarchal patterns and the sense of its presence being more associated with how *men* operate was something Jung subscribed to (1953/1966: paras 306–28) and implies he saw change and growth as inevitably upward, or forward-moving, in its nature.

That is not to say, of course, that he downplayed the value of the feminine. Instead, the feminine had a pivotal role in addressing the imbal-ance in the modern psyche, as Jung (ibid.: 306–27) perceived it. This imbalance, arising from an overemphasis on scientific methodology as the source of truth, the raising up of rationality and the limitations of the hero myth (with its counterproductive emphasis on the need for the masculine to 'conquer') results in a kind of withering away of the health of the psyche.

Disconnection from the fullness of the instinctive depths and the range of expressions of self come to be a hallmark of this crisis of being. More than this, Jung is referring to a crisis in the masculinised, post-Christian psyche of western man. Jung came to recognise the need for a reconnection with the 'goddess' of the feminine in order to revitalise the fading numinosity of Christian symbolism (Jung, 1952/1969). Here we see the collective parallel with his identification of *anima* as the 'source' of soul for men.

As Rowland has argued, Jung uses the *trickster* archetype to build his strategy for rescuing the hero archetype from its increasingly wooden place in myth-making for our times (Rowland, 2005: 186–91). Jung identified the trickster as not just the mischief-maker who unlocks the change process but also as having the capacity to transform 'his' own sexual identity, suggesting that he can change into a woman and a mother (Jung, 1954/ 1968: para. 472). This is not the hero of yore – the knight who slays the dragon and wins the princess, or the outlaw who defends the lives and values of Christian civilisation.

In our story, Jack is maybe a step nearer to trickster than to hero, as he is just a boy and only becomes resourced to outwit the giant through the culturally counterintuitive step of selling the last object of value belonging to his mother for a handful of beans. His heroism arises through being willing to 'trick' his foe rather than conquer him face to face. He is able to destroy the giant by coaxing the latter out of the world 'up there' and onto the bridge into mundane reality represented by the beanstalk. The archetypal 'giant' of the tyrannical father, the abusive senex figure, is literally brought down to earth and killed by being exposed to the wounded reality he has created by killing Jack's father.

The significant parallel with Jung's theme of the feminine healing the masculine via the trickster is evident, and implies the importance of dethroning the overpowering and at times destructive phallus of patriarchal western culture. The boy's positive anima – or, as I will come on to characterise it, *alive* version of anima ('erosima') – has enough energy and guile to do this.

This last point needs to be considered in the light of the problem inherent in Jung's formula for the psychic renewal of western civilisation: his clear implication that the feminine has a crucial role but that this is *in the service* of resolving a crisis in a predominantly masculine world, for example through offering access to a more pluralistic and relational way of being that the culture it has already defined itself to be. This raises the question, as Rowland puts it: 'Can modernity be healed by, in some sense at least, standing still?' (op. cit.: 320).

Jack's capacity as a boy to dethrone the tyrannical masculine suggests an emphasis on the resolution of the 'problem' of one-sided masculinity through trusting in the presence of the trickster to move between male– female, *anima–animus*, and free up the alchemy of this, rather than seeing the feminine or anima energy as being a kind of *antidote* to imbalance in the masculine. This sort of archetypal 'problem' gets addressed through drawing on something in the masculine 'I' of Jack which is able to let go of normative attitudes associated with the hero, intermingled with a trusting of the value of the feminine (as personified by the transactional value of the cow, the fateful revelations and encouragement of the fairy, and the benevolent protection of the giant's wife).

So, rather than 'the feminine' being there to 'sort out' the problem of modernity, what happens between Jack and the giant implies that deep change in our collective and individual expressions of being human can come through 'tricking' ourselves out of fixed ways of looking at ourselves and each other. This thought leads me to query the exclusiveness of Jung's most prominent formula for how change can come about – the transcendent function (Jung, 1916/1969).

This query arises from the sense that this formulation depends on the same need for the feminine to provide the *eros* missing from masculinised western culture, as perceived by Jung. Transcendence of this impasse via the confrontation of the masculine *by the feminine* is the only way forward for Jung. There may be an internal logic to this route towards resolution but it leaves out other ways in which meaningful change can happen; for example, that the original state of play could not, of itself, provide a solution without this encounter happening.

So, the immanence of the internal or external situation I find myself in cannot, of itself, provide the answer to whatever psychic tension or dilemma I am faced with – there has to be a splitting into opposites, a wrestling of these together, then a waiting for the new to emerge. I suggest, though, that *some* intrapsychic as well as real-life situations may require this approach, while other situations require a more mindful and less active approach. This is the approach of *wu-wei* (allowing the process), of staying with not-knowing, of silence. There is a focus on the here-and-now; the time and place we are in, not where we could be; staying with the *immanent* rather than trying to activate the *transcendent* – or maybe activating the latter by properly honouring the former.

The *immanent function* comes into play when we allow ourselves to stay put and not try to force change that is not ready to happen. This is not just another way of talking about *nigredo* – the darkest hour before the dawn – it is saying that change does not have to take a noticeably active form. It can be the careful acceptance of how things are, the willingness to stay and work on a relationship, or the acknowledgement of a need to accept the limitations found in any life. Change of different sorts – psychological, spiritual – can then happen. The formulation for *the immanent function* is:

1   I notice something in me is pushing for change.
2   I 'look' closely (immanently), with this feeling without acting on it.
3   I remain mindful but inactive in other ways with it, noticing how it evolves, considering psychological, spiritual and ethical implications.

There is overlap with the *transcendent function* here, as this often involves allowing change rather than forcing it. The difference, I suggest, is in *attitude* – with the *immanent function* we are, like in an Eastern religious attitude, just staying with what we experience of a feeling or a thought, not intending an action or outcome to arise out of it.

The other dimension of working with the *immanent* relates to *shadow*, and not reaching for the *transcendent* as a way of avoiding our own messy, dirty stuff or what we are fearful of. Instead, the *immanence* of the inner or outer problem is walked towards, not away from. This formulation offers a counterbalance to the one-sided belief that life is dominated by action, change and separation. Staying with and waiting on what is in front of us are features of the *immanent* and flesh out options for our relationship to the future: stay on the ground, go up into the air, or move comfortably between the two. Like many things worth doing in life, the latter takes practice, but eventually moving between the two can become a 'both' rather than an 'either-or'. The beanstalk represents this potential to bridge the *transcendent* and the *immanent*.

This possibility hangs between the perpetuation of the *immanent*–female versus the *transcendent*–male gender equation. Here a woman naturally embraces, even *creates* the *immanent*, e.g. in the way she can literally 'give birth' to the here and now (and what is more immanent than a newborn baby?). Likewise, a common assertion I hear in the consulting room, from women in heterosexual relationships, is that male partners do not focus enough on what happens at home, suggesting it is 'she' not 'he' who tends to hold more of the *immanent* in family life.

A man's tendency 'not to focus on home' points to a closer embrace of *transcendence*: to look outwards, upwards and forwards rather than at what is going on right here, right now. This links to the speculation that men are more likely to be one step in the future, 'waiting to become', and they may be more prone to a sense of discontinuity between present and future, struggling to manifest what belongs in the present, rather than averting their gaze from it – 'it' taking many forms but most obviously 'home'.

For intimate relationships, this juxtaposing of *immanent* versus *transcendent* realigns the balance between holding, preserving and nurturing relationships and changing, transforming or ending them. It values the psychological significance of both for better understanding our responses to being in relationship. It also represents an attempt to provide a more pluralistic and fluid way of thinking about change at both collective and individual levels, allowing for development to happen in an 'either/or' (transcendent or immanent) or 'and/both' way – with the latter a development on from the former.

Gender complexity as emergent

There is a link worth drawing out here to the scientific and philosophical concept of 'emergence'. Emergence theory suggests that 'systems are emergent when activity or behaviour that lie on one scale produce patterns of behaviour on a more complex scale' (Solomon, 2007: 280). This observation, applied to the internal workings of male–female relationships, speaks to an apparently growing momentum in the diversification and complexity of being male or being female, with more roles having an interchangeable quality, and the freeing up of the right to express sexuality, or even change sex.

The historically predictable male–female relational dyad is evolving into a more complex, emergent level of relational possibilities, where a range of ways of thinking about gender – social constructivist, feminist, archetypal, neurobiological, relational – contribute. Another key factor in this emergent 'cocktail' are the respective 'territories' of women and men – areas of influence on how each gender responds to the world around them, and on how they identify with their gender. These territories have been established historically through a range of societal and archetypal influences. This includes tendencies for more established *immanent* (women) and *transcending* (men) ways of perceiving and relating, including still influential role templates which we might find ourselves slipping into.

These 'territories' evade close definition and are usually unconscious, apart from when we turn and notice these influences on our gendered sense of self. The screen between them and our conscious awareness is what stops us from finding a more satisfactory formulation for gendered relating. The power of these 'territories' is fuelled by the collective quality of them, and the way group male and female behaviours and attitudes seem to become more distinct and polarised than those found in individual men and women. The emergent level arises from what happens when the hidden territory comes into view (like a kind of pre-conscious) and intermingles with our individual experience of 'being a man or a woman'. These considerations will be factored into the model offered below, after some necessary reflections on Jung's initial *anima–animus* formulation and its place in this model.

Experiencing *anima* and *animus*

While Jung's prizing of feminine, soulful, *anima* qualities for men reflected the beauty of this idea, his awkward development of the idea of *animus* in women – in its negative form presenting as judgemental and illogical (Jung, 1953/1966) – has tarnished the conceptual framework he built around this dyad. However, it provides a valuable clue in making us aware of the tendency in the human psyche to not be able to (or choose not to?) 'see' the gendered other in a clear or balanced way. In this respect, the 'screen' which blocks the view into the 'territory' of who a man or woman really is is provided by the equivalent of the workings of what Jung labelled *negative animus* (i.e. the tendency to make hasty and imbalanced judgements). When we overgeneralise about the other gender (e.g. 'men never help around the house' or even 'all men are bastards'; or 'women cannot read maps' or even 'all women are sluts') and make derogatory or even sexist statements about them, this tendency is at work, leaving us struggling to see what is really going on, individually or collectively.

This leaves us unable to see what aspects of being a man or being a woman really are *shared*, or *different*. So, in the model, not seeing (negative) and seeing (positive) are seen as deriving from Jung's ideas on *animus* but they apply as much to a male *collective* capacity for prejudice or skewed thinking as much as anything women, *collectively*, might fall prey to. I ascribe new terms to make this distinction between 'not seeing' and 'seeing': *thanimus* (after *thanatos* – Greek for 'death' – combined with *animus*) and *erosimus* (after *eros* – the life instinct – plus *animus*).

The flip side of this is that, collectively, *anima* becomes associated with *connection*; where there is a positive, warm, sometimes erotic, engagement between men and women this arises from positive *anima*: *erosima*. Where the connection breaks down, this emerges from a more negative *anima*, which I am terming *thanima*, and the gender electrics either short-circuit or flip over into a negative charge. Again I am using this reading of negative *anima* collectively to name how relations between men and women generally either flow well (*erosima*) or do not (*thanima*).

The ways I am proposing to utilise *anima–animus*, therefore, are twofold: the first has a more *collective* (not *individual*) resonance and involves a correspondence to the trend in post-Jungian (Mathers, 2001: 85–6) circles to utilise Jung's notion of *syzygy*, and yoke together the two as available to both women and men (e.g. *anima* as soul and eros in both men and women).

This enables the use of *negative animus* (*thanimus*) as that which creates the blocks and stereotyping prejudices around the 'screen' between *collectively inspired* perceptions and attitudes towards the other gender, and *positive animus* (*erosimus*) as having the potential to enable us to properly 'see' one another – men really 'seeing' women and vice versa. It may be that the screen is lowering in this era of more open perspectives on what women and men can be and do.

Anima in this reading comes to represent collective influences on relationship, so where there is a general cultural influence of 'disconnect' in male–female relating then *thanima* (*negative anima*) is at work, such as when there seems to be a significant degree of relationship breakdown across a society. Where this is showing signs of repair then one could say *erosima* (*positive anima*) is having an influence.

The other way of using *anima–animus* is at the individual level. I believe that there is real value in holding onto Jung's original formula at this level, not because it does not have its flaws (and embarrassing ones at that) but because valuable nuances and possibilities are lost if we ascribe the yoked *anima–animus* in a blanket way to the individual experiencing of both men and women. This latter approach is certainly safer as it avoids confronting the prejudices and mismatches of Jung's original model, but it runs the risk of failing to honour the real possibility of distinctions between men and women in how they perceive and relate.

A gendered model of the psyche – principles

My approach to establishing this model involves taking Jung's map of the psyche and reworking it with further gendered aspects. This task could easily fall into a hyper-intellectualised attempt to reify the 'presence' of gender experiencing, and concordance or difference, in the human psyche. A more productive, not to mention *real*, approach is to keep all aspects of the psyche *active*. So, for example, when one is speaking of 'the self' it is 'as a verb rather than a noun' (Young-Eisendrath, 2004: 5). I 'self' when I move into active, authentic engagement with life, rather than the *self* 'making' this happen. That is not to say that this purposive centre of who we are or the other archetypes of the psyche identified by Jung – ego, persona, shadow, *anima* and *animus* – cease to have an archetypal *presence* in our unconscious; it is more a recognition that these live through our feelings, thoughts, instincts, intuitions and actions, through what we do, how we relate and the workings of our inner world (dreams, active imagination etc.).

The same principle applies to 'gender experiencing'. We express our own gendered dimensions of who we are – and the more conscious we are of them the less the risk of the more problematic aspects of them happening *to* us, in the way Jung described a complex gripping or 'having' us (Jung, 1934/1969: para. 253). That way, the influence of social and archetypal imprinting on how we are as a woman or as a man gets filtered by our awareness and then lived out *in our own way*, rather than acting like a microchip in a computer which determines what we will do.

The second principle which informs this model refers to the unconscious, 'territorial' level to being a woman or being a man, which is based on thousands of years of evolution of *collective* gender difference, plus the emergent influence of *individual* variation. This acts as a backdrop to our struggles with gendered relating, rather than as a determinant of 'what must happen' in our relationships and roles.

This principle describes areas of gendered experiencing which may be peculiar to, or preponderantly more prevalent for, women or men. It also leaves the possibility for the unknown – what we do not understand or 'see' about distinctions between being a man or a being woman. These hard-to-define territories operate behind a kind of 'screen' between what we see of our own identity and what we cannot see (or can only see dimly). This approach recognises how centuries of cultural conditioning may have shaped what emerges from 'behind the screen'. It also does not rule out the opposite – that the cultural to and fro between feminine and masculine may be a product of a genuine struggle between deep archetypal formations of the masculine and the feminine – father (sky) and mother (earth).

It seems likely that we use the 'screen' between our individual gendered identity, and the more archetypal versions of masculine and feminine, to avoid something elemental in ourselves which might overwhelm us if we do not defend against it – the uncontained, primitive expression of our human, sexed (male or female) nature. So, we sublimate (Carlson, 1990: 549), those aspects of our gender identity which may have socially unacceptable sexual and aggressive aspects (e.g. converting male aggression into tribal sporting activity and affiliations), possibly burying valuable unlived aspects with them.

I am also thinking here of Jung's formulation on ego and self, i.e. our ego will choose whether or not it truly listens to the deep, purposive, guiding of self, or whether it ploughs its own, risky furrow (growthful and/or destructive). In respect to gender we are driven by biological and deep psychological factors; *and* we also have a choice as to how we live our lives as man or woman. The former has some 'self' qualities – there are biological and psychological potentialities just 'there' to live out as men or women. We still, though, have a choice in what we do with at least some of these powerful influences.

It also seems that there is something protective going on here, as if the visceral sexual and aggressive manifestations of our gendered instincts could otherwise overwhelm us and our capacity for relationship. We could also fall into the 'static' masculine and feminine highlighted by Hill (1992: 5) as a way of trying to deny the instinctive power of these manifestations. The screening off of these aspects of 'archetypal gendering' helps form our socially 'acceptable' identity but may stop us getting into balanced or 'right' relation to the presence of our own gender and that of the 'other' gender.

The key thing for us as individual human beings, I suggest, is to distinguish between our felt sense of gendered experiencing (what it feels like to be a man or a woman) and what might programme us into operating in a socially and historically constructed 'gendered' way. As with all unconscious processes, when we do not notice what is influencing us, difficulties can arise. When we *do* notice shadowy aspects, we can actively work with unresolved tensions inherent in gendered *reality's* intertwining with gendered *illusion*. This intertwining reflects the double bind with fantasy, imagination and illusion: we can get trapped in versions of 'reality' which oppress us – or we can draw on them to consciously enrich our humanity.

Inter-gender and interpsychic gender experiencing: a model

This model includes aspects of gendered 'being', such as the 'screen' alluded to and my adaptation of *anima–animus*. It reflects how gender difference becomes more influential at a collective level and more illusory at an individual one, and how ego functioning as a woman or as a man includes *personas* we adopt and our capacity to notice *shadow*. Our conscious experiencing gets influenced by what is 'behind the screen' in *male* or *female* territory, for example *puer–senex* (men) and *puella–wise woman* (women)

Table 2.1 The Jungian model of the psyche as filtered through gendered
experiencing

INDIVIDUAL PSYCHE	HIGHER GENDER ILLUSION	LOWER GENDER DIFFERENCE
MEN	**ARCHETYPAL**	**WOMEN**
'What being a man is like'	Ego	'What being a woman is like'
	'Being-in-the-world'/persona	
	Erosimus ('seeing' the other gender) (c)	
	Struggle with continuity/discontinuity (between*)	
	Personal shadow	
————SCREEN————	Thanimus ('not seeing') (c) ————SCREEN————	
Erosima/Thanima (i)		Erosimus/Thanimus (i)
Male territory	**Shared/overlapping territories**	Female territory
puer–senex*		puella–old woman*
	Erosima or Thanima (c)	
	(men and women in, or not in, good relation)	
———————————————————self———————————————————		
Transcendence ——————————————— Immanence		
	Transcendent vs Immanent functions	
	Shared archetypal territory	
Archetypal masculine ——————————————— Archetypal feminine		
COLLECTIVE PSYCHE	**HIGHER GENDER DIFFERENCE**	**LOWER GENDER ILLUSION**

(i) = individual
(c) = collective

archetypal polarities unconsciously influence how '(dis)continuous' our sense
of self is. *Anima and animus* collectively interplay with both genders but, like
Jung, I see *anima (erosima/thanima)* as more powerfully constellated individually in men and *animus (erosimus/thanimus)* as more influential for
women than *anima*. These influences are elucidated in the following chapters.

Concluding comments

The discussion has mapped out ways in which gender can be conceptual-
ised, and I have begun to sketch a post-Jungian model for describing its

meanings and influences. A distinction between 'women's territory' and 'men's territory' has been made, to denote the possibility of difference: archetypal, historical, cultural – whether constitutional or socially constructed. This will help us think about where acknowledging difference has value or not.

Acknowledging the 'unknown' dimension of what we mean by 'gender' is vital. What Foucault (1992: 10–11) calls 'arts of existence' – valuing the work involved in staying with difficulties or contradictions – applies particularly here. This chapter has, I hope, illustrated the scale of the challenge involved in pinning down what 'gender' is. One could concretise it in neuroscience, or deconstruct it in feminist and postmodern discourse, but neither suffices by itself. Rather than trying too hard to define 'gender', acknowledging its pervasive influence on how we live feels a more pertinent reference point for exploring it.

Chapter 3

Gender electrics: Eros, thanatos and currents from the past

The unconscious is the ever-creative mother of consciousness
(Jung, 1954: para. 207)

Relationships can get caught up in misunderstanding, disappointment and hostility, as well as opening avenues for expressing loving care, desire and close connection. There is a 'third' area between women and men (or in same-sex relationships) where any or all of these things may occur. This area is a living alchemical presence which interlocks with, but also constellates something additional to, the relational dyad.

This parallels the way the space between psychotherapist and patient, as described by Ogden (1994), acts as an 'analytic third', or becomes Jung's 'third' in the analytic relationship, constellating a new presence alongside the conscious and unconscious processes of each of them (Marshak, 1998: 59). Working from the premise of a 'relational third' between partners in close relationships, this book attempts to peel back the layers of this domain in forming, experiencing and ending relationships. In this chapter I tentatively construct a model for understanding where the early development and experiencing of males and females may accord, or diverge, in ways which can have profound impacts later on this relational 'third area'.

The area I am describing is an influential, shared state of unconsciousness, informed by Jung's borrowing of Levi-Bruhl's *participation mystique* (1912/ 1952) – although this usage has been criticised regarding the relationship between subjective experiencing and objective reality (e.g. Anderson, 1999). Klein (1946) designated this concept as projective identification. We put aspects of ourselves we unconsciously want to be rid of into the other, who feels and acts them out for us. Or it could be described in *anima–animus* terms as projection of negative or positive versions of these contrasexual 'inner figures' into the other.

Jung describes projective identification in alchemical terms:

The doctor becomes affected, and has as much difficulty in distinguishing between the patient and what has taken possession of him as
has the patient himself . . . The activated unconscious appears as a
flurry of unleashed opposites (such as hate and love) and calls forth an
attempt to reconcile them so that, in the words of the alchemists, the
great panacea, the *medicinia catholica*, may be born.

(Jung, 1954/1966a: para. 375)

He proposes that projective identification – within a relational context –
can have a purposive function:

I do not, of course, mean the synthesis or identification of two individuals, but the conscious union of the ego with everything that has
been projected into the "You". Hence wholeness is the product of an
intrapsychic process which depends essentially on the relation of one
individual to another. The relationship paves the way for individuation
and makes it possible, but is in itself no proof of wholeness.

(Jung, ibid.: n. 16)

However, this depends on a person coming to see what it is they are
projecting so powerfully into the other, and then owning and integrating
these contents. So often in relationships things get stuck because either, or
both, partners do not get to this point. This is where couples therapy can
have such a valuable role to play.

When projected aspects of ourselves we prefer not to acknowledge are
unconsciously 'put into' the other, then 'I' cannot see 'you' fully because all
I can see are the projected, underdeveloped aspects of me in your perceived
feeble, irrational or unreasonable behaviours. These projections have a
shadow quality to them, and one question I want to hold onto is whether
shadow could be said to have a *gendered* quality at key points of difference
or tension in close relationships between men and women. This relates to
the idea I introduced in Chapter 2 of there being distinct *female* and *male*
'territories' which get polarised in such moments.

I want to highlight the influence of these 'territories' in the developmental
paths of girls and boys as they travel through puberty and adolescence to
become women and men, with their different rates and foci of maturation
provoking reactions and projections. Likewise these 'territories' may show
up in how the counterpoint of *immanence* and *transcendence*, already
alluded to, gets bounced between men and women at points of significant
tension in relationships.

More potentially life-enhancing connections may be made between men
and women, or boys and girls, but the unconsciousness of the third area
between them may block access to these through gendered forms of *shadow*.
This is nothing new in terms of Jung's emphasis on our needing to notice

what of us we may 'give up' to the gendered other. In his often essentialist frame of reference this might refer to a man's soulful (*positive anima*), loving, relational characteristics and potentialities being projected into an idealised woman, or a woman's wisdom (*positive animus*), objective insights and creativity getting 'put into' the idealised man (Jung, 1953/1966).

So, our relationships give us the chance to help each other notice blind spots arising from our *shadow*; we can hold parts of the other for them while they notice, wrestle, and hopefully take ownership of them. Like Buber's (1923/2004) 'I–Thou' relationship, this is a full, vivid relationship to another which enables each individual to see and confront themselves via both *really seeing* the other, and being able to withdraw and own their projections. Here, the unconscious 'third' between a man and a woman has a more fruitful, purposive quality.

A post-Jungian developmental approach to gender

Approaching the construction of a framework for understanding man–woman relating based on a developmental model requires a heavy dose of caution, and attention to the problems inherent in trying to schematise the often fluid and opaque delineations around gender and sex. It also requires a sound basis for hypothesising about what might be shared and what may be different.

The attempt to construct this acts as a crucible for an alchemical struggle between essentialist and constructivist ways of looking at gender. The ways in which constructivist can become essentialist almost without us noticing, and vice versa, have already been touched on in Chapter 2 and can be seen in terms of Jung's *enantiodromia* principle, derived from the pre-Socratic Heraclitus (Kahn, 1979).

I hold an awareness of this as consciously as I can without becoming bogged down in anxieties about being too essentialist in my theorising. My aim is to fashion something authentic and credible about gendered development from frameworks such as Freud's psychosexual model (1920/1991) and Klein's (1946), Winnicott's (1962), and Lacan's (1966/1977) reworking of this. I will also refer to the valuable commentaries of Kristeva (2004), Chodorow (1978), and Benjamin (1988), particularly in how they resituate the places of girls and boys, as against more phallocentric models of early development. The work of Fordham (1957) and other post-Jungian thinkers will also be brought to bear on this enterprise.

If I get even part of the way in illuminating distinctions between the development of boys/men and girls/women, then I will have achieved something worthwhile with this book. The essentialist versus constructivist dichotomy will provide a valuable tension between the fixed and the variable, the old and the new, the orthodox and the radical, which I hope can free up thinking about gender.

The working hypothesis here is that there may be some key differences between being a woman and being a man, for, as in any piece of research (and I see this book as research into ideas, information and phenomenological experiencing around gender), it helps the focus of the project to set up such a hypothesis and see if it stands up. However, I am not taking an overtly 'essentialist' position or intending to theorise from certain 'givens' about differences between man and woman, though the biological 'givens' around reproductive and other body/brain-sex distinctions have to be given their place.

Conceptually, I prefer to work with the idea of male and female 'territories' as it suggests there are two large but loosely boundaried psychological spaces which over many millennia have come to be associated with what is fundamental to the felt presence and expression of 'being a man' and 'being a woman'.

As mentioned earlier, these *may* be pictured as 'sky' for men and 'ground' for women, as implied by the mother left on the ground, and the boy up in the clouds in *Jack and the Beanstalk*. This female/ground and male/sky split may, as I have already argued, be to do with the masculine/ transcendent–feminine/immanent split inherent in the Abrahamic religions. However, these two 'territories' could equally be just as well portrayed as sitting alongside each other, like two halves of an old country which have evolved into two separate but still intimately linked states.

Some definitions and assignations of 'being female' and of 'being male' can be helpful in distinguishing between what it is like 'being a woman' as compared with 'being a man'. Highlighting these distinctions can help identify what may be shared, or may free float, between men and women. This project therefore hopes to make a contribution to the valuing of these aspects and their freer availability in relationships.

This enlarging shared territory between men and women in westernised societies is more than just border territory; it is more like a shared state or country forming in the midst of the conjoined male and female territories. This 'new state', to use geo-political terminology, has far to go before it finds its natural boundaries, or forms a stable relationship with the two old countries it is emerging from.

It is also important to acknowledge the significant diversity in gender relations across and within westernised societies. There remains a heavy influence from less reconstructed traditions, intermingled with overt attempts at establishing more 'androgynous' approaches.

Influences on the developmental model

Classical Jungian perspectives are not often associated with the construction of detailed developmental models. Jung was generally less interested in outlining specific steps in life and more interested in archetypal patterns than, say, the stages in psychosexual (Freud, 1920/1991), cognitive (Piaget, 1955) and gender identity (Kohlberg, 1966) development.

As Levinson *et al*. (1978: 4) argue, Jung's developmental interests settle more comfortably around adulthood than childhood, with his emphasis on the midlife shift, after which, for Jung (1933), a 'turning inwards' after the extraverted work of the first half of life begins. However, there are aspects of the *anima–animus* and *shadow–persona* archetypal polarities, for example, which lend themselves to a more schematic utilisation.

As Main (2008) points out, there has been a long and lively debate in the Jungian world about 'development', where this term is applied broadly to refer to ways of understanding how we come into the world, grow and become adults. The tensions between what Samuels (1985) labelled the Classical, Developmental and Archetypal schools of analytical psychology make it possible to view childhood through a range of lenses: mythological, archetypal and prospective influences intertwining with whatever psychosexual, neurological and cognitive patterns may also be at work.

This reflects my own approach. I recognise how multifaceted the development of the individual is, both in terms of what may 'unfold' from the innate features of a child at birth and in how relational and wider environmental factors can interfere or redirect human experience and growth. In the light of this, the valuing of complexity is important, as is 'the view of the psyche or its development as a self-organising or self-system' (Main, 2008, 76).

So, in this chapter, a post-Jungian take is offered on the developmental, or unfolding, processes (whichever end of the telescope one wants to use to look at them) and the threads which may inform these – in particular the evolving presence of *anima–animus* as the earlier stages of the life cycle proceed. I will use the terminology already introduced in Chapter 2 to assist in this task – applying Freud's notions of life instinct (*eros*) and death instinct (*thanatos*) so that *anima* gets characterised as either the life-enhancing and at times erotically tinged *erosima*, or as the resistant, hostile or deadening *thanima*; while *animus* is likewise split into *erosimus* and *thanimus*.

This approach is set out with reference to consonant stages and concepts from models already alluded to. I will refer to Erik Erikson's (1950) stage polarities and to Levinson's model for the life cycles of men (Levinson *et al*., 1978) and women (Levinson and Levinson, 1996). I also refer to Kohlberg's model for developmental stages in gender identity (1966) for its obvious relevance but also to provide, alongside Piaget (1955), a recognition that the dynamics of development do not happen in a hermeneutics based only on unconscious processes, which depth psychology sometimes runs the risk of implying. Cognitive and social processes, with their emphasis on *conscious* awareness and activity, are also key aspects of gendered development.

Kohlberg's 'gender consistency' theory defers to Piaget's stages of cognitive development (1955), such as in the latter's view that the child won't have grasped the principle of 'conservation' (i.e. things do not change even if they appear to look different) until it is seven years old. Full gender consistency is attained around then, so if a boy has long hair (contradicting social convention), he is still understood to be a boy. The conclusion arrived at by a child at an earlier stage would be 'long hair equals girl' even if the hair belonged to a boy.

This process, for Kohlberg, begins with an emerging awareness from around the age of two that 'I am a boy' or 'I am a girl' ('Gender Identity'). From around three, it is understood that gender remains fixed – girls realise they will grow up to be a woman, and boys realise they will grow up to be a man ('Gender Stability'). Then the stage which completes gender awareness ('Gender Consistency') follows from seven through to twelve.

It is pertinent to set these alongside Freud's psychosexual stages: Gender Identity parallels the Anal stage, when, as Erikson (1950) characterises it, there is a struggle for autonomy versus falling into shame or doubt; 'Gender Stability' arises as the child moves into the Oedipal struggle, which culminates at the end of the Phallic stage in either resolution of psycho-sexual identity or an unresolved, unstable sense of this; and 'Gender Consistency' more or less parallels the Latency stage, perhaps fixing the outcome of this struggle, plus the influences of social constructions of gender, into something more rigid and patterned.

Although cognitive models of development can seem somewhat pre-scriptive and limited in their recognition of the influence of unconscious forces, they provide an important rooting of developmental theory into the *thinking* and *perceiving* aspects of a child's development. It is also in this respect important to recognise what Mathers terms 'the Self's meaning-making cognitive ability' (Mathers, 2001: 216).

In other words, I am referring to the capacity of the deintegrative and re-integrative (Fordham, 1985) processes of the self to be consciously expressed in our information processing, perceiving and thinking. This informs how we may each wrestle with the tension inherent in our individual lived experience between the essentialist and the constructed versions of gender. This applies to young children, too, as they pass through overlapping stages of aware-ness, testing the reality of what they have been told 'makes' them a boy or girl, sometimes activating their 'Transcendent Function' (Jung 1916/1969) to help them make something new and individual from this tension.

The cognitive processing of what can be noticed around feeling, bodily sensation and instinct, combined with the impact of relationships and environmental factors, is very important in how we make sense of our gender identity. I propose to factor in the tension between cognitive, affec-tive, biological and other archetypal influences and describe what the outcomes of this struggle might be for differences or similarities in male–female experiencing of reality, and of relationships between them. If gender role is only a construct, for example, what dynamic forces might help sustain this? Likewise, if aspects of these roles are genuinely rooted in something deeper, how might we describe the archetypal forces – or differing 'territories' – this arises from?

This model is not 'integrative' as such, as the differing ways in which human development, and the intrapsychic and relational patterns associated with different stages of it, do not lend themselves easily to this. The purpose of the model, theoretically, is to pull in Jungian concepts in a way which could shed light on distinctions in gendered development.

The classical Jungian emphasis on archetypal presences can, I suggest, bring greater depth and colour to purely developmental schemas when this is used in an active way, e.g. with *anima* and/or *animus* actively constellating in our way of being at different stages, rather than being seen as fixed personalities of the psyche.

This more constructivist approach suggests that such 'figures' are manifestations of my engagement with self, others and the world, rather than autonomous characters which impact on me. This allows for their presence in the conventions of psychoanalytic- or object relations-based stages. They come in and out of them, sometimes decisively influencing what we 'do' with the changes we experience in and around us.

In this model, I will also refer to Lacan's pivotal psychoanalytic model (1966/1977) for understanding the roots of gender identity, so as to lay the foundations for a formulation of the proposed model for understanding how the paths of development between females and males may diverge. These will then be elucidated more fully in Chapters 4 and 5.

The health warning for this project is obvious but needs stating. The psychic contagion of stereotyping of men by women, and vice versa, has been highlighted already. It is pure *negative animus* territory. To take another central image used in this book, the 'giant' risk looms large over any attempt at delineating difference between men and women. In this sense it could evoke at worst a paralysing fear of persecution for 'saying the wrong thing'. On a less dramatic level, it leaves, as I can testify, a nagging anxiety that everything one tries to say about it is shadowed by a kind of self-conscious avoidance of shooting oneself in the foot. It is a giant which lumbers around in the background, occasionally threatening to slide down the beanstalk and 'name and shame' any hint of stereotyping.

Nevertheless, the value in opening up and speculating about possible differences in an informed and sensitive way, makes these anxieties worth living with. These could be characterised in me as a man as a fear of invoking *negative anima* (*thanima*) in how I write, and *negative animus* (*thanimus*) in women readers in particular. This fear, I suggest, may reflect the presence of recently established and highly charged taboos in western society about generalising about gender difference.

These taboos may be rooted in a fear that if debate about difference is given too much air to breathe then the hard won gains of feminism, and the fulfilment of a widespread valuing of pluralism and individual freedom in relationships, will be lost. If we accept that men and women are different in definable ways then won't the ghost of patriarchy rise up and drag us back into outdated modes of relating and perceiving?

In fact, it only seems to be in the populist publications of our times that this idea of difference is given room to breathe. *Men are from Mars, Women are from Venus* (Gray, 1992) is the obvious example of this. Its championing of difference may lapse into simplistic assertion about possible differences – e.g. 'Just as women are afraid of receiving, men are afraid of giving' (ibid.: 60) – but at the very least, its huge commercial success implies there is a widespread hunger to explain, or at least find a satisfactory story about, differences between women and men. This 'hunger' may well reflect a kind of collective brainwashing by the overarching social constructions of 'gender' which shape our environment. Or, it could also imply the presence of a well-founded collective *intuition* that there are real, but difficult to define, differences between who 'I' am as a woman or as a man. It is the presence of this second possibility which motivates the discussion.

This possibility in turn implies that this intuition is archetypal, i.e. something which we all carry with us. I speculate that this sense is present from birth, and our deep confusions about gender identity and difference arise from this sense of us 'not being able to put our finger on' it, but somehow 'knowing' it is there.

In this respect I would like to suggest something about how archetypes, especially as these apply to *process* or *life experiences*, influence our intuitions about ourselves. If archetypal influences carry any meaning in a gendered way – i.e. in some regards women and men are influenced in different ways by archetypal processes – then it plays out in our intuitive responses to each other, as well as in the inner patterns of expectation we may live by.

This point becomes more significant if one factors in the *possibility* that the archetypal intuitions of men and those of women may fundamentally differ in some respects. These differences inevitably can lead to disagreement and disappointment as well as a more nourishing sense of stimulation and complementarity. These 'gendered archetypal intuitions' *could* feed how women and men experience themselves (and life).

Arising from the discussions in the previous chapters there are three main areas in which I tentatively suggest women and men generally engage with life differently – based on my own experience as well as experiences conveyed to me by women and men (in clinical and other contexts). These are, I postulate, constellated in a long-lasting way by the archetypal, relational and environmental influences found in the different developmental paths taken by each gender. These areas of predominantly experienced differentiation – bearing in mind *individual* women or men may experience life in different, even opposite, ways – are:

- *Location in time and space*: Men *may* generally experience a more driven relationship to their 'becoming' complete and fulfilled in the future. This can lead to a sense of discontinuity where the 'felt sense' of the path they 'should' be on is not experienced in the present. On the other hand, the experience of being a woman may be more about being 'complete in the present'. There may also be distinctions in how space and location are experienced.
- *Ways of projecting*: The suggestion here starts from the classic formulation of Jung's (1953/1966) that men project their feminine aspects onto women (*anima* projection) and women project, via their *animus*, their masculine aspects onto men. However, I am interested in the possible differences in how this is 'lived out', how it is experienced, as this may well have a profound impact on how men and women experience 'otherness' or 'sameness' in each other.
- *Authority and personal power*: The differences in how men and women experience their own authority or lack of it have obvious environmental and social influences, such as long-established patriarchal ways of perceiving and organising society. However, I suggest that the ways a man might emasculate a woman's sense of her own power are different in a more fundamental 'territorial', maybe *archetypal*, way than how a woman might emasculate a man's sense of his own power.

I will trace back these proposed differences to formative developmental 'stages' or 'processes'. I use these terms loosely as it is not always helpful to assign fixed markers to human development. In this respect I appreciate the way Michael Jacobs (2006) has written about Freud's psychosexual stages as being more usefully seen as 'modes'. For example, adults can fall into a 'latency mode' when their capacity to learn or develop is stultified unconsciously by circumstances which reactivate the quality of experiencing they might have felt during certain periods of childhood.

In this respect the familiar Jungian notion of a complex – made up of constellating factors which incorporate early experience, archetypal factors and the current situation – relates to the possibility of so-called 'stages' of development being re-constellated by current circumstances. This is how negative *anima* (*thanima*) and *animus* (*thanimus*) may be brought to life in heterosexual relationships. A partner's behaviour and attitude re-constellating experiences of stuckness or rejection, say, from earlier in life can influence us to be hostile or withdrawn in the present if we do not consciously challenge such tendencies in ourselves. Whether it is possible to identify specifically *gendered* complexes which can be activated for men 'only' and for women 'only' *because of the presence of the gendered 'other'* is a speculative question which lies beneath this observation; a question to hold in mind even though a definitive answer is unavailable.

Mapping gendered development: From birth to the pubescent moment

The broad patterns of early development are set out in this section with reference to the developmental schemes of Freud's psychosexual model, Klein's radical adaptations to it, and Lacan's framework for describing the emergence of the child into the 'Symbolic Order', among others. This approach will lay the ground for incorporating *anima* and *animus* from a developmental perspective.

I start from the premise that when an infant is born, a girl or a boy has an unconscious awareness that *she* is either 'the same as' mother or *he* is not. I am suggesting this in respect to the way Klein (1945) postulates that the child (of either gender) is instinctively aware from birth of what formed them – i.e. the mother–father sexual union. She argued, based on her observations of the symbolic play of children (which carried hallmarks of destructive and sexual instincts) that Freud's theorising on the oedipal stage should apply right from the beginning of life. Likewise, I suggest this presence of the oedipal from the start strongly implies there is a felt difference in a girl's relation to mother, compared with a boy's relation to mother. This difference, I suggest, operates at many levels, but fundamentally it may be possible to speak of the main distinctions residing in the '*unconscious knowing*' and '*conscious experiencing*' of the individual. The possibility of the presence of this 'felt difference' resonates with ideas about how we represent and integrate the presence of significant others in our internal lives (Martin-Vallas, 2005).

Unconscious knowing

This term refers back to Klein's idea of the infant having a kind of archetypal (though she did not use this word) awareness within her or his inner phantasy world that they are the products of the union between mother and father. The oedipal struggle, with its emphasis on wrestling with the same-sex parent to try to 'win' exclusive union with the opposite sex parent is played out in Klein's formulation within the child's internal phantasy life (Klein, 1945).

In the unconscious life of the nascent infant, Klein suggests, the overwhelming aggressive and erotic energies present from birth get channelled into the intrapsychic relationship with introjected part-objects and later, whole-objects. So the infant's oedipal struggles with the internalised versions of the parents would be with, for the boy, the part-object of penis or whole-object of father; while for the girl it would be with the part-object of breast or whole-object of mother. In this sense, I am suggesting, there is a fundamental identification being made between girl–mother and boy–father. Although they are intrapsychically at loggerheads, it is their very similarity which generates this basic, defining, struggle: '*You are the same as me, so I must fight you to get the object you have union with.*'

Conscious experiencing

I also suggest, because of the nascent presence of the oedipal struggle in the newborn child, that bodily sensation and feeling may provide a degree of *conscious* experiencing of 'sameness' or 'difference'. This may be reinforced by the general differences (rougher/smoother or hairy/not hairy) often manifested between men and women.

When an infant boy reacts to the touch of his mother's fingers or lips, for example, this is infused with a different tone, a differing erotic or aggressive quality, compared with what a little girl may experience; because what the boy and girl are unconsciously seeking out in the contact with mother is fundamentally *different* – the boy seeks an eroticised union with her, while the girl seeks both full identification with what she represents as well as a kind of 'victory' over her in 'winning father'.

This formula works in reverse for the relation with father. It is worth noting the suggested ambivalence in the gender identification with the same-sex parent, as pointed out above, particularly in relation to how that might be *felt* and *sensed*: 'I am the same as you, and I want to *be* you; but feelings and sensations arising from your presence and touch also remind me I want to be me, and to have the object you have.'

This brings the power of *envy* into the equation. To want to destroy the good object (e.g. mother) because one can bear neither the possibility of someone else having her, or the knowledge she may derive pleasure from herself, generates, according to Klein, a cycle of phantasy: I feel envy; unconsciously I *destroy* mother; I believe I have destroyed her; I feel guilt; I seek reparation towards mother; I feel envy towards the restored introjected mother; I destroy her again; and so on (Klein and Riviere, 1937/1964). This cycle remains as an infant moves towards the depressive position, when she or he gradually realises mother is made up of 'good' and 'bad' rather than the previously split sense of the paranoid-schizoid position (Klein, 1946).

I want to suggest that envy may in subtle ways be directed differently by boys and by girls. Both, I would suggest, experience envy towards mother, as she is the object of adoration for both, as well as fear in respect to her overwhelming power to remove herself, or the part-object which is central to the early experiencing of the infant – the breast. However, I propose that the infant girl, following on from Kristeva (2004), has formed a bond with mother which in a way places her sense of self *inside mother* (i.e. inside her *introjected* mother as an object). Meanwhile, a boy's envy is more about the love and desire for the object from *outside* the introjected mother.

Map of gendered development (1): Birth to pre-pubescence

I will now lay out in diagrammatic form the proposed staged map for gendered development in order to further furnish my discussion. Having highlighted the value of Klein's location of oedipal energies at the start of life, I also stay with Freud in the sense of acknowledging his psychosexual stages as retaining value in helping us to outline the movement through, and beyond, broad stages of development. In turn, these refine the experience of the child in struggling with the 'real objects' – the parental 'giants' who are around them – and the meanings, desires and other responses evoked by them.

My proposed model illustrates commonalities as well as proposed distinctions between the developmental pathways of boys and girls. The place of *erosimus/thanimus* (girls) and *erosima/thanima* (boys) are highlighted as contasexual influences on the overall disposition of the psyche – i.e. as moving in either a life-enhancing or a 'deathly/depressed' way – rather than Jung's counterpointing of *eros* with *logos*.

Ideas from Winnicott, Kristeva and Fordham will be woven into the discussion arising from this model, which will focus particularly on pre-oedipal, oedipal and latency phases. The pubescent, later adolescent and early adult phases will be further explored in Chapter 6.

In laying out a schema with reference to Freud's psychosexual stages I recognise the problem inherent in Freud's model – the possible leanings towards assumptions about where the power in gender relations lies, i.e. with the male *phallus*. As Frosh puts it: 'Many masculinist assumptions are endemic to psychoanalytic theory itself, thus vitiating any claim it may have to give a gender-free account of sexual difference' (Frosh, 1994: 13).

However, Freud's model, with its 'masculinist' problematic, stands as a valuable reference point for wrestling with the problem of 'gendered paradigms'. It highlights how binaries between male and female experiencing can generate different 'positions' on developmental difference. This applies of course to me – my maleness generates a subjective thread to my theorising. This is a dimension of the model I have done my best to counter through the range of ideas I have applied, but remains an important consideration as I navigate the reader through my proposed developmental schema.

Birth to 18 months: The primary oedipal phase

Our coming into life and its link to mother is symbolised in a rich array of archetypal images and themes, well documented in Jungian (e.g. Neumann, 1955) writing. We cannot get into life without experiencing the pain and disorientation inherent in the initiation *in extremis* which the birth of a

Table 3.1 Map of gendered development (1): Birth to pre-pubescence

Birth–18 months/2	Late infancy 18 months/2–3	Arriving child 3–6	Latency 6–10	Pre-pubescence 10–11
		Male		
Gendered 'otherness' of mother	Envy	Peak of erotic bond to mother	Conscious: loyal to father Unconscious: desire mother	End of *anima* conflict results in
Embodied *anima*: Oral struggle	*Erosima and thanima* struggle re autonomy	*Oedipal erosima and thanima* struggle	Certainty of 'I as a boy'	1. Rebirth of *erosima* 'I can move ahead and relate and create' or
Shadow		Penis	*Anima* sleeps	2. Rebirth of *thanima* 'I am
Breast–anima +ve/–ve	Anus	Castration anxiety	Forming of identity and friendships with boys	stuck and cannot relate and create'
Envy: Erotic over relational		Vagina		
		Both		
Oral	Anal	Phallic	Libido falls into latency	End of early *anima* or
Early attachment-patterns	Early attachment-patterns	Oedipal conflict: *Collective animus*	Socialisation Same-sex friendships	*animus* conflict Emerging pattern ('set for life') of relating
Self de/re-integration	Self de/re-integration	*The law of the Father*		to self, others, time and space
Gender un-aware	**Has gender identity**	**Gender stability**	**Gender certainty**	**Gender consistency**
Trust vs mistrust	Autonomy vs shame and doubt	Initiative vs guilt	Industry vs inferiority	Identity vs identity diffusion (1)
Internal part/whole object relations	Anus	Penis Symbolic Order	No/little eroticised activity	Initiation rites

continues

human infant provides. The huge, almost apocalyptic, quality of this experience (Rank, 1993), perhaps comparable only to the similarly inscrut-able experience of *dying*, appears to render any question of whether this is experienced differently by a baby boy or a baby girl as rather facile.

It is worth holding this 'absurd' hint of a question in mind, however, in the light of the parallel 'unknown' question of whether a girl inside the womb might *in any way* experience this period of preparation for 'entering the world' differently to a boy?

Table 3.1 (continued)

Birth–18 months/2	Late infancy 18 months/2–3	Arriving child 3–6	Latency 6–10	Pre-pubescence 10–11
		Female		
Gendered 'sameness' of mother	Envy	Peak of erotic bond to father	Conscious: loyal to mother	End of animus conflict results in:
Embodied animus: Oral struggle	Erosimus and thanimus struggle re autonomy	Oedipal erosimus and thanimus struggle	Unconscious: desire father	1. Rebirth of erosimus 'I can move ahead and relate and create' or
Breast +ve/–ve			Certainty of 'I as a girl':	2. Rebirth of thanimus 'I am stuck and cannot relate and create'
Animus envy: Relational/ erotic	Anus	Penis Penis envy Vagina	Animus sleeps Identity and friends (girls)	

'Naive' questions like this are useful (however empirically 'unknowable' the answers may be) because they can draw out tensions inherent in our struggle to understand what may 'make' a boy or a girl, and I would invite you to notice your responses to them. Are the birth experiences of all infants more or less similar (taking into account all the frightening variables which can impact on a baby in the womb)? Or do the archetypal influences of the feminine and the masculine in any way intermingle with the balance of the 'X' and 'Y' chromosomes to impact on this? Does the passage into life get influenced by the quality of *anima's* presence for a boy baby, and likewise by the quality of *animus's* presence for the nascent girl?

Having flagged them up, I want to put these questions on the 'back burner' as we look at the pre-oedipal phase of infancy – in Freud's psycho-sexual terminology, the period incorporating the oral stage of 'taking in' of early experience, and the anal stage of withholding and expulsion. I will explore this and proceeding phases of human development in order to see if it is possible to gain a clearer picture of where some primitive sense of gendered identity may find its roots, referring again to Klein's theories on early infantile development to help flesh out at least the *possibility* of an instinctive presence of awareness of self as predominantly *male/female*.

I will also refer to Winnicott and his powerful evocation of how the newborn child experiences her or his environment, and the dangers of any sense of self being broken up or profoundly undermined by 'primitive agonies' (Winnicott, 1960), and consider whether 'good-enough mothering' has differing hallmarks for the care of infant boys as compared with girls.

Winnicott's model for how the infant deals with the gradual move from *absolute* to *relative* dependence (Winnicott, 1963) can be related to

Fordham's model of *the deintegrating self* (Fordham, 1985) and how the emerging 'way of relating' to objects such as mother or father (and the environment) may or may not differ between the infant girl and the infant boy. Lacan's 'mirror phase' (1966/1977a) will also be considered. His ideas on how we start from a distorted or disconnected sense of who we 'are' via our first encounters with the image of our body in reflection offers a valuable template for understanding the projections we produce about the other gender. Our image of self is based *on the reflection* more than who we really are, and so our gendered identity also gets heavily influenced through encounter with 'other' males/females who reflect our gender back to us.

Freud addressed the questions surrounding sameness and difference between development of baby boys and girls as a corollary of his theorising about the psychosexual basis of human psychological functioning. For Freud, there were significant commonalities. However, he viewed the way a small boy would unconsciously relate to his sexuality as being very different to how a small girl would, though the shared infantile aim lay in 'obtaining satisfaction by means of an appropriate stimulation of the erotogenic zone which has been selected in one way or another' (Freud, 1920/1991: 101). The whole *tone* of that search for getting this stimulation is reported by Freud as distinctive when it comes to male and female experiencing and activity. He proposed that 'the sexuality of most male human beings contains an element of *aggressiveness* – a desire to subjugate' (ibid.: 71).

Alongside this clear implication of male sexuality as aggressive in its expression, there is a focus on 'possession'; the boy is in possession of the penis – the physical and symbolic representation of sexualised phallic power. The corollaries of this – the boy's fear of castration, as well as the girl's envy of the boy's possession of the phallus – arise in proceeding psychosexual stages, but seem to stem from what Freud perceived as a split between the inherited unconscious experiencing of self for girls and boys from the beginning of life.

In the oral stage the exploration of one's thumb, mother's nipple or a blanket edge through sucking, rubbing, swallowing or expelling via the mouth incurs certain implied areas of difference, according to Freud. For the boy there may be a need to experience feelings of *subjugating* the object through the labial *possession* of it as, say, the nipple of his mother remains in his mouth and secretes the warm, filling milk. As Freud describes it, the emerging awareness of the sexual dimension of this experience for the infant and the satisfaction this brings separates itself from the hunger for nourishment (Freud, 1920/1991).

To take these themes of a need for *subjugation* and *possession*, one could suggest the foundation for a boy or man wishing for romantic and sexual relations with another is a craving for a return to the delicious feeling of being filled, complete, triumphant; a moment of transcendence even, as experienced in the *subjugation* and *possessing* of mother's nipple, breast and milk. *Erosima* is supremely alive in this moment as the infant boy repeatedly embraces and consumes the adored contrasexual *other* – a moment yearned for over and again throughout life.

Boys, girls and envy

Returning to the question of *envy*, I want to highlight the way Freud perceived its place in the psychosexual 'forming' of gendered identity. As indicated, this is overtly skewed towards the boy and away from the girl; the latter automatically envies the former's possession of the phallic prize – the penis. Freud even went so far as to suggest the sense of *lack* for the girl generates a castration complex, which is imbued by the absence of any vaginal sensation until puberty (Rycroft, 1995). This misapprehension seems to have been fuelled by societal incomprehensions about the nature of female sexuality, as well as about the potentialities inherent in women generally that were around in nineteenth and early twentieth-century Europe – an area Karen Horney (e.g. 1967) took Freud to task over.

The notion of penis envy is pivotal in Freud's model to the assignation of difference between female and male. The difference in the place of castration – of the penis, or what it represents symbolically (e.g. erotic pleasure generally, or a compulsion to prove they have a suitable substitute for the penis) – is part of this equation. It translates for boys more as dread about it happening, and in girls more as the sense it has already happened to them, and the *lack* they are left with.

Freud also asserted that, for the boy, a kind of envy would arise in relation to his growing awareness of the nature of the female body and a woman's capacity to bear children. The boy notices he cannot experience his body like a girl experiences hers, nor be the container from which the ultimate creation springs – a new human life – like a girl can. This pertains more to the boy's negative oedipal complex than the pre-oedipal phase of Freud's schema (Freud, 1924).

However, I am also incorporating Klein's way of looking at early unconscious processes. This concertinas all of Freud's stages into her initial phase of *birth to depressive position* (the attaining of a more balanced sense of mother and self as mix of 'good' and 'bad' via a reconciling of the splitting between *good breast–bad breast*). A boy may unconsciously envy 'what the girl possesses' from birth (and vice versa).

If these processes are translated into *anima–animus* language, penis envy (and her castration complex) could be seen as a girl's *thanimus* response to the lack of a phallus and the *eros* energy associated with it – an amalgam of feeling acutely what one does *not* have alongside anger towards what the other *does*. For the boy, there is a converse *thanima* anxiety about the feared loss of *eros* energy, which would follow on from castration, and the loss of the phallus.

Alongside Freud's original formulation, the seminal application of *envy* in a more general, pervasive way by Klein (1957) needs to be factored in. As well as perceiving the nature of penis envy as being more complicated than Freud suggested, Klein argued that envy itself is 'one of the fundamental and most primitive emotions' (Segal, 1979: 139), possibly an *a priori* potential presence in the psyche.

The baby realises that the source of her or his physical and emotional nourishment – mother's breast – is not in but outside of him or her, and this generates envy. The general equation here is that the infant child would rather destroy the good (part) object than live with its goodness being outside of her/his control. This apparently archetypal destructiveness, which operates in the child's inner world of phantasy (the 'ph' denoting Klein's emphasis on an inner world where part-objects like the breast, or whole-objects like mother, get introjected and wrestled with unconsciously), is for Klein a necessary stage towards the reparation with the inner mother which comes about after envy and gratitude have been allowed to struggle with one another before being adequately integrated. As implied, when envy is present to an excessive degree, it sets up a pathological difficulty. In classical Jungian language it is a complex with *thanima–thanimus* characteristics: defensive, hostile, judging and over-sentimental.

For the purposes of our discussion, a question is raised as to whether any of the ideas explored here can be reliably distinguished in gendered terms, i.e. whether there are unconscious processes which take distinctive forms in females as compared with males (or vice versa). Further inquiry needs to be made into how psychosexual and/or archetypal structures of 'becoming human' arise in infancy and whether there might be any reliable patterns which differentiate between boys and girls.

However, at this stage, the application of *eros/thanatos* to *anima–animus* is worth further consideration with respect to the notion of *envy*. As described, it may be useful to think of Freud's idea of a girl's penis envy (and her castration complex) as a hallmark of *thanimus* (negative *animus*), and the boy's castration complex as a reflection of *thanima* (negative *anima*). In both cases, *contrasexual* energy is experienced in a fearful and defensive way.

My suggestion is that the nature of the pervasive *envy* that Klein writes about may be influenced in its form and activity by *whether it is a girl, or a boy, who is unconsciously gripped by it*. The envious destructiveness of the boy towards the feeding breast is influenced by *thanima* to attack not just the loving, nourishing source in his phantasy, but also the more erotic dimensions of his relationship to mother, which her breast carries. The later complicated emotions of the love life of the adolescent and man are characterised by how this envy is channelled. So, if the envious attacks on mother's breast are so uncontained as to leave him with a powerful legacy of erotic (*eros*) and destructive (*thanatos*) unconscious activity, then after 'anima goes to sleep' (during the latency period of around six years through to puberty) she may well explode back into life in a similarly uncontained way when adolescence arrives. The energy which is generated by the 'storm' of these early envious attacks may return via highly charged sexual and/or aggressive acting out in the teenage years.

The pre-pubescent moment

Applying to both genders, 'the pre-pubescent moment' refers to the episode leading up to puberty ('just before the dawn'), where the body and overall apparatus of the psyche is preparing itself for this pivotal sea change in the nature and lived experience of the child. Based on my clinical experience with both women and men (and children and young people of both genders), something profound happens at this stage which can either enable the freer expression of self (*erosima/erosimus*) which defines how the adolescent sexuality of the person will be expressed, or bring on a kind of 'death' (*thanima/thanimus*) where the energies of the psyche get stuck in atrophy.

I will return to the 'pre-pubescent moment', but the suggestion I am making here is that the problem of envy in the pre-oedipal stage impacts at this point where the experience of puberty is mapped out; it may be defined by unbalanced, extreme versions of *erosima* or of *thanima*, or more commonly be a muddle of the two which finds ways of working itself out in a variety of relational, sexual, social and creative ways.

This stops adolescence from being experienced in a fully lived way, or can even leave a person caught at this pre-pubescent stage as they pass into adulthood. For the boy, the *erotically* charged problem of envy towards mother/breast remains unresolved. Unconsciously he feels as if he has destroyed the (part) object of his erotic desire and has not moved on from this through the reparation available in the depressive position. The role of father is crucial, too; while I am focusing here on the implications of a boy's unconscious attacks on the breast, his identification with phallus as symbolised is also important.

For a girl, meanwhile, the destructiveness is aimed at the breast within the nascent forming of a more *relational* bond with mother. As I will go on to explore below through the writings of Kristeva (2004) and Chodorow (1978), the erotic is present but the way in which a girl can seem to become mother's relational 'partner' and successor means envy acquires a differently layered quality to it. Here, the girl's envious attacks on the breast echo the possibly more bisexual characteristic of female sexuality. By this I mean the way, alongside the *erotic* desire (in a heterosexual sense) of the girl for the phallus of the masculine (father's penis etc.), there is a patterned pull into a deeper *relational* bond with mother.

As I will shortly go on to describe via the arguments of the writers mentioned above, the infant girl becomes an identificatory object for mother, who may then reproduce her role and way of relating in various ways, moderated by how consciously or otherwise the maturing girl and woman works through the imprint of this early bond. *Mother identifies with me and I identify with her*. It is a fundamental, relational bond, which I will pick up later in the book as throwing up problems lived out in relations between men and women and in how domestic life is 'ordered'.

In terms of the workings of *envy*, the destructiveness towards the breast therefore becomes an attack on something which, for the girl, is instinctively felt as part of her. She therefore splits this attack in ways the boy does not. On the one hand she destroys a version of the bad breast which represents the potential of it to share itself elsewhere or simply enjoy its own riches without her. On the other hand she 'gobbles up' the aspects of the breast which represent the 'good' relational feeling (the specialness of the mother–daughter bond) tinged with the erotic. I propose that this difference provides a speculative explanation for why girls seem 'better prepared' for puberty because the relational base with mother survives this process.

Erosimus is better preserved and protected while it 'incubates' during latency compared with e*rosima*, which in a sense has been laid bare by the encounter with the introjected breast during the pre-oedipal phase, without the relational depth of connection available to the girl. This is not to minimise the potential difficulties for the girl; the narcissistic quality of mother's relational embrace of daughter can sometimes be overwhelming, or the unresolved envy in her can also set up a more destructive pattern for the girl – both of which can generate pathological problems for her in later life (Chodorow, 1978).

However, the presence of the relational bond, as I will further expand upon, offers the girl more of an alignment between *relational* and *erotic* flow as she arrives at the 'pre-pubescent moment', compared with the split between the two which is the trend for the boy in relation to mother. Nevertheless, unresolved, or disproportionate, envy in the girl still contributes significantly to the outcome of this 'moment'. Here, *thanimus* dictates the way in which *animus* operates via puberty – an adolescence characterised by withholding of *eros*, perhaps taking more aggressive or self-destructive forms (e.g. self-harm), or attempts to compensate for the absence of *erosimus* by trying to 'make perfect' the body as an object of desire (through eating disorders such as anorexia or bulimia nervosa).

The question raised here surrounds the place of father and/or phallus – and the possibility of envious attacks on the penis as an internalised part-object. The way this gets worked through – or not – is, I believe, fundamental to the potential of *erosima* and whether this gets 'fertilised' or remains stillborn (as in the clinical examples given in Chapter 4), and I will return to this and its impact on the pre-pubescent 'conception' of *thanimus* or *erosimus* later in this chapter. Suffice it to say, like *anima* in the boy, the way *animus* goes on to manifest in adolescence and beyond – either exploring self via sexual, relational, social and creative experience, or being withholding or destructive in relation to these psychic potentials (or a mix of the two) – gets strongly influenced by this 'moment' of becoming.

As indicated, I want to offer some counterbalance to Freud's phallo-centric psychosexual model by bringing in Julia Kristeva's important ideas about the origins of female sexuality. Freud implies that male sexuality and therefore the general experience of being a boy or man – other than with gay or 'inverse' (Freud, 1920/1991: 46) sexuality – is characterised by a movement towards having, or keeping, subjugation and possession over the sexual object (whether this be a whole person, an erotogenic zone or perhaps some representation of sublimated phallic power such as found in material wealth, a job or any other status symbol). But his reading of female sexuality is clearly associated with *lack*, with *not having* the phallus and therefore not having anything 'to subjugate with'. Here *subjugation* and *possession* are replaced by the envious craving for this power.

In my adaptation of Jung's contrasexual formula the infant girl may first experience *thanimus* in terms of lack, envy and therefore disappointment. What she gets from mother's nipple is physically filling but sexually not so. This is not to say the girl obtains *no* erotogenic stimulation from sucking mother's breast, or satisfaction from filling up with mother's milk. Rather, while the infant boy may experience phallic fulfilment through an experience of subjugation and possession of mother, the girl is reminded of what she and the mother have between them, but crucially also what she does *not* have (but the boy does).

While the boy embraces *erosima*, she gets to swallow the milk of *thanimus*. However, this equation has more to it than a one-sided experience of *lack* – there is an experience of *lack* for boys, too. This is where Kristeva's take on infantile female sexuality helps in offering something compensatory to Freud's downgrading of the quality of girls' early experiencing.

She begins from a critical stance on Freud's insistence on the 'primacy of the *phallus*' (ibid.: 308) in the development of early sexuality in both males and females. She notes how Freud later came to notice the intensity of the relationship between mother and daughter and how this seems to be 'encysted in preverbal sensory experience' (Kristeva, 2004: 2) and may act as the foundation for a more established relational, and bisexual, orienta-tion in girls and women.

This last comment seems important to me as it points to something which happens at an earlier stage than the oedipal/phallic. What Kristeva also argues for is a re-evaluation of the presence of mother in the forming and establishment of the girl's sexuality. In her view:

> Infantile sexuality, which is not that of the *instincts* but that of the *drives* understood as psycho-somatic constructions, pre-existent

biology-and-meaning, is thus formed from the outset in the newborn's interaction with his two parents and *under the ascendency of maternal seduction.*

(ibid.: 2, emphasis added)

Kristeva argues that the imprinting of an infant's sexuality, awaiting the unfolding in its *archetypal* potential, can be activated by *either* the pre-dominating presence of mother, or the involvement of father (or mother's desire for him). This 'seduction' takes place in what she characterises as the 'primary oedipal phase' (ibid.: 1), which refers to birth to around three years old, i.e. through the oral and anal stages.

For the girl, Kristeva observes, orificial excitation tends to predominate over the clitoral, and this refers to an imprinting of what she describes as 'the excited cavity of the inner body' via an introjection of the seductive mother (ibid.: 5). This introjection is, Kristeva argues, given greater force by a noticing of resemblance between daughter and mother.

There is also a gradual process of psychical imprinting going on, and in the phallic/secondary oedipal phase a tendency to prize or idealise relational representation (and/or romantic love) over and above erotic excitation becomes established. This process for Kristeva is consolidated by a feeling of a link between the *sensory* reality of the internalised psychic object of mother and the *outer* reality of mother's presence, both of which act as a necessary compensation for the experience of being invaded by mother' as her first unconscious object. The apparently more powerful identificatory processes between mother and daughter, as opposed to between mother and son (where son may become a phallic substitute for mother), lend themselves to the eliciting of the intimacy of the mother–daughter relation.

Another factor in drawing the little girl powerfully into the relational domain of mother may be what Abraham observed as a distinctive 'early vaginal blossoming of the female libido, which is destined to be repressed and which is subsequently followed by clitoral primacy as the expression of the phallic phase' (quoted in Falzeder, 2002: 527).

Abraham suggested that the female oedipal complex arose from a vaginal reaction to the intuited presence of father's penis. Here one can suggest a real distinction between the psychosexual pathways of boys and girls – girls having two seats of primary sexual experiencing compared with boys: vagina and clitoris, the latter of which becomes the focus of genital stimu-lation as oedipal feelings take hold, safely channelling taboo urges for vaginal experiencing in relation to father. This also provides a link to mother as the taboo engenders a refocusing on the relational, for which the pre-oedipal template with mother has already been well established. Mother and daughter can thus link together to defend the taboo.

This is where the boy's experience of *lack* may be felt, not only in the more limited genital 'options' open to him. Intimacy between the boy and mother at this formative stage, I argue, lays the foundation for a pattern of an experienced 'split' for him. While the girl comes into the closest connection with mother through the process described by Kristeva (2004) above, the boy's psychosexual (and social) formation is in a crucible of desire for, and sensory intimacy with, mother, but *not* in the seminally relational way the girl experiences.

Chodorow's (1978) observations tend to reflect the sense of a subtle, but nevertheless profound, difference in the formative experiencing of the pre-oedipal – or as Kristeva (op. cit.) characterises it, 'primary oedipal' – phase. She drew on a range of studies on how gendered differences in this phase arise from conscious and unconscious relations with mother (e.g. Chodorow, 2001) as well as a close analysis of where Freud's initial formulations (1920/1991) accrue unhelpful emphases on a phallocentric reading of infant development.

As far as the infant girl is concerned, Chodorow (1978: 109) suggests that mother's 'symbiosis with daughters tends to be stronger . . . [and] . . . to be based on experiencing a daughter as an extension or double . . . [with] . . . cathexis of the daughter as a *sexual* other usually remaining a weaker, less significant theme.' On the one hand this can generate an identification (in the extreme, as a narcissistic extension of themselves) with daughter which threatens to swamp her capacity to establish a separate, distinct sense of self. On the other, the kind of psychic daughter–mother intimacy alluded to by Kristeva is also a potential relational 'prize' for the girl which can remain available to her for a lifetime.

For the infant boy, meanwhile, something different happens. For mothers, 'sons tend to be differentiated . . . and mothers push this differentiation' (Chodorow, 1978: 110) and 'maternal behaviour, at the same time, tends to help propel sons into a sexualised, genitally toned relationship, which in its turn draws the son into triangular conflicts' (ibid.). This leads into the equation of Benjamin's – described in Chapter 2 – whereby the boy establishes who he is via 'discontinuity and difference' from mother (Benjamin, 1988: 75).

Gender and 'recognition'

For Benjamin, a crucial concomitant of this breaking of the identification with mother relates to her thinking on the place of *recognition*. Benjamin prioritises the intersubjective, conscious, human need to be recognised; for *you* to acknowledge and feed back a nourishing sense of who *I* am to you – stemming from Hegel's (McTaggart, 1964: 11) original position that *I* can only get a full sense of my value in the reflection of it in the response of the other. Benjamin also describes the converse need to *really see* the other person: 'The idea of mutual recognition is crucial . . . it implies that we actually have a need to recognize the other as a separate person who is like us yet distinct' (Benjamin, 1988: 23).

As well as the importance of recognition being something about what is sought 'between' the child and mother (or other primary caregiver), there is a parallel significance in the child's need to *recognise themselves*. In this respect, this is an opportune moment to refer again to Lacan's 'mirror phase', from six to eighteen months (Sarup, 2002), and its value for making sense of the (secondary) oedipal (or phallic) phase as it impacts upon being a girl or a boy.

Essentially this phase is based on the infant's seeking out of a sense of identity which has some kind of coherence. When the child begins to notice their image in the mirror, and is aware that they are a *separate* human being in their own right in relation to the parent who may be standing behind them, or lifting them up, they become identified with the *image* they see of themselves in ways which are distorting and problematic.

For Lacan this means the little girl or little boy can never truly be 'themselves'. The identity they have perceived as 'theirs' from what they see in the mirror establishes a tendency in them to 'seek and foster the imaginary wholeness of an "ideal ego"' (Sarup, ibid.: 65). This tendency is hallmarked by a spirit of anticipation, a constant feeling for who they could or should be. As this formula implies, this is a self-recognition which is really an illusion, and which sets up a relation to self which cannot be fulfilled as it implies there is an ideal point of completion which we arrive at in the future – as if, to borrow Jung's language, individuation might be a state we *arrive* at and perfect, rather than his more real portrayal of it as a process of *becoming* and struggle (Fordham, 1985a: 34–40).

This pinpointing by Lacan of where a universal tendency (and source of unhappiness) might arise reflects my observation that *continuity* and *discontinuity* (the sense of how *continuous* or not our sense of self might be – past to present to future) is fundamental to our mental health and wellbeing. The extent to which our image of self coheres with reality, or is a distortion of it, will impact on our capacity to hold a reliable enough 'timeline' of self.

So, if my image of who I was at, say, four years old, evolves contiguously into my image of self at seven, and then again at twelve and then seventeen (etc.), then I am describing an experience of self-recognition which is more or less *continuous*. If, however, the connectivity in my sense of how I have evolved between these points is hard to maintain or incongruent, then my self-image originating in the mirror phase is helping to generate a deep sense of *discontinuity*, something I argue that male development, with its splitting of the *erotic* from the *relational*, may be more prone to.

I want to make a couple of observations regarding possible, generalised differences in how patterns arising from the false dichotomy of the mirror phase may arise for the infant boy compared with the infant girl, and relate these to *anima–animus*. The infant boy sees 'in the mirror' a version of himself who carries the promise of an impossibly full embodiment of *erosima*. Here, a pact is made with the future which cannot be fulfilled in reality, but instead sets up a degree of anticipation which has a rather shaky relational base. Father represents this idealised endpoint, while the quality and nature of the erotically based tie to mother has a powerful influence on how the trajectory of a boy's, and then a man's, journey is lived out.

This is where *thanima* can cause havoc with a man's sense of continuity, particularly as the relational base is not there in the way it generally is in the container set up between the girl and mother early in her life. The girl will recognise herself more in mother than will the boy, and if the *erotic* and *relational* have become estranged by experiencing mother as an unreliable or deadened presence then for him the idealised future self can act like the moon when a child tries to catch the lunar reflection in the water with their net – a constant, repeating experience of gold slipping through his fingers. While Jack captures priceless treasures and brings them home, the boy, and the boy in the man, may never get to enjoy this experience.

For the infant girl, meanwhile, the first acquaintances made with the physical image in the mirror can be seen as a kind of idealised projection of *erosimus*. She also sees a body and a face which she imagines reflects her capacity to arrive at her fullest potential. In her case, though, this could be read as an idealised image of fulfilling her physical and erotic potential – within the holding of a *relational* frame of reference, as pointed towards in the formative developments in her initial, and initiatory, relationship to mother (Kristeva, 2004; Chodorow, 1978).

In her unconscious anticipation of this happening in reality, *thanimus* provides the pattern of unfulfilled anticipation to the trajectory of the girl's life. In this respect, the deathly, destructive version of *animus* provides the discontinuity between an idealised future self and an ongoing struggle with a more faulty version in the present. What I would argue brings the girl closer to being at ease in the present is the relational connection with mother (where this forms in a non-pathological way).

Jung has set out ways in which the archetypal power of mother can imprint on the daughter in unhelpful ways, such as what he termed the 'hypertrophy' of the maternal aspect, so childbirth becomes the only goal (Jung, 1938/1968: para. 167), or comprehensive 'identification' with mother (ibid.: para. 169) results in the daughter losing her own sense of identity. I would prefer to see these as the kinds of phases a daughter can go through before integrating them within her own developing sense of what of mother she wants to emulate and what she wants to place in the background. In the same way a son may pass through phases of ardent love and loyalty for mother. This smacks of a willingness to sacrifice himself as son-hero, or conversely to fight tooth and nail to be free of her all-encompassing influence (Jung, 1912/1952).

However, I think the prospect of the girl 'becoming mother' is distinctly more *immanent* than the prospect of the boy 'becoming father', as while the latter requires a long journey towards successful identification with him 'out there' (sometimes with less than helpful connotations of *transcending* home and family), the deep bond twixt mother and daughter, and its relational base, is usually already made by the time the mirror phase identified by Lacan begins to influence things.

Where mother is concerned it seems that for the little boy the significance of 'being distinctive' from mother is more radical than for the little girl; to some degree he becomes defined by how he is *without* her. Benjamin suggests that the boy goes on to try to reconcile this need to be separate with his need for recognition by moving into a stance characterised by the drive to subjugate and dominate 'mother', via doing so in his relations with women (Benjamin, 1988a: 77).

For the girl, the recognition received from mother and, as daughter, how she recognises mother's distinctiveness, could be said to act as a signifier of her own individuality *within* the loving dyad formed between them. While the place of father and the impact of the mutual 'recognition' between him and daughter is important, I suggest that these pivotal 'equations' between mother and daughter on the one hand, and mother and son on the other, more profoundly influence the configurations for patterns of male–female relating later on in life.

We are talking about a combination of deeply set (archetypal?) influences, but open to the fluidity of 'here-and-now' relating and *recognition*, as well as to the more remote (but nonetheless *present*) influence of societal shifts in parenting and socialisation, such as the growing involvement of fathers (where a two-parent dyad for the child is available) in the early care of the infant. This combination of influences lays the ground for the lifelong (and in some ways collective) frame of reference for familial relations in the 'territories' of being a man or being a woman. There is an emerging implication that beneath the historical hegemony of patriarchal influence there are deep patterns at work, which take a psychosexual form in their early demarcation between the experiencing of a male and of a female.

So, the mother–daughter bond is cemented in the primary oedipal stage, and creates the roots of what later perpetuates the 'territory' associated with being a girl/woman. This includes the ways in which her unconscious *envy* towards the introjected version of mother may get counterbalanced within the powerful relational bond formed between mother and daughter, as described. These influences are then complemented by the input of patriarchal forms channelled through a girl's (*th*)*animus* experience of the 'law of the Father' – which I will come back to in the following section – to 'locate' females within this 'territory'.

By implication, this early dynamic also significantly informs the locating of boys within the territory of 'being a boy and a man'. The infant boy, as argued above, falls outside the relational 'psychic bonding' of the girl and mother, but an erotically based (*eros*)*anima* bond to the latter remains. In terms of the place of *envy*, the introjected mother presents his inner world of phantasy with the roots of the very split he then lives out later in his conscious and unconscious struggles with relating. That is, it is relationship as well as erotic fusion/penetration that mother holds the key to. The notion of another having her, or of her deriving pleasure and connection with those capacities in herself, leads the infant boy to destroy or devour her over and over within that phantasy world. On top of this there is the propulsive force of the need to separate, to recognise mother as *fundamentally* other to him, in order to become himself.

The boy's journey towards the reparative possibilities of the depressive position are thus hallmarked by the split between craving erotic and relational connection with mother (and experiencing the envious destructiveness which goes along with that), while also feeling a need to be separate. The territory of 'being a boy and man' shares the erotic dimension but the relational dimension is dependent on the quality of this *anima* bond. The examples in Chapter 4 will, I hope, convey what happens when this relationship is dominated by deadly *thanima* rather than living *erosima*.

As well as the Jungian hallmarks in her description of this process (archetypal imprinting, compensation, and a profound *participation mystique* with bodily, sexual, and psychic dimensions), Kristeva's (2004) portrayal of the crucible of female forming offers some powerful pointers for a post-Jungian model for early, gendered, development which informs the idea I am working with around the 'trajectory' of *anima–animus* forms in girls (and boys). This portrayal receives general accord from Chodorow's (1978) impression of how mothering patterns may be transmitted to daughters while sons get impelled towards a more split position in relation to mother. Benjamin's ideas on the role of mutual recognition, described above, and how this may have a formative influence on patterns of gendered relating, also contribute to the emerging picture around these proposed trajectories.

Applying Erikson's notion of the tensions inherent in the pre-oedipal stage, one could say, assuming the deep bond with mother has been installed in the ways Kristeva and Chodorow outline, that *trust vs mistrust* – Erikson's (1950) proposed internal conflict within the infant in the oral stage – is not such a prominent struggle for the girl. It may be more relevant to describe the girl's struggle at this stage as being between *permission to be* and *fusion with (or smothering by)* mother.

On the one hand this reflects Erikson's apparent bias towards the male experience of child development (Chodorow, 1978), and on the other it highlights the possibility that this is indeed a more problematic situation for the little boy. As he does not experience mother in this deeply embedded relational way, but rather experiences the relational dimension of his connection with mother via the powerful eroticism between them, then the question of whether he can trust *love*, and the *world* he finds himself in, can depend on the stability and strength of the *erotic* bond. This idea, in turn, will be modulated by consideration of the presence and role of father, which I will make some observations on below regarding Winnicott's (1958) 'nursing triad'.

Erikson's formulation for the anal stage is of a struggle in the infant between *autonomy* and *shame or doubt*. Again the male bias can be felt – Erikson seems to be describing something akin to Benjamin's observation that the boy has to split off from the relational dimension in order to begin his long journey towards real autonomy. If he does not feel he has the space or permission to carve out this opportunity, then he is faced with a difficult battle which exposes him to the possibility that he may doubt his individuality, lose his self-esteem, and be perceived as failing. These uncomfortable, sometimes debilitating, states seem to resonate strongly with some of the clinical examples from men I give in Chapter 4.

The struggle for autonomy does apply of course to both girls and boys. However, I suggest that for girls, assuming the secure base of the original relational daughter–mother bond has been made, this phase again has firmer ground for them. However, the presence of father, or whatever is represented by him (e.g. his absence), brings with it *doubt* about the boundaries of the intrapsychic and relational worlds she inhabits. This also raises the possibility of *shame* if she feels she may not be acceptable to 'father' or the empty space left by his absence.

These possible patterns in early development for the girl or boy are, as I keep stressing, generalisations which cover a multitude of variation. However, in concluding this section on the primary or pre-oedipal phase, which is of such critical importance, they offer us a map with which to explore origins of later gendered forms of experiencing and relating.

Winnicott and Fordham: Ego integration and gender

Finally, I want to bring a couple of other influences to bear on this discussion. First, Winnicott's emphasis on ego integration suits our discussion well because, for girls and boys, how fully this arises from the body and 'absolute dependency' (Winnicott, 1963) on mother (or the primary caregiver) will have implications for their sense of self, including their gendered experiencing. His axiom about the prerequisite of 'good enough mothering' (Winnicott, 1962) for ego integration to occur healthily brings with it a question – what is 'good enough' for the girl as against 'good enough' for the boy? Answers may be suggested from the discussion so far, when taken alongside his observation that the stable offer of love and a holding environment enable the infant's ego to emerge and integrate naturally within the container of her/his bodily self (Winnicott, 1962).

Good-enough mothering for a girl would be all of this as filtered through the relational fastness established with, and by, mother. Within this the girl gradually finds her autonomy through having her feelings of omnipotence allowed and nurtured before she discovers her capacity to be alone – playing and exploring with a feeling of separateness while mother looks on. For the boy, the same principles apply but the need for the boy to define himself, through relational distancing alongside a craving for erotic union with mother, means the 'good enough' in this case involves a feeling of *both* possibilities being available.

Here, though, things become more complex as we consider Winnicott's assignation of the 'nursing triad' as being significant to the provision of the 'good enough' (Hawkins and Shohet, 2000). Winnicott's formulation for this was based on a traditionalist reading of the roles of mother and father. Here the primary dyad is between mother and child, and father makes up the triad by *supporting the mother* so she can give to the needy infant what she or he needs. My reading of this is that it is less a triad and more a kind of linear system in which father and baby are rather remote from one another, and father only relates to the child via the mother.

This is not wholly what Winnicott meant, as he did not deny there is a relationship between father and child, but the theory is 'of its time' in presuming father does not have an elemental role to play in the early ego development of the child (unless mother is not around to bring up the child, and so he has to act as a mothering substitute).

It seems an equation which has its roots in the oedipal triangle, with its locating of father as the parental figure who waits his turn to enter the developmental drama sometime after the domination by mother of the first acts of the story. I suggest a fuller and more accurate reading of early experience needs to incorporate the presence of father from the very start. *Animus* is alive (*erosimus*) in the psyche of the girl right from the beginning and she seeks out the physical embodiment of him, usually in father, from that point. The boy, too, seeks out the embodiment of his otherness to mother, not available through her presence, which also symbolises his sense of what is distinctive about *him*.

This is a version of *animus* which in a boy is his sense/image of himself as a 'he'. Up to this point I have fought shy of the current post-Jungian vogue for 'yoking' *anima* and *animus* together as a combination which gets 'installed' in both genders, so they are available in some way to both boys/men and girls/women. My rationale for this is not because I fundamentally disagree with this approach, which provides for a more pluralistic (not to say less stereotyping) application of Jung's initial formulation, but rather because I think something is lost in starting from this position.

The ways in which the life of *anima* in boys and *animus* in girls may inform their development are harder to arrive at when we stay with an all-encompassing partnering of the two which may throw up any combination of influences in girls or boys. I want to argue that the 'same-sex' inner figure (*animus* in a young boy and *anima* in a young girl) takes a back seat, but is nonetheless there to stabilise the emerging sense of self-identity around her 'girlness' and his 'boyness', rather than generating erotic, sexual aspects of self, as Samuels (1989: 103–4) suggests; which I argue arise from *contra-sexual* influences in the psyche.

Returning to Winnicott's triad and the place of father in ego integration in the earliest stages of a child's life, I will turn to Fordham's model to help flesh this out. His model needs to be seen in the light of more classical Jungian ways of looking at early ego development, notably that of Neumann (1955). The latter takes an archetypal perspective on the influence of mother – as an experience of the Great Mother, who is overwhelming in her presence and influence. Neumann describes ego development as passing through an initial 'uroboric phase', where the lack of conscious differentiation from mother is the hallmark, followed by the 'matriarchal phase', where the ego plays a passive role in the face of the huge imprinting of the great mother on the situation of the child. From here, the child's aggressive fantasies begin to allow the ego to emerge in the heroic sense of overcoming these overwhelming influences. The long path of individuation has only just begun, as the child gets their first glimmers of their separate identity and begins to let go of the closed world around mother and them.

This approach, based on Jung's (1940/1968) premise that the child does not as such have their own unconscious, but is possessed by the unconscious(es) of the parents, raises many questions about the apparent ways very young children seem able to influence their environment. Fordham took a very different starting point – his observations on this from his child analytic work.

In Fordham's model, the baby arrives in the world ready to begin the individuation process, and the self is active in initiating contact with the environment through a process of *de*integrating – that is, putting 'out' aspects of the self in order to make contact with and receive experiences which can then be *re*integrated. An obvious example would be when the baby is hungry and makes this known by crying (where the crying is a *deintegrate*). When he or she receives the feed from mother's breast this provides a *reintegrate* which contributes to the developmental process of which the emergence of the *ego* is the prime deintegrate which enables the child to cope with life's demands.

Applying Fordham's terminology to early gendered experience, there may be a gendered dimension to how the deintegration–reintegration process is experienced in connection with mother. For the girl, the early relational bonding with mother, as an experience of 'sameness', may be experienced through the deintegration of her relating capacity (eye contact, a smile etc.) being met with a predominantly *relational* reintegration experience (returned eye contact or being scooped up by mother) tinged with the underlying erotic aspect of the sensations evoked orally and then anally.

For the infant boy, meanwhile, the predominant deintegrating aspect of his look, touch or reaching out will be *erotic*, with oral excitation a strong feature in the early days of his bonding with mother. There will also be a lesser, but nonetheless present, quality of relational experiencing in the ensuing reintegrating experience.

In both cases the *deintegrating–reintegrating* process will be primarily towards mother, because of her defining presence as the source of the baby's being (where she or he has emerged from) and nourishment (food and love). Father, if around, will come into play to varying degrees of availability. As time passes, I suggest, the difference between the experiencing of a little girl or a little boy becomes sharpened around a growing awareness of when a *reintegration* from mother or father conveys a feeling, thought or bodily sensation of *sameness* (daughter–mother; son–father) or *difference* (son–mother; daughter–father). Here, *mirroring* (Shwartz-Salant, 1982: 45–50) also suggests itself as a key phase of self-validation which may have a gendered dimension. The boy's mirroring by mother has an element of *difference* in the returned smile, look or touch, as does the girl's mirroring by father.

So, we get a sense of the emerging distinctions in the *gendered* selfhood of young girls and boys. Winnicott's nursing triad illustrates the primacy of the contact with mother and how this might differentially impact on a boy, on the one hand, and a girl on the other. The individuation process begins in this context, and to borrow Fordham's terminology, the deintegration–reintegration process is begun with mother and then gets fed into an interplay with mother, father and the general environment. This reflects the implications arising around the nature and quality of the differentiation in how boys and girls begin to relate. Put simply, girls relate *towards* mother and what she represents and boys *desire* her and what she represents, but also experience 'relating' as a movement *away from* her. The development of these differences will emerge more fully in the following section.

The secondary oedipal phase (3–6 years): Phallus and the oedipal conflict

As the child moves into the 'phallic' or 'secondary oedipal' phase the imprinting of the dyad with mother becomes less *figure* and more *ground* (Perls, 1969). The predominantly *relational* presence of mother has become embedded for the girl and the mainly *erotic* version of mother likewise for the boy.

Also, within Freud's classical formulation, the young child is moving towards a more integrated experience of her or his sexuality, with the masturbatory emphasis settling on the genital area (Freud, 1920/1991: 102–8) and the place of *phallus* becoming pivotal to the influence of penis envy (girls) and the castration complex (boys).

As the dynamic becomes more overtly triangular, the presence of father (or the space left by his absence) acquires a powerful significance. Here we are more fully in the territory of Jack's struggle – between the domains of mother and (dead or giant) father. In Freud's familiar formulation, the boy comes into conflict with father over the erotic 'treasure' of mother (lending an interesting libidinal slant to the gold coins, eggs and harp Jack steals from under the giant's snoring nose).

For the girl, Jung's use of the 'Electra complex' (Scott, 2005: 8), after the mythological figure who encourages her brother, Orestes, to kill her mother, Clytemnestra (after she arranges for the death of her father, Agamemnon) reflects the equal significance for the girl of her libidinal desire for father, which mother is experienced as blocking access to. One aspect of this story I want to highlight is the way Electra gets her brother to kill mother. Here, one could say, the daughter needs to use the aggressive, deadly masculine – *thanimus* – to do the dirty deed, though the impetus for the act arises from her thwarted *erosimus*, which desired union with father.

This raises questions I will return to about the source and characterisation of aggression in both men and women, i.e. does it arise predominantly from 'same-sex' energy/libido (*thanima* in girls/women and *thanimus* in boys/men) or 'contrasexual' energy/libido (*thanimus* in girls/women and *thanima* in boys/men)? Alternatively is there value in looking at aggression as having a 'yoked' *anima–animus* quality? The presentation of interpersonal aggression may have significant areas of variance between the 'territories' of men and women, alongside commonalities, so bracketing this complex and possibly nuanced (in terms of gender) area as arising in *yoked* terms seems insufficient.

In the Kleinian reading of this dynamic, as we have already observed, these oedipal dramas have already occurred – or rather began occurring – right at the beginning of life, with the tiny child 'unconsciously knowing' about the sexual congress of mother and father as their source of origin. As I have argued, this 'knowing' may well also incorporate some kind of deep awareness (unavailable to consciousness, but 'there') of their sex. This is surely implied by Klein's positing of the activation of the oedipal complex from the start of life, as how could a boy get into this struggle with introjected representations of 'father/phallus' without such *gnosis*, and likewise the girl with introjected 'mother/breast' part-objects?

Warren Colman (2006) has provided a skilful reading of *anima* and *animus* in respect to the oedipal drama in the lives of younger children. He describes the contrasexual other in terms of an identification with the adored parent (so *anima* is mediated by mother for the boy, and *animus* by father for the girl). Using this model, Colman proposes how *anima* and *animus* can be enabled to perform their full roles in the individuation journey of the person – as bridges to the unconscious – by being freed from these oedipal identifications. This can therefore become a theme of therapeutic work. Likewise, I propose the tackling of *thanima* or *thanimus* manifestations can be a therapeutic focus.

The other key set of ideas relevant here are those of Lacan (1966/1977) and his notion of the *Symbolic Order* and *the law of the Father*. In Lacan's system for understanding human realities and modes of engaging with the world he envisages three 'Orders' (Sarup, 1992): the *Imaginary Order* incorporates the realm of phantasy and image, evolving into adulthood from the mirror phase onwards; the *Symbolic Order* refers to the ways we symbolise our experiences and feelings, primarily via the conventional language systems of the societies we inhabit; and the *Real Order* relates to what in reality is hard to express (e.g. sexual experiences and contact with death) but nonetheless carries the greatest of impacts upon us.

In moving into the *Symbolic Order*, it is the father's symbolic place which Lacan sees as crucial. *The law of the Father* is how Lacan (1957) ascribes the fundamental principle which governs this process, and it is a principle which carries a stern *senex* quality around prohibition. All the desire and struggle to have sexual congress with mother (by the boy) or father (by the girl), as activated by the oedipal conflict, is banished to the depths of the unconscious.

Father symbolically comes to represent the imposition of the incest taboo, and this is established via a kind of *quid pro quo* in which the child unconsciously subscribes to this taboo (and the breaking open of the more narcissistic and incest-tinged quality of the mother–child dyad) in exchange for being admitted and accepted into the wider world of language and social intercourse. Referring back to Lacan's observations on the *mirror stage* (see above), the child comes into the oedipal drama already alienated from a full sense of who she or he 'is', attached instead to seen, thought and sensed representations of self. This split between the *Real* and the *Imaginary Orders*, or rather the superseding of the former by the latter, is pivotal to the way, according to Lacan, the *Symbolic Order* operates. By learning to use language, words (or names) come to represent and even replace the *Real* objects and subjective experiencing in the life of the child as the source of meaning (Lemaire, 1977).

I will speculatively convert this formula into the language of *anima–animus*. The application of *the law of the Father* within classical Jungian parlance suggests it is *animus* which assumes the pivotal role in moving the child further into life by breaking the exclusivity of the mother–child bond. The inevitable double-edge here is that while *erosimus* provides the 'masculine', life-giving impulse for this, its deadening counterpart, *thanimus*, provides the strict prohibition around the potential acting-out of incestuous desire. It also creates the 'screen' which splits, through sublimation, the child away from their deepest erotically driven feelings and fantasies and takes them into a world of signifiers and linguistic symbolisation, where they can take their place within the *Symbolic Order*.

If this translation of the Lacanian framework for understanding the outcome of the oedipal struggle holds any water, then the place of *animus* energies, in boys as well as girls, becomes very important. This suggestion tallies with the model I set out in Chapter 2, where I suggested that where *anima–animus* gets yoked so as to be available in some form to both genders, then *anima* finds its life (and deadness) in the realm of *relationship*, while *animus* is more to do with what we can and cannot *see* – i.e. it either frees up conscious awareness or it freezes and closes down this awareness (hence my placing of *thanimus* as a kind of gatekeeper of our capacity to 'see' the reality of the gendered Other).

I would extend the idea of 'yoking' in this context to suggest that *anima–animus* are at their most vividly present *together* in all of us at the oedipal stage. In the heat of the unconscious struggle to 'win' the opposite-sex parent the two sides of the contrasexual psychic arrangement in the psyche bring all their energies to bear on the fantasy of erotic union with mother or father. In this sense, *eros* is in full flow; in the boy the reins are mainly taken by *erosima*, and in the girl by *erosimus*, though in both cases the influence of the more deadening versions of both will vary according to the vicissitudes of the relationships (inner and outer) experienced thus far.

In the girl's case *anima* energy and 'soulful' meaning is encountered, I suggest, in the revelation of the presence of father's *anima*, which mirrors back to his daughter what her *animus* (or rather *thanimus*) has not let her see while she was gripped by the reflective gaze of mother. The girl has a fuller experience of her *anima* energies as the dominant *animus* loses its grip on her psyche, temporarily.

A parallel process occurs, I suggest, with *animus* in the boy. When father 'comes on the scene' *animus* energy becomes available more fully. The fixation on mother and his *erosima*-driven craving for intimacy with her gets challenged not just by father's presence and what it symbolically represents, but also the proddings of his awakened *animus*, which reflects back a longing for father, too.

In both cases, the more 'collectively yoked' *anima–animus* is drawn on to offer some complementary energy and enable the loving but possibly claustrophobic 'warm bath' of the dyad with mother to be exposed to the more variable currents of life's atmospheres as symbolised by father. This tallies with the sense I am working with that the wider, deeper, 'territories' of girl/woman versus boy/man experiencing are at times exposed to deeper archetypal processes, which operate beneath the life of the individualised presence of *anima* (boy) and *animus* (girl), and which require the power of the *syzygy* – the conjoined energy of feminine/masculine forces – to bring about profound shifts in the life cycle.

Here again I find the *Gestalt* terminology of *figure* and *ground* helpful in visualising what may be happening. I suggest that once the movement into the *Symbolic Order* is in full flow, the yoked *anima–animus* fades back into the 'ground' and the struggle between the boy's *erosima* and *thanima* resumes the focus as 'figure' in the foreground, and the equivalent battle between the girl's *erosimus* and *thanimus* comes back into view.

As feminine/'mother' *anima* energies generally fade when girls or boys move into the latency stage, generalised *animus* energies consolidate the emergence of the *superego*. 'Law', standards and attitudes, whether imbibed from father, mother or both, become inscribed in the psyche of the child, including unhelpful *animus* messages of certitude and judgement (i.e. when these are burdensome rather than offering helpful boundaries and guidance) – with all the implications this may bring for the child's self-concept and relationships with others. 'How to behave as a girl' or 'acceptable behaviour for a boy' become consolidated as frames of reference as each moves into the latency period (starting at around five or six years and continuing until ten to twelve years).

Kohlberg's (1966) notion of 'gender consistency' is useful here, as it may well be that children become fixed upon the 'certainty' of their 'girlness' or 'boyness' during this period, which is broadly associated with primary/junior school age, because the superego requirement to be 'definite' about what is right and wrong is filtering through with real force to the psyche of the newly inducted member of the *Symbolic Order*. The need to be 'definite' translates into a sharper definition of 'my gender identity' and gets reinforced by identification with same-gender friendship groups.

So, as our individualised *erosima–thanima* (boy) or *erosimus–thanimus* (girl) expressions 'go to sleep' in this period of latency, the *collective* imprints of *anima–animus*, which sit somewhere between the realms of social learning (Bandura, 1977) and something more archetypal, such as the impacts of our parental complexes, begin to induct us into a *Gendered Symbolic Order*. To be accepted as son or daughter, the child also needs to be accepted as boy or girl, and same-gender friendships act as *signifiers* of this fact, as do all the paraphernalia going with gender difference in that age group – e.g. boy versus girl clothes and fashions; girl versus boy sports and activities; boy versus girl 'tribes', such as cubs and brownies. The felt sense of being a girl or being a boy gets wrapped up in, and experienced through, these identifications.

This is a crucial stage in the establishment of the male and female 'territories'. The children inducted into the *Boys' Symbolic Order* or the *Girls' Symbolic Order* are unwittingly sustaining these age-old 'territories', and they will keep at least one foot in the *Order* or territory associated with their gender identity for the rest of their lives, unconsciously bolstered, I suggest, by the differing boy/girl patterns associated with the initial relationship to mother.

As implied, the individualised expression of *anima* or *animus* 'goes to sleep' during this period before reawakening more fully (or perhaps being 'stillborn') at 'the pre-pubescent moment'. As well as incubating, there is a sense of our individual *anima* or *animus* expressions of the erotic and the relational 'licking their wounds' after the tough oedipal battle has inflicted its first and most impacting wounds on the psyche. There is a degree of inner reorganisation going on, preparing for the rebirth of our contrasexual inner figures. If the wounds from the oedipal struggle have a deeply fearful, confusing or deadening quality to them (perhaps because mother, father or both have become internalised as sadistic, unpredictable or unavailable in their responses to our needs and desires) then the rebirth can have all sorts of connotations, from the eruption of an insatiable sexual appetite through to a deadly psychological stillbirth.

The pre-pubescent moment and beyond

This point of change seems to have a defining quality for the individual. The way it 'happens' seems to both reflect the key features of a person's early experiences, and set the scene for how adolescence and early adulthood will be negotiated. A number of patients I have worked with have pointed to pivotal shifts in their sense of self and relationship to the external world around this time. From a man I worked with who associated a loss of a sense of direction in life with the age of ten, to a woman who linked her current dislocation from meaningful relationships to an unexpected change of school in her last year at primary school, there seems to be something about the end period of the latency stage through to puberty which determines how we feel about ourselves in crucial ways later in life.

As indicated in my 'map' of gendered development (pp. 68–9), I want to propose that something critical happens around the age of nine to twelve which defines gendered identity and our prospective sense of self – *who I am going to be* – not least in the sense of what we can take with us from our first decade and what we leave behind. This is particularly pertinent, I suggest, in terms of our life force, our *eros*. What my clinical experiences suggest is that the 'pre-pubescent moment' both reveals and sets up the pattern of how far into life we are going to be truly 'born'. In Jungian terms, this is a moment when 'the violence of the Self' (Huskinson, 2002) takes charge and cuts across our previous ways of understanding self, and determines how much our teenage years, for example, will consist of a struggle to survive, or, if we are lucky, lead to liberation of our autonomous identity.

The man I referred to above experienced a seemingly mystifying loss of confidence in his identity at the age of ten and wandered through his teenage and early adult life like someone, as he put it, 'who has lost his memory, and wanders through his home town asking everyone he meets, "where am I?"' He was looking for the magic beans, and somewhere inside himself he may have known where they were, but he could not recall where they might be. His unconscious had swallowed the memory up – but why? Likewise, the woman I referred to had no idea why a change of school in the last year of her primary education years had thrown her so far off balance, why she had fallen from the beanstalk just when she was starting the long climb up to the world of adulthood.

I suggest that at this time *anima* and *animus* have been slumbering through the latency period, incubating themselves in order to prepare for the full rebirth of the *twins* inherent in each. For girls, this involves the rebirth of *erosimus* and *thanimus*. *Erosimus* carries the life force and holds characteristics which will enable the girl to embrace the shift into womanhood in a wholehearted way, including a sense of self-as-woman which facilitates in turn a freed-up, healthy way of relating to men. *Thanimus*, on the other hand, carries the death instinct and thus tends to want to draw the girl away from embracing her emerging womanhood. This also gets reflected in a more rigidified *negative animus* quality, which seeps into attitudes towards men and tarnishes her relationships with them later in life.

Likewise, in a boy, *erosima* has a quality of both awakening him to his future potential and gendered identity (self-as-man) and helping him make the bridge across from boy to man, which I would argue is less easy to define than the bridge nature explicitly offers the girl, via the beginning of her menses (Casement, 1995), and hence of puberty. For a boy, the physiological change associated with being potentially able to parent – marked most obviously by his first 'wet dream' or masturbatory ejaculation – can come at any time between the ages of twelve and sixteen (or even later).

As Casement (1995) argues, anthropological studies demonstrate (e.g. van Gennep, 1960) how the certainty of the place of the start of a girl's menses in her passage into womanhood has long been ritualised (sometimes in brutal ways), but how social and physiological versions of puberty do not always converge. Casement (ibid.: 4) helpfully characterises how 'this lack of convergence is more common in rites pertaining to boys . . . [because] . . . physical puberty is largely a matter of public opinion as its onset is less marked and more gradual.'

This is, I suggest, one of the contributory factors to the potential for 'discontinuity' in the male psyche – a discontinuity which can often be traced back to this pre-pubescent phase. The other twin emerging from early *anima* in the boy, *thanima*, is the very influence likely to jump on any sense of potential discontinuity and exacerbate it to the point where it becomes a defining characteristic as a boy tries to get himself moving into male adulthood. Inevitably, if *thanima* is in the ascendant then his ways of relating to women will be affected. He may struggle to *be* himself with a woman, just like a woman in the grip of *thanimus* will likewise feel caught in questions of 'how to relate' to men. In both cases love and sex may well be dragged into faulty, disappointing, even toxic territory.

The central idea here, to recap, is that ahead of puberty *anima* and *animus* retreat into undifferentiated versions of themselves during latency before being reborn as split. In both cases they again 'give birth' to twins – one a life-enhancing *eros* version, and one carrying deathly, destructive *thanatos* characteristics. The predominance of one over the other will depend on who the person *is* (i.e. the genetic and environmental influences), their early psychosexual and relational development and attachments, the wider collective messages about gendered identity and, I suggest, the ways in which the Self has chosen 'to do violence' to their identity and experiencing prior and up to the pre-pubescent 'moment'.

Concluding comment

The discussion in this chapter has sketched out ways in which the psychosexual and relational influences in the formative years of life may have divergent characteristics for males and females alongside the commonalities of development. As well as illustrating the complexity inherent in making sense of psychological, environmental and possibly archetypal influences on being female or male, this exploration has highlighted the evolving impact of contrasexual influences in the psyche. *Eros* and *thanatos* wrestle for dominance of *anima* in the boy and *animus* in the girl. The implications of this struggle will be demonstrated in the clinical explorations of the next two chapters, where the oppressive giants of *thanima* and *thanimus* have slid down the beanstalk to blight individual lives.

Chapter 4

Thanima

If one's head is not pointed in the direction of the Giant, he is there and gone before one knows it

(Monick, 1987: 38)

The discontinuities of development in the male psyche are the focus for this chapter. Jack's predicament in the *Beanstalk* story could be characterised as how to move from 'inadequate son' to 'potent son'. Male development can get caught in a limbo between pre-pubescent 'waiting' and adult 'becoming', leading to a brittleness in the maintenance of potent, grounded, adult relationships. This is pertinent to understanding male 'territory' and can shed light on the dynamics which get 'en-gendered' between women and men.

This discussion analyses how men may experience and articulate inner deadness and disintegration. I will incorporate thinking outlined in Chapter 3 on how *anima* works for boys and men and its polarised versions of *erosima* (*anima's* life-giving form, often erotically charged) and *thanima* (where *anima* is charged with deadness, hostility or fragmentation – or all three).

There is more focus on *thanima* than *erosima* here and on what might engender feelings of 'discontinuity' in men. I suggest that this feeling state is a product of a combination of perceptions or thoughts about how to 'be' (including how to 'be male') and emotional states which refer back to very early experiences of self and mother. Analyses with men whose narcissism and disembodied relationship to their own presence dominate clinical work form one reference point. These analyses were sometimes experienced as 'dead', and the question of how psychic deadness and impotence can be worked with is considered. I draw on a range of disguised examples from my clinical work with men, as well as utilising literature on how women analysts might experience working with men. I consider how the *puer–senex* archetype can illuminate the stark realities of a man's early experiences, particularly in how mother's presence is felt, as well as in how the presence or absence of father is experienced.

The *puer et senex* archetypal polarity (Jung, 1940/1968) played a key part in Jung's reading of the lifelong struggle for the man – and the boy within the man – with the problem of becoming ungrounded. The *puer* is the 'eternal boy' (and *puella* is the 'eternal girl') who never wants to grow up, like Peter Pan. This gets reflected in behaviours or fantasies which are unrealistic, overly idealistic, naive or avoidant. Jack is a *puer* as he does not seem to know how to grow up. At a deeper, unconscious level, however, there are forces at work which enable him to do so.

The obvious example is his naive exchange of the cow for a handful of beans – this counterintuitive trade-off leads to the release of the fecundity within the beans, and the bridging of earth and sky by the beanstalk. In a clinical context this implies the hidden potential of the unconscious to *compensate* for the often debilitating influence of *puer*. The childlike, playful and aspirational qualities of *puer* can on occasion link the boy or man to his deeper potential and liberate him from stuckness, either through consciously breaking through inner rigidity, or stumbling upon a breakthrough via the kind of naive intuition described in the story. This potential is illustrated in the story by the role of the sky – Jack has to go 'up there', in a classic *puer* move, not to escape, but to find the solution he is seeking. However, the focus in this chapter is on *puer's* more problematic aspects, and how it can conspire with *thanima* to deaden or subvert fuller engagement with life.

Senex (see, for example, Sharp, 1991: 109–10), meanwhile, represents the more solid, authoritative power of the father (or king). In its healthy form it provides the grounded counterbalance to the flaky, childlike, *puer*. However, Jack encounters a tyrannical version of it in the giant, who is violent, abusive and greedy. He eats people (especially 'Englishmen', illustrating how vulnerable Jack is to his father's fate). We can see the giant's unappealing characteristics as Jack's projected rage and self-destructiveness. His father has been murdered, and in a boy's fantasy life this is, according to Freud (1920/1991), not unlike what happens during the oedipal conflict between son and father over mother. There may be ungrounded feelings of triumph at having 'killed father', a link to Arlow's (1961) model for understanding this story as a mythologising of an immature ego's wish to kill father without there being any consequences.

The fear and guilt associated with 'killing' father to get mother is represented in the story by how father gets blown up to giant size and in turn does not just want to kill Jack, but actually eat him up. So, there is a fantasy here of becoming nothing more than fodder for father ('crushed bone' in his bread), to compensate for having 'killed' him, and possibly returning to being just one of the millions of spermatozoa swimming around in father's testicles.

Jack's *puer* problem – he is unable to grow up quickly as his mother needs him to – is reflected in where his capacity for healthy maturation has become inaccessible; his 'giant' tyrannical father's balls have it, and there's a sense that he has to wrestle with (or trick) father in order to get this back. Intra-psychically, introjected father has become a figure of tyranny and terror – wholly negative *senex* – which thus makes the task for Jack to get hold of his positive, grounded, *senex* energy a difficult one.

This *puer–senex* problem is characterised here in terms of how *thanima* (negative *anima*) can grip the unconscious development of some boys and men, keeping them from dealing with this problem through deadening their capacity to recover the giant's treasure. In turn, this can bring oppressive, emasculating, and other potentially destructive qualities to bear on how they relate to themselves and others in *conscious* ways.

I also propose a theoretical and clinical bridge between *puer* and *narcissus* to frame how a man may unconsciously strive against psychic fragmentation by clinging to an identification to both – in order to remain intact in the face of being caught in a pre-pubescent state which reflects an insecure attachment to mother. I will describe how male analysands may find a more grounded embrace of reality via a gathering use of empathy and potency in the transference–countertransference, helping them to begin to leave a 'dead' (*thanima*) version of relationship with mother behind, and to come to an intrapsychic settlement with the 'dead' version of father, if this is the legacy they hold instead, or as well.

Discontinuity in the male psyche

It is difficult to successfully describe within a post-Jungian framework a picture of how the development of the male psyche can be disrupted by discontinuities in early attachments. However, several themes which have arisen from work in which I have been engaged with male analysands may illuminate this problem. They include: suffering in relation to feelings of being split, frozen or having a sense that one's identity has a discontinuous quality; a presence of 'deadness' in the transference-countertransference; a disconnection in the relationship with the body, or not being healthily 'embodied'; the presence of an idealised, dynamic and potent – but elusive – self and of a weaker, passive version of self, which is disregarded in a '*shadow*' sense, or even despised.

Where something has fractured or failed in the making of the early bond with mother – or with both father and mother – these manifestations of loss and despair show up in analytic work in certain ways. A theoretical framework to elucidate this problem includes playing with the idea of a bridge between the archetype of *puer* and the myth of *narcissus* to better understand the unconscious strategies used by men to bolster the fragile defences of the self against disintegration. These can show up in the consulting room in a range of ways – narcissism, depression and repressed rage to name but a few. These presentations can also be seen as manifestations of *thanima*.

Such presentations of fragmentation seem to point to hard-to-reach pathology which may be peculiarly 'male'. The backdrop to these clinical presentations is some archetypal features of human development which are difficult to understand and to impact clinically. They seems to loom particularly large in the case of men for whom there is a lack, or significant diminution, of an active inner dynamics; men for whom a more passive relationship to life arises out of something depressed, indifferent or rejecting in the *vas* of early relations, which perpetuates itself as somehow 'inevitable' in adulthood. Absence of a genuinely potent 'father within' is a common element in the equation. However, I also believe that our notions of what 'potency' is are rather confused, because of misunderstandings about the meaning and presence of parental (personal and archetypal) power and how this is incorporated by a boy.

I have noticed that anxieties about personal authority can be central to how male analysands locate themselves in the world. In examples I give in this chapter, this feeling of personal authority seems to float free from its moorings – if it had any anchorage in the first place – resulting in a discontinuity in the presentation of the self that I have not noticed so frequently in female analysands (in the following chapter, female 'versions' of pathology, equally as problematic, will be proposed).

The range of clinical experience with men that I draw on is broad in terms of age, social status and sexual orientation, but all present elements of the *malaise* hinted at above – the struggle to find a correlation between inner confusions, and their own place in life. These are men for whom *thanima* undermines their grounded sense of self through deadening or disorienting their feelings and capacity for erotic, as well as assertive, self-expression.

One could say that *thanima* energies flow in through the gaps left by the weak *puer–narcissus* bridge suggested above (this is not, after all, the powerful, erect beanstalk). A theoretical model to link these themes together will be developed via the bridging of two of the most commonly used notions in analytical psychology for describing the discontinuous male psyche: the archetype of *puer et senex*, and the myth of *narcissus* and its clinical presentation as narcissism. In my clinical work I see how men with identity discontinuity unconsciously 'build' this *puer*–narcissism bridge as a survival mechanism, a deep defence against *thanima* and the potential for disintegration it can bring.

Analytical theories of male identity discontinuity

Jung, of course, made very few references to narcissism, the irony being that much of his thinking about how people can fall into states where they avoid embracing life reflected this concept. Jung seemed to regard the term as unhelpful where it got affixed to any attempt by an individual to build their individuating sense of self by confusing it with self-knowledge (Jung, 1963: para. 709). Although he recognised its presentation as a primary source of pathological 'self-love' (Jung, 1964: para. 204), his ideas about the *spirit* archetype enabled him to establish a different kind of platform for describing the phenomenon involved. In his elucidation of the meanings of alchemical processes, Jung evoked the kinds of dual, or split, states commonly described in psychoanalytic literature. This *archetypal* route into giving these states definition lends what is elsewhere termed 'narcissism' a less overt status in analytical psychology, but one which captures the crucial place of the self in its efforts to reinstate its significance when empathic parenting has been lacking in early life.

This archetypal approach does have its limitations, though. Jung's model drawn from the *Rosarium* (Jung, 1954/1966a: para. 401) has enormous value in, for example, its metaphor of *nigredo* for psychic deadness in the transference–countertransference. However, in my experience, strictly applying the sequence laid out in Jung's model of the unfolding archetypal transference does not always reflect what seems to be going on. In one case, the analysis seemed to begin with *nigredo* – as it seems had the analysand's life – before dreams came to play a more prominent role, and an awakening 'ascent of the soul' began to happen, followed by a more alive engagement with the world. Eventually, the archetypal backdrop to the work – a kind of false *coniunctio* between the figures of mother and priest – became clear from various dream images, confirming how a 'mother church' complex was at the heart of the deadness, as if he had been 'baptised' into discontinuity and deadness at the beginning of his life. This deadness was a powerful signifier of fractured attachment, a profound discontinuity.

Thinking on male development within the post-Jungian framework also offers useful pointers to understanding how men might unconsciously process deadening early experiences. Efforts to identify archetypal facets of the masculine are useful, such as the presence of the 'oedipal boy' and the 'divine boy', which can remain predominant as signifiers of immaturity (Moore, 1990: 15ff).

Perhaps of more clinical relevance is the emphasis on father as an inner object in the child's development (Samuels, 1989: 66ff). This is of particular import for a boy when taken in relation to how he introjects aspects of mother. Bovensiepen (2000) usefully expands on the impact of the internal parental couple on the boy's psyche, particularly as he confronts the bridges between latency, adolescence and adulthood. Bovensiepen draws on Meltzer's (1992) distinction between identification with mother (*intrusive*) and with father (*obtrusive*) to argue that for the boy to get lost in the former without experiencing the more active identification with father can leave him caught in a 'claustrum' – or a state of 'pathological projective identification' (Bovenseipen, 2000: 13). This model is most relevant to some of the clinical imagery (cave, box, etc.) that comes up in this chapter.

Balint's work on the 'basic fault' (1968: 18–23) has helped me to think about what may have initially generated the sense of disintegration in my male analysands. The 'basic fault', which may occur in the most formative stages of the mother–infant relationship, offers a portrayal of the critical schism in the inner world which can later be reflected in a sense of emptiness and passive acceptance of life's vicissitudes. Balint applied his concept to the early development of both men and women so it is impossible to use it alone to base assertions about the gender-specificity of a 'male' pathology of discontinuity. However, Benjamin's (1988: 75–6) formulation of the roots of specifically male identity, referred to in Chapter 3, helps to clarify this.

Drawing on Stoller's (1975: 99) analysis of gender, Benjamin observes that 'the boy develops his gender and identity by means of establishing discontinuity and difference from the person to whom he is most attached' (Benjamin, 1988: 75–6). The boy, unlike the girl, has to dis-identify from mother in order to be free to grow. This throws up all sorts of enduring conflicts about power – should he submit or dominate, or maybe try to 'share' feelings of power? These conflicts remain charged with the presence of mother if this dis-identification misfires, resulting in a *recurring* sense of discontinuity, which infects the 'here and now' – rather than being a necessary stage of separation which has been experienced and left in the past. This infection gets reflected in how *puer* often takes centre stage with *senex* waiting in the wings to supply its grounded sense of personal authority, a wait that can be lifelong.

Emerging from internal waiting and/or deadness is a difficult and painful process for both analysand and analyst. Ogden (1995: 699) writes of a process 'in which the patient's experience of deadness . . . [was] . . . transformed from an unthinkable thing in itself . . . into a living, verbally symbolized experience of the patient's (and my own) deadness . . . Deadness had become a feeling as opposed to a fact.' Through the evolving transference onto the analyst, the analysand re-experiences, and becomes more conscious of, the deadness; *thanima* is experienced as a psychic fact within his psyche. The countertransference also makes a version of this deadness available for the analyst to work with, and to eventually be recognised by the analysand as a feeling state, not the fixed reference point for all experience.

As Eigen (2004: 14) points out, the analyst working with a clinical 'forcefield' of deadness needs to 'find his own anti-growth sense . . . [in order to make] . . . room for the patient's.' This can provide an uncomfortable challenge, requiring the analyst to allow deadening aspects of his or herself (*thanima* or *thanimus*) into consciousness to furnish the countertransference with its full context, without slipping into enactments of the feelings which may arise. This then acts as a vital beginning to bridging the sense of discontinuity, as it gives due recognition to the central importance of the deadness, rather than leaving it outside conscious awareness.

If disregarded it may even 'kill' the analysis by slowly strangling any life out of it. The probability of it provoking corresponding *thanima/thanimus* responses in the analyst, e.g. sleepiness or lack of interest, is strong. As Eigen suggests, once the analyst notices what is happening, the deadness can be afforded its vital place in the work and the dead side of the analytic relationship can be used as a resource rather than a drain.

Another important concept which informs an understanding of the roots of male identity discontinuity is Green's (1986: Ch. 7) idea of a dead mother complex. This arises, Green postulates, when mother experiences a drastic sense of detachment from her infant, a kind of bereavement which is likewise experienced as a catastrophic loss for the child, and is another way of describing the installation of *thanima* in the little boy (or *thanimus* in the little girl). After doomed attempts to repair mother's feeling state the infant's ego employs a desperate defence against the trauma that has two features: 'the decathexis of the maternal object and the unconscious identification with the dead mother' (ibid.: 150–1).

The child has had to psychically 'kill' the introjected mother as protection against the pain of the loss of maternal love, but will inevitably remain in unconscious identification with the dead mother as a way of preserving some kind of relationship to what happened and was lost. In analysis, the resultant presentation of depression and deadened affect manifests the presence of this complex. The long-term impact of this in terms of narcissistic wounding and the installation of a deep-seated deadness (*thanima* or *thanimus*) will clearly be profound, irrespective of the gender of the individual. This applies also to the implications arising from the work of Ogden and Eigen. It needs to be taken in conjunction, however, with the patterns around discontinuity and deadness in men which I will elucidate. Together, these insights provide theoretical and clinical underpinnings for my discussion.

Suffering the legacy of discontinuity

In my clinical experience I have noted a common expression of male pathology: alongside inner splitting or 'freezing' of being is a sense of discontinuity – a feeling of ordinary development having been disrupted, and re-experiencing this disruption in the present. This brings with it a legacy of disorientation, anxiety and suffering in interpersonal and intrapsychic life.

The *OED* (Allen, 1991: 333) definition of the adjective 'discontinuous' is: 'lacking continuity in space or time; intermittent.' For some men, this statement carries a relevance more profound than this straightforward definition may have intended. The healthy development of the male psyche requires the upholding of an unconscious belief in the 'linear', 'forward' or 'upward' trajectory of its becoming. When this is cut across or undermined, a legacy of *feeling discontinuous* develops and becomes part of the furniture of the psyche. The irony of Benjamin's observation above is the implication of 'discontinuity' as a *healthy* goal for men when it involves a 'good enough' dis-identification from mother. If this attempt fails, then the struggle for the 'discontinuity' of separateness turns in on itself, becoming a psychic burden and a *saboteur* of efforts to develop a stable and engaged life.

Here one could say the positive discontinuity of *erosima*, bringing life enhancing qualities of autonomy and trust in self while being able to enjoy the benefits of relationship to others, has flipped into the negative discontinuity of *thanima*. This shows up in a variety of ways – in a constant striving for an idealised life, job or relationship, for example, or in a recurring feeling of inner collapse which repeats in social or intimate interactions. Nostalgia can be another expression of the *malaise* – repeatedly revisiting a time (usually pre-pubescent) when everything was 'fine'; before things changed, permanently, for the worse.

These men may come to analysis as a means of finding – or rediscovering – the path they instinctively feel they 'should' be on; men who see themselves as trying to improve and prove themselves, feeling they are pulled down by a 'lower self' which they wish to overcome or even discard. Whatever form this discontinuity takes, it arises from deep, dark roots to become intimately bound up with a man's striving for a clear identity.

There is often a fixation at a point earlier in life where the apparently linear progression from childhood to adulthood was irrevocably truncated – maybe through a traumatic attempt to bridge primary and secondary school, or the collapse of a sexual relationship in teenage years. Both are possible manifestations of something having 'misfired' at the 'pre-pubescent moment', where *anima* energies in boys reawaken, in this case with *thanima* in the ascendant.

This sense of having left a key element of self behind, or of not being whole because of a crucial break in the 'timeline' of life, presents in a variety of ways: through attempts to control the analysis (as a compensatory strategy to counter a deeply felt loss of control in life), intellectualisation, or somatising of the problem (e.g. in sexual dysfunction such as impotency or post-ejaculatory depression, where discontinuity is manifested in breaks between desire, bodily functioning and outcome – satisfactory consummation is unavailable in the present and merely a forlorn hope for the future).

There can be a sense of being in the presence of a psyche which, through its use of narcissistic defences against disintegration, and adoption of a *puer* position in life, has formed a membrane to hold itself together and protect against impingements. There are also echoes of the 'protective shell' (Tustin, 1990: 189) of an autistic defence, alluding to the ideas of Baron-Cohen (2004) on how autism may be seen as an extreme presentation of the male brain.

Baron-Cohen's assertion that the male brain tends to be geared up for systematising and cognitively understanding experience – more than feeling it and empathising with it – links to the male presentations of discontinuity I refer to above. Bearing in mind there is much about 'brain-sex' we do not know, the male brain may rely more on a linear path in order to 'become' fully adult than does the female brain. If this systematised, deeply embedded, expectation of 'progress' (forward, upward, transcending) is disrupted or broken then the impact is powerful and long-lasting, as neurological expectations have been critically disrupted.

It is important to reassert the dangers of overstating congenital gender difference, and see Baron-Cohen's contextualisation of such difference as being a variable which shifts in degree and form depending on other factors surrounding genetic and environmental influences on an individual man or woman. Bearing these points in mind, the implication remains that the female brain anticipates a less linear line of development because the ground it begins on in life with mother is more secure than the male's; the little boy's *erosima–thanima* problem depends on the quality of the erotic bond more, so may be less sure of itself in the very early stages of life.

The ramifications for female development will be explored in the following chapter, but one speculation relates to a possible distinction between how definite the physical and psychological markers of puberty are for girls compared with boys. Generally speaking, the onset of first menses at the start of puberty, and therefore an embodied awareness of their ability to conceive, brings them into the fold of womanhood in a definitive way. In turn this affirms the early daughter–mother contract described in Chapter 3, a bond which held out the promise from mother: 'if you identify with me now, you can "become me" after puberty', a promise fulfilled for many women when they have children (a promise which can have limiting, even suffocating, connotations for women, too).

For boys, meanwhile, the dropping of testicles, first wet dream and awareness of the capacity to father a child comes at a time which is more difficult to predict. Meanwhile, the less bodily rooted, less defined, nature of the early father–son bond contributes to the sense that the *rite de passage* from boyhood to manhood – unless explicitly marked by some kind of familial or social ritual – is more implicit than explicit, and therefore more elusive in relation to a male sense of continuity and identity.

These observations complement the proposed distinction between the male need for a straight-and-narrow road and the female capacity to manage without it. The early bond with mother usually means the road is already there for the girl and does not need to be 'found' in the same way.

The male brain may have evolved a more rigid and therefore more fragile range of responses to deep relational disruption, particularly with regard to mother because of deep uncertainties set up by the greater dependency of the little boy on the erotic bond (*erosima*) to her, as opposed to the predominantly relational container offered to the little girl. This is exacerbated by a less certain same-sex identification with father *and* a less well-defined 'border crossing' into adulthood.

Clinical examples of *thanima* waiting and deadness

Men sometimes speak in the consulting room of the wish to be more alive, regarding themselves as not having properly lived. They believe they have watched the world go by rather than having dived into the stream of its risks and pleasures. They want to take the plunge before it is too late, and throw off whatever has kept them in a moribund relationship to life. I have also worked with women who have been prey to a feeling 'life has passed me by', but the quality conveyed has not been quite the same – perhaps because of the differing nature of the influences of *thanima* and *thanimus* on trajectories of males and females respectively. I will elucidate this distinction further in the following chapter.

One man's dream symbolised the problem of inner deadness clearly. There were two adjoining houses – one was lived in and well kept, the other empty, boarded up and dilapidated. This image of a split self described the way the more alive side of him was being held back from embracing life by the other, like dry rot spreading from the decaying house to the well-preserved one. In the analysis this perspective showed itself in a kind of hopelessness; he said the analysis would not make any difference. At other times, the more vibrant 'house' showed itself in a determination to find an expression for a wish for something new. It was as if there were two versions of *temenos* competing to define the direction in which this man's psyche was headed. The more active version was eventually expressed through a career change after the analysis ended, perhaps having 'deposited' enough of the deadness within the container of the analytic relationship to free him of the feeling of being beholden to it.

This kind of difficulty was more pronounced with a man, in his later middle age, who brought a deeply felt belief it was too late for life to assume any kind of tangible meaning. He came to analysis hoping I would help him come to terms with what he had missed. One exchange between us conveys how frozen his sense of his own presence had become:

Analysand: 'I feel it again.'
Analyst: 'What?'
Analysand: 'Everything . . . stopping.'

Analyst: 'Can you describe what this is like?'

Analysand: [long pause] 'It's like . . . everything in me freezes . . . ice . . . ice all around me . . . I can see you through the ice . . . like I'm a caveman who's been frozen for thousands of years.'

Analyst: 'Waiting to be free?'

Analysand: [sob] 'Yes, yes . . . and the world . . . time . . . just keeps rushing past . . . like it always has.'

A strong conviction had taken root: nothing would change – life would hasten towards its end without him having agency over events. Inevitably this conviction came into the transference. Working with his projection of the depressed parental dyad onto me did make some impact on this, but the sense remained of a soul hibernating while life went on around him.

Other male analysands have appeared to constellate the sense of time within having stood still, but their solution seems to be to project forward into the future an idealised time when they will 'become'. This can present in the consulting room as a transference onto the analyst as the heroic parent who will enable them to escape from the frozen present. This 'future' is seen as a time when the man can be potent, heroic, and win the love of his life – like a little boy dreaming of being a prince, or a Beckham.

A man I worked with seemed caught in a temporal projection forwards, imagining the day his ex-lover returns to him, knocking on his door and begging forgiveness, while in reality he was struggling to feel his *own* current presence in life. Here, being 'patient' becomes a state of mind. A voice within says: 'If I am a good boy I will become a man.'

Another response to suffering induced by having to be interminably 'patient' is the expression – or withholding – of rage. While some men seem to fall into presentations of passive-aggression (e.g. a man longing to beat up a colleague after taking on work he could not say 'no' to) others act out a deep frustration with life by literally attacking people they care for. Men who get into a fight because 'at least something is happening' may feel a fleeting, skewed sense of being alive. At times domestic violence against women carries a dangerously displaced expression of *thanima* rage against feelings of deadness.

In describing how men may suffer – and make others suffer in the process – a picture emerges of something coming to a standstill, and the boy inside the man struggling to get things moving. Often the boy is not big or strong enough, wrestling with the broken key he hopes will open the door to adult aliveness. As a result of this internal object relationship, the boy and the man become united in a deeply felt passivity in the face of being locked out of life.

'Deadness' as a presentation of 'discontinuity' can infect an analysis, if not 'kill' it. When felt breaks in connection and relationship in an analysand's history reconstellate in the transference–countertransference, the work can come to a standstill. With one man, the lifelessness in the consulting room became so stultifying that an image of a box emerged in my mind, as I struggled to stay alert. This man had spoken of feeling 'trapped' in his life. The frustration and lethargy I experienced in my own countertransference gave me a sense of being 'boxed in'. This led to a feeling of suffocation and of restricted movement. The work between us seemed to be enclosed and flattened.

A flavour of this is conveyed in the following vignette: The analysand had been talking about something he did at work the day before which demonstrated how 'shy' he felt. I found myself drifting into a sleepy state, noticed it and pulled myself back and said: 'You believe you can't assert your views at work?' Silence fell, he averted his eyes from me and seemed to 'shut down', his head slumping forward. His shoulders came up as if he was about to sigh. He stopped himself, reminding me how I had stopped myself getting sleepy – my countertransference was picking up how his efforts to remain outside of a lethargic despair required constant vigilance on his part. His body seemed to freeze in this tense position. He then looked at me and nodded his head slowly before it dropped and stilled again. I felt as frozen as I sensed he was.

Sandler and Sandler describe this as the analysand's unconscious strategy of casting the analyst in a role complementing their constellation of inner objects. This blends with the analyst's personal tendencies to create in him 'a compromise formation between his own tendencies and his reflexive acceptance of the role that the patient is forcing on him' (Sandler and Sandler, 1998: 53).

My deadened and enclosed aspects, conjoined with the deadening parental figures he was unconsciously demanding I adopt, helped to maintain the 'box', until his dreams began to open up a contrasting source of material – compensating for the flatness and emptiness of the interactions between us. The parallel between the 'box' and the 'caveman' in the earlier example is also worth noting. It offers an allusion to something womb-like – a hint of where *thanima* possibly trapped the little boy within an intractable waiting for *erosima* in the relationship with mother. These speculations would require further clinical data to substantiate the notion of the captivity of some men's psyche being identified with the womb.

Another speculation which may merit further exploration is that such men may be carrying a 'dead' transitional object. Here Winnicott's idea (Dell'Orto, 2003) of how a child latches onto a toy, a way of relating or an image which enables her or him to separate from mother healthily by 'carrying around' this substitute for the relationship, is turned on its head. The deadness in the early relationship with mother (the victory of *thanima* at this critical stage of development) results in a 'dead' transitional object, meaning the healthy repositioning of self in relation to mother – and wider society and culture – has not been constellated, and instead the imaginal, feeling and instinctual legacy left in the unconscious is of something stuck, absent or 'dead'; another way of understanding why men may struggle to make the 'transitions' life can demand.

Clinical examples of disembodiment

Feelings of detachment or estrangement from the body can also feature in the lives of men who experience a disabling sense of discontinuity, leaving them less able to articulate emotion in dialogues with others or with self. A corollary of this sometimes seems to be a loss of agency over aspects of physical being and functioning.

Some men find their sense of discontinuity presenting in their sex lives. The play on life and death is relevant here, sexual expression becoming haunted by *thanima* via the little deaths of erection dysfunction, premature ejaculation, or post-ejaculatory depression. This somatised malaise is like a curse arising from confusion and ambivalence found within a man's relationship to mother. His attempts at preserving aliveness (*erosima*) in the face of the 'dead mother' tend to be erotically *stuck* rather than *charged* as he strives to connect with some inaccessible aspect of mother via a loyalty which can sometimes permeate his love life (e.g. by foregoing relationships with other women). This boundless loyalty can show itself in an approval-seeking transference. To move beyond such disembodiment represented by sexual difficulties would be for a man to turn his back on mother – and supersede his lifelong loyalty to a 'meaning which remains in abeyance in the psyche while awaiting its revelation' (Green, 1986: 172).

In the clinical setting, I have sometimes found myself picking up the awkwardness felt by such male analysands in my countertransference reactions, and have had to overcome a kind of protective embarrassment towards the details given of difficulties experienced. Over time it has been possible to form an alliance against the self-consciousness in the room, as the capacity for trust, acceptance and humour builds – an emerging positive transference in the face of the deadness.

This enables the male analysand to become more active in his efforts to channel erotic and sexual energies towards relationship. Often I experience this as a need for me to be active and provide the phallic energy missed from the relationship to father. While this could be seen as an enactment, the analysand's fear of re-owning what he has projected onto me is so great it has forced me into enacting it for him.

There are other ways in which discontinuity for men may get somatised, e.g. through becoming overweight, underweight or ill (or through drug dependency). However, a common theme seems to be a dissociation from the felt presence of the physical self. The lack of an embodied identity in the world is a symptom of a failed – or at best vague – embodiment in the fleshly home of the male psyche. *Thanima* has short-circuited healthy embodiment.

A more common presentation of feelings of impotence in men is a chronic difficulty in taking risks, confronting problems and generally taking initiative. The lethargy which may intervene between intention (or hope) and action, can stem from an unconscious belief that action is too dangerous, too threatening to the still-dominating connection to the lost or fractured attachment. One male analysand had converted this complex into a belief in the future as hopeless, so he envisaged he would experience the moments before his death as an unfolding revelation of everything he had failed to do. Rather than his life flashing before his eyes, it would be the life he had *not* lived. Here, the discontinuity is projected into the future as ultimate suffering at the very point his consciousness is 'snuffed out'.

Physically he experienced this dread – reminiscent of being visited by the 'Ghost of Christmas Future', where Scrooge is shown his untended grave, and his memory is despised and banished (Dickens, 1843: 69–70) – as a lethargy which left him inactive in response to inner urgings for action. This man gradually came to tackle his fears of a wasted life in the future by being more active in the present, after a process of engaging with the deadness in the room. A dormant son–father dyad became *ersosima*-active in the relationship and his capacity to challenge me made new thinking, and action, possible.

Two selves: The idealised and the rejected

In order to rationalise their feeling of temporal discontinuity some men describe their identities as being split into a 'higher'/'lower' or 'superior'/'inferior' duality. The aim becomes to 'get rid of' the negative version of themselves. This seems to be an attempt by the ego to banish the feelings of being split, rather than falling into the chasm which has opened up. Men who are living with such a legacy construct a 'timeline' of their life history, particularly in identifying key points where things seem to change for the worse.

This refers back to my idea in Chapter 3 about the psyche being 'ripe for splitting' at the pre-pubescent stage of individual development, and how this can get rationalised by a person telling themselves nothing will ever be the same because of what happened 'back then'. They hold themselves together by maintaining a belief in a 'higher' version of self (a 'transcending me') which offers a *puer*-like hope of sanctuary in the future.

One example of how discontinuity threw up the sense of a split self is an author who suffered writer's block and came, through analytic work, to see a split in himself, represented by two figures he imagined counterpointed to one another. First, there was a Shakespeare-like version of himself who wrote fluently and with great skill (given concrete representation by a statuette of the bard on his writing desk). Second, there was a depressed version of his father, who had had a tough life working in the coal mines since his teens. Inevitably, this man identified his depressed states of mind, when he could not write, with this figure.

I found myself taking father's part to counterbalance the Shakespearian idealisation, and moderate the sense that this man seemed to *love* himself when he wrote (*erosima*) and loathe himself when he could not (*thanima*). The split between his scope to follow the vocation he wanted and his father's self-sacrifice left the man with a powerful tension between wanting to recover something of his father and wishing to banish his presence from his psyche.

The discontinuity for this man seemed to relate to a time in his teens when his father fought for his son's right to write. His father had surrendered to a bleak working life at a corresponding time in his *own* life – a powerfully paradoxical discontinuity shared by father and son. At the close of our work this man said he had placed a picture of Dad on his writing desk alongside the figure of his muse.

This kind of splitting into versions of self which are in conflict takes on a 'male' quality, I would suggest, when archetypal ideas of father are imprinted behind them; the need to be 'strong', 'decisive', 'authoritative' and so on (whether these are seen as genuinely archetypal, or as social constructs, or both). The internal pressure is to despise and 'be rid' of aspects which contradict these.

Bridging discontinuity

A common feature in my analytic work with men is of something critical happening at the pre-pubescent stage (or 'moment'). As suggested, it is as if the psyche is ripe for splitting at this time – if the latent legacy of a *thanima*, fractured early attachment to mother is there. The presence of a potent father figure (internal or external) would also seem to be a factor in enabling the boy approaching adolescence to take his own potency and experiment with it among his peers. In the cases described in this chapter this was largely absent; instead, teenage years were often isolated, potency getting turned inwards rather than out into the world. This could be a narcissistic strategy for survival or an incubation of potency for a later 'becoming', or both.

So how might the boy, and then the man, survive and try to build a better life for himself in the face of discontinuity? The archetypal *puer et senex* dyad (Hillman, 1979a: 3–53) offers one template for the adequate movement of the male psyche through life's staging points – i.e. healthy development as being the capacity to leave childhood behind while remaining able to 'play', before taking on the role and authority of father (whether becoming a real father, or in internalising *senex* characteristics in a grounded and balanced way).

So what might the male psyche do when this trajectory collapses? What archetypal resources are available to the psyche to repair or replace the road it 'should' have been on? As the men here described presented features of narcissism and of *puer*, it is worth considering if the male psyche which feels discontinuous may be striving to bridge the two together as a way of moving across the gap thrown up by discontinuities experienced early in life and repeating in the present.

Here, *thanima* generates two attitudinal 'sets': a *puer* combination of ungroundedness and timelessness (Tatham, 1992: 21–8); and narcissistic self-referral and aggrandisement. The attempt to bridge these two attitudes comes through perceiving the *narcissus* myth and the *puer* archetype as positions on a continuum (the first mainly directed inwards and the second outwards) which offer a kind of flexibility, however limited, for such men to oscillate between in their efforts to cope. I want to explore how the male psyche may try to reorganise itself when the *puer et senex* 'route map' gets irrevocably lost – like someone driving through unfamiliar territory when the map he has been given is useless.

It needs to be stressed – as Narcissus is not an archetype *per se* – that I am referring to a *puer*-narcissism *continuum*, not an archetypal polarity. The position taken at any time by the male psyche will draw on the two 'ways of being' – identification with *puer* and/or narcissism – to generate personas, e.g. 'loyal son', 'heroic son', 'martyr' and so on, to provide some sense of identity.

A man may exhibit *puer* features (Hillman, 1979a) in a lack of groundedness, a 'flitting between' (courses, jobs, relationships and friendships) and a tendency to fly high before crashing down. Such men often seem to be asking straightforwardly for a grounding analysis. My responses to how earnest and unrelated such men can seem include: a difficulty in remaining focused; impatience and irritation; and fatigue – all possible countertransference reflections of their difficulties. These *puer* aspects have challenged me not to take my own 'flight' from remaining fully in the room.

Narcissistic features in these analysands present as a need for me to mirror back their overriding sense of having been misunderstood and undervalued, and to offer succour to their belief that they really were more valued than they thought. One man brought a dream in which he looks at his face in the mirror but there is nothing there. This pointed to the deadness in the transference–countertransference and how it seemed to mark a shift in his awareness of others as *persons* in their own right (Levinas, quoted in Lowenthal and Snell, 2000) not just as objects for him to (narcissistically) utilise. It also graphically portrayed his painful struggle to have his own identity. As Jacoby (1985: 29) points out: 'The . . . [narcissus] . . . myth deals with the drive for self-knowledge and self-realization.'

Here is an important link between narcissism and *puer*, for the eternal pre-adolescent in this analysand had needed to 'see' the image of his elusive 'fallen away' power reflected in the constellation of relations he experienced in the transference. This deadened the work for a period, but was also a necessary stage of self-validation in establishing his relationship with me, enabling a freeing up of his symbolic life while his self-referring aspects stared into the mirror of his transference onto me.

Hillman's pointer to *puer* as carrying a 'distorted . . . transcendent function of the family problem, as an attempt to redeem the parents' (quoted in Moore, 1990: 227) also seems particularly relevant to constructing of the 'bridge' between *puer* and narcissism. When the dynamics in the parental dyad become overly moribund or antagonistic, a child unconsciously attempts to 'solve' the problem (Mitchell, 1988), but this saddles the child with something much bigger than he can manage and it inevitably gets distorted. This is like *Jack's* 'giant' predicament of dealing with the loss of his father plus his mother's depressed and impoverished state.

His identification with the 'eternal child', plus his narcissistic defence of it, unconsciously act as the family's attempt to 'bridge' a gap between the parents. So, the bridge between *puer* and *narcissus* can, unlike the beanstalk, be the boy's doomed attempt to build a bridge which works for the family too.

I suggest that the kinds of presentations of male discontinuity set out in this chapter reflect where archetypal polarities of transcendent versus immanent are stretched to breaking point within the individual suffering involved. So, in his failed *puer* attempt to reach the sky (father) a man cannot resolve his problem by transcending, or 'solving', it. Likewise, by falling into narcissistic styles of relating to himself and others, he is attempting, but failing, to embrace a grounded, immanent experience of being loved (mother) by loving himself.

Neither 'father/sky' nor 'mother/ground' gets satisfactorily located or related to. Here, instead of providing a real solution through bridging mother and father, *thanima* generates an illusory beanstalk. When someone tries to climb up from the bottom to the top of it they fall (*puer*). If they are at the top trying to climb down, they remain stranded up in the air with only themselves as company (*narcissism*). The deadness is a meeting point between these two positions, suspended in mid air, between ground and sky.

Seeing the analysand's deadness as a product of an introjection of the feeling and sexual life of the parents helps in understanding the lack of lively affect in the analysand or in the transference–countertransference. The absence of narcissistic mirroring (Schwartz-Salant, 1982: 65–6) due to the deadness experienced in early parental relationships can set the tone of his inner life as self-referring and intellectualised, requiring significant others – e.g. a partner – to be his 'mirror'.

The *puer* aspect of the *puer–narcissus* bridge is represented by his efforts to break out, to fly above this intense difficulty by such behaviours as self-referring intellectualism. In contrast, the narcissistic aspect of the bridge is represented by the erection of a defensive shield which protects him against the unbearable realities of unmet needs and the 'otherness' of significant objects, rather than a healthy narcissism (Gordon, 1993: 272).

In the examples given, the *puer–narcissus* bridge often seemed entangled with *shadow*-enfeebled, 'inferior' and darker areas of the psyche given refuge 'beneath the bridge'. This is where the collapsed structure of the *puer–senex* pole has fallen. From one end of the bridge *puer* takes flight through the darkness. Hillman (quoted in Moore, 1990: 227) also writes of how the 'neurotic foreground obscures the archetypal background' of the *puer* complex. The picture is completed by the figure of *narcissus* at the opposite end of the bridge, who stares into a black or empty mirror (like in the dream example).

From my clinical experience, I have noticed that a reliance on a narcissistic stance to defend the core of the self often goes hand in hand with the *puer*-like seeking out of new life. It would be imprudent, however, to postulate that behind all presentations of *puer* there is a narcissistic defence. However, what emerges as a pattern is the way this powerful linkage can play a role in a man's attempt at forming an identity in brittle circumstances. This in turn seems to require a clinical approach that allows for repeated revisiting of the refuge of memories from adolescence and earlier which carry some vital sense of self. Meanwhile, unseen, the archetypal processes can come to life and then show themselves via dreams.

Father and discontinuity

Often, the male analysands referred to spoke of their fathers as 'less than' they might be – to a degree where the sobriquet of 'good enough' would not apply. In some cases this is internalised as images of father as uninspiring or even stifling (as in the 'dull' image of father described by the writer). In other cases father is experienced as weak (one analyst described his as seeming like 'a little brother') or brutal, or the son feels there has been some kind of collusion by father with mother's deadness towards him – e.g. where father has not 'stood up' for him in the face of unempathic interventions by mother. In another case father's apparent sense of his own weakness led him to try to 'team up' with the son to show him he is 'on his side'.

As already argued, the *mother–daughter* as an identificatory dyad is usually established in a more fundamental way at the start of a little girl's life, compared with the *father–son* dyad, which seems to have a less rooted or predictable starting point. There is no guarantee for the boy or man that he will be able to rely on this identificatory dyad to help him find his potency and sense of self in a context where *thanima* rules his relationship with mother.

One analysand vividly illustrated relational uncertainty about father in a dream where father hands him a partridge from out of the Christmas tree.

The partridge carries connotations (in its mythological link to Aphrodite) of an attitude that is flighty, self-deceiving and destructive (Tatham, 1992: 100–2). The dream portrayed the dark side of this father–son relationship, with its implied handing on of a legacy of *thanima*-possession and *puer*-identification.

This illustrate how the *puer–senex* pole may fall into abeyance from the angle of the father–son dynamic. When this combines with a freezing of the early relationship with mother, this can generate an archetypal constellation around the male psyche which makes the healthy kind of obtrusive identification with father that Meltzer (1992) writes about unavailable and the boy is gripped by the intrusive identification with mother, promoting a deadness in his engagement with the world.

Men working with women analysts

The examples I have given are obviously seen through the eyes of a male analyst. It is important to counterbalance this with consideration of how a male analysand can grapple with the impacts of *thanima* fragility and discontinuity in the presence of a female analyst. While it is generally true that both male and female analysts constellate (or 'become') *mother* in the transference at some stage, and *father* at another, I suggest that there will be some differences in how this is manifested. There is a kind of 'secondary reinforcement' to same sex-transference (male analyst and father transference or female analyst and mother transference) as the bodily presence of a man or a woman reinforces this. If, on the other hand, it is a different-sex transference (female analyst and father transference or male analyst and mother transference) then the transference will not be so rooted in the *immanent* bodily presence of the analyst. So, there are versions of *thanima* constellation in the male analysand–female analyst dyad which shed valuable light on our discussion because the bodily female presence of the latter brings mother more *immanently* into the therapeutic dynamic.

I am going to refer to a couple of examples provided by women analysts from relevant literature which help to tease out how *thanima/erosima* show themselves through common features of the transference–countertransference. As a starting point, the quality of the erotic transference is of particular importance in relation to the role of *erosima* or *thanima* in founding a little boy's sense of self from within the very early attachment to mother. How this shows itself in the transference/countertransference will tell us a lot about the unconscious 'living out' of *eros* in a man.

Guttman argued that 'fundamental images of women' (quoted in Schaverien, 2006: 213) are brought to bear in an *archetypal* way on how male analysands perceive a woman analyst. Guttman formulated a model for how a man may experience the 'woman analyst as mother'. This is applied to 'asexual' aspects of mother such as nurturant, suffocating/

engulfing and withholding aspects and also 'sexual' aspects, whether 'posi-tive' or 'negative' (Guttman, 2006). In the light of the critical role of the erotic in early experiencing of mother by a boy, I would question the distinction between 'sexual' and 'asexual' here. The male analysand encounters a rekindling of the early relationship with mother, which, *as a whole*, has an erotic dimension, when he comes into the analytic space, and this may be more pronounced if the analyst is a woman rather than a man.

Joy Schaverien's important paper on 'Men who leave too soon' (Schaverien, 2006a) provides some powerful insights into how men may (re)experience this dimension of *erosima* in the presence of a woman analyst, who comes to represent whatever aspects of mother once constellated the erotic for them. Schaverien points out that some men leave analysis before an erotic transference has fully developed – instead there is a 'moment' where the presence of the erotic begins to come into awareness and the man removes himself from the analysis rather than facing up to uncomfortable or overwhelming feelings such as one of smothering dependency.

She concluded that men often leave before the work has run its course because of this fear of dependency or of the power of 'undifferentiated sexual and aggressive impulses' (ibid.: 19) which grip and overwhelm before the early-child needs have a chance to show themselves. In these cases, the 'beanstalk' which enables movement between feeling too near, or too far, in relation to mother, is once again just an illusion which generates a 'flight' response from the therapy.

Schaverien (ibid.: 22) goes on to report from her experience on how men tend to either get into a kind of collegial or competitive stance with her, *or* become dependent in an erotic and rather helpless way. The fear of intimacy, accompanied, perhaps, by a craving for it – i.e. desiring mother while also fearing being 'swallowed up' by her – is a hallmark of the early male experience of mother (put another way, the little boy's *erosima versus thanima* struggle), and what Schaverien helpfully describes here is how this can get acted out within the therapeutic relationship between a female analyst and a male analysand.

She also highlights that the struggle the man experiences with this can also have an aggressive component, as he wrestles with the conflict between wanting intimacy and defending his separateness. At a relatively undiffer-entiated level, this can generate difficulties within the therapeutic relation-ship, as Marie Maguire (1995) has highlighted. Maguire gives a powerful example of a piece of clinical work with a man who oscillated between an overbearing determination to prove his heroic qualities, through to sharing murderous fantasies which she, as the analyst, inevitably felt uncomfortable or threatened by. The dominance of *thanima* in this man rendered him potentially dangerous.

He was, in the language of our story, oscillating between Jack's despera-tion to prove to mother how heroic he could be (including erotically) and the giant's murderous, overblown rage and sadism. Chasseguet-Smirgel's (1986) observation that the scale of a man's tendency to be violent is in proportion to his difficulty in accepting mother's capacity to procreate, is telling as a description of an *erosima* wound.

On the other hand, this male analysand's attempts to convey his heroism, sexual potency and capacity for violent overpowering of the other were ways of reacting to, or covering, the depth of the humiliated, raw and vulnerable feelings emanating from his early experience. Maguire describes how through working on his internalised relationship to father as well as his intense envy of the reproductive capacity she and other women possess, he arrived at a point where he could say: 'I don't feel I am waiting to grow up any more. I've become a man' (Maguire, 1995: 91).

One could suggest that in working with his intense and unresolved *erosima–thanima* energies with a woman analyst the full acuity of his early feelings surfaced more readily than if the analyst had been male. There was an intense and even potentially dangerous period where *erosima* manifested in an uncontained set of fantasised erotic 'performances' (the analysand sharing fantasies about seducing her) and *thanima's* presence implied a murderous rage which was close to the surface. However, the analytic 'beanstalk', like the one in the story which sprung up between mother's world 'down here' and father's world 'up there', did slowly take root in the consulting room, enabling a healthier conjoining between appropriate and warm erotic expression (rather than narcissistic rage) on the one hand, and a capacity to respect and relate to the loved (m)other (rather than a *puer*-like, distant, 'sky-god' rage) on the other.

Another relevant contribution from Maguire (1995) is her contextualisa-tion of male aggression as being a 'double-edged' (phallic) sword. This follows Klein (1928/1975), who noticed that boys tend to externalise their aggression more, with socially powerful, but destructive, consequences. Maguire parallels this situation with how men may be described as belong-ing, historically at least, to 'the more highly valued sex' (op. cit.: 96) from a social/hierarchical perspective.

Whether this remains the case could be contested, but her point is that this raising up of 'the man' in western society has acted as a good *quid pro quo* for men, enabling them to project feelings of inadequacy or vulner-ability onto women and to avoid the infantile roots of these. Inevitably, such avoidance generates a psychic fragility beneath the veneer of socially identifying with set models for 'being male'. Maguire describes a 'fault line' (ibid.: 96) arising in men, which reflects a difficulty in achieving differ-entiation from mother. This line of thought resonates with the central theme of this chapter. All men, even those who have worked most fully on this process of differentiation, and have been offered a healthy experience of its moderation by their mother, live with this fault line to some degree.

Archetypal maleness? The place of phallos

One other area which needs to be factored in before I draw together the strands of this chapter concerns the question of whether there is, alongside the powerful impact of mother/the feminine on the formative influence of boys and men, an *archetypal* presence in the unconscious which, even if, say, a boy has no father (or male equivalent) present in his early life, may generate a sense of male identity and distinctiveness. The archetype of *phallos* offers just such a presence in the psyche, where *phallos* refers in this context to the male experiencing a key 'point of reference. Sinew, determination, effectuality, penetration, straightforwardness, hardness, strength – all have phallus giving them effect' (Monick, 1987: 9).

However, referring back to earlier arguments on the fluidity and ubiquity of masculine and feminine energy in the psyches of each person, whether they are 'sexed' as male or female, we need to recognise that phallic imagery and identification crops up for women, too. In the following chapter I will refer to this, and how notions of the 'phallic mother' (including how *animus* may come to represent *phallos*) can influence the inner and outer lives of women.

However, the emphasis in this chapter is on the availability or otherwise of archetypally phallic energy in boys and men, particularly for those who have not been fathered in a concrete sense. For them it seems as if the awareness of this energy within them is a kind of 'search for the lost chord' – something they sense is there but cannot pin down consciously. In my own experience, growing up after my father died, and as the concrete memory of him faded, I remember (particularly in my teens) a presence of father/phallic energy 'out there', somewhere in the ether, but not finding it easy to name, locate or use. In *Jack's* case, his unconscious intuition of something else 'out there' apart from what his mother represented leads him to the old man, who 'holds' the phallic energy for Jack – though the 'bag of beans' could be said to be more the shape/form of testes, with the 'sperm' (beans) inside, rather than the conventional penis/phallus shape. The beanstalk itself, as discussed in Chapter 1, is a rather obvious phallic symbol, shooting erect up into the sky and making the 'land of the giants' available. When Jack meets the fairy at the top of the beanstalk he also encounters the truth – when she tells him his father was murdered by the giant and the latter embezzled his inheritance. So, here are two dimensions to the phallic energy Jack had been missing – access to power (the kingdom in the sky) and to truth. Now, via the beanstalk, Jack is able to recover both when he outwits, and then kills, the giant.

A critical factor which enables this kind of archetypal process is what Monick (1987: 23) describes as 'phallic autonomy'. So although, for example, social and familial convention can act to restrain a man's (or woman's?) sexual activity, in the end phallos is capable of acting out its drives and desires irrespective of this. This is the same principle as that of the autonomy of the unconscious. In other words, the presence of phallos can be a bit like the presence of an autonomous complex at work in the psyche: 'Erection points to a powerful inner reality at work in a man, not altogether in his control' (ibid.: 9). This last point raises questions about a man's responsibility for his own drives, sexual and aggressive, and highlights the need to be alert to the danger of a kind of ethics-free zone around a man's drives.

Nevertheless, without some kind of 'breaking out' of phallic energy, whether this be via talking back at his parents, staying out late or sometimes getting into potentially compromising sexual situations or aggressive conflicts, the boy may find himself unable to appropriate his version of phallos for himself. Whether – as Freud and others argue about castration anxiety – the phallic is initially possessed by mother and has to be wrestled away by her in an application (to use my terminology) of phallic *erosima* energy is a moot point. Here, the boy's *erosima* connection is healthy and infused with life, so therefore it is 'ok' for him to get into a wrestling match with her, rather than where *thanima* predominates and the deadness or uncertainty in the relationship does not give him a feeling of 'permission' to do this.

Monick (ibid.: 45) provides an interesting take on the possibly hampering impact of discontinuity in the male psyche. He also characterises this problem in terms of the unconscious attempts of the boy to solve the problem in a *linear* way. So, if the boy is caught by not having freed himself from mother, then while he tries to move forward, he may in reality find himself sliding backwards, as he cannot separate his love and commitment to mother from his craving for autonomy. In this sense there is no 'sideways' move available, or scope to change the angle of the trajectory he is on.

A dream from a male analysand I worked with illustrates this well – he is on a train moving forward on a straight track, but when it arrives at the station, he finds he is back at the station he started from. I have touched on theories about how the male brain may tend to categorise and fix meanings more than the female brain. The metaphor of the railway track – once you are on a train you can only go backwards or forwards – seems a good one for how boys and men may deal with the 'problem' of differentiating from mother.

On a train you cannot, like in a car, take advantage of myriad opportunities to take a left or right turn; and when you come to a junction it is the person in the signal box who decides if the points should change to shift you onto another track. Discontinuity – whether manifested in feelings of fragmentation, alienation or being 'stuck on the track' – is the consequence of this predicament, which has a hallmark of the ego having surrendered its capacity to determine authentic direction for itself.

The way through this predicament, as Monick points out, is to acknowledge 'psychological thinking is paradoxical as well as linear' (ibid.: 54). This is where therapeutic or other reflexive frameworks can offer a man the opportunity to get hold of the *autonomous* presence of phallos in his psyche and develop more flexible ways of perceiving himself and his life. In this sense, the power of 'the phallic mother' can be overvalued (Kulish, 1986) and what Hillman (1975: 84ff) describes as the 'naturalistic fallacy' of the unconscious as being commensurate with 'mother' or the feminine limits this potential for flexibility.

So, it is important to acknowledge the presence of *phallos* as the energising resource in the boy or man for activating *erosima* energies which free up his relationship to inner mother and whoever he projects his versions of mother onto externally. This, I suggest, is the 'magic beans' for the boy. They will be there somewhere, irrespective of how stuck he might feel.

Concluding comments: Confronting discontinuity – the wait for the Great Mother to give up her dead

This chapter has explored some key themes around the impact of *thanima* on the male psyche, and how this can show up in analytic work. I have suggested that the presence of deadness in the transference–countertransference with a male analysand can be read as a signifier of a *death* at the start of life, where *thanima* has won out over *erosima* in the early attachment with mother. This then leads to discontinuity in the male psyche. In response to this, there is commonly a formation of a *puer–narcissus* bridge through which the psyche holds itself together and tries to negotiate life.

This particular response may be specifically male, as boys, unlike girls, have been forced to break with mother, and if potent father/phallic energy is unavailable, they are unable to repair the 'break' and can suffer in the long term from a discontinuity which continues to haunt them.

In terms of working therapeutically, there are two key aspects of the analysis of male identity discontinuity. The first is noticing the deadness which appears as a feeling of 'absence' in the room through countertransference responses such as feeling the impulse to 'run away' from the work or breathing getting heavier as an 'airless' quality comes into the room. I noticed, as I began writing the closing section of this chapter, a real struggle with 'writing about deadness' – the stifling power of *thanima*, perhaps?

The second clinical aspect of work with these men is to be able to bear the presence of *puer's* imploring for escape from the land of the dead, by pulling the work back into that dead space, however flattening and claustrophobic this can feel. By noticing what is happening and asking the analysand to do the same, the deadness is exposed. The full extent of its influence on the feeling, thinking, physical and erotic life of the man is revealed. The *nigredo*, which a man may have been living with all his life, comes into the open, and unconscious influences become more apparent. In analysis the re-experiencing of the deadness allows the story of a 'lost life' to come forward. The enlivening influences of *erosima*, with its capacity to enable the man to contact *phallos* energy in his psyche, brings the possibility of some fresh integration and change.

There is a sense that some of the men I have described are 'dead' inside. In order to reclaim something of such a man's life, the constellation behind his deathly 'baptism' into life needs to be exposed. Where dreams reveal this backdrop – as in the archetypal mother–priest dyad at work in the case referred to earlier (p. 97) – this begins, in alchemical terms, the mercurial process of *purification*, as the alive elements which had been incubating since early life begin to become available to him. The containing and potent aspects of the analyst play a key role in enabling these archetypal factors to come into the foreground.

The presenting 'deadness' from these clinical examples shows what happens when there is discontinuity in the development of the male psyche. The *puer–senex* relation falls into disrepair and there is a mismatch between where a man feels he *should* be in life and where he actually *is* (reflected in the oscillation between *puer* and *narcissus*). Clinical practice becomes a struggle to hold what is left of the link between *should* and *is*. This involves pinning down reality and not allowing a whimsical attachment to what is lost to stop the work being grounded. If the work falls between both, it is like standing with a foot on either side of the threshold between boyhood and manhood – an ambiguity which allows the deadness to take hold.

The passing through *nigredo* opens up the possibility of further shifts. Although the sense of discontinuity – which results in internal waiting, deadness and disembodiment – can be profound, life can begin to return, and *erosima* begins to take its revivifying place in the foreground of psyche's life, via a gradual opening of authentic modes of relating in the transference–countertransference, and away from the reliance upon the life-saving but false bridge built by *puer* and *narcissus* to rescue the self from disintegration.

In relational terms, the following speculation arises. Male 'territory' in relation to women seems to be hallmarked on the surface by (in its less conscious forms at least) a quest for certainty and the linear mapping of past, present and future. Meanwhile, underneath there is a deep fissure, a crack in the psychic bedrock where the wound(s) incurred by the effort and pain involved for the boy in splitting from mother – in order to allow 'male territory' to form – can be found.

The quality and impact of this process both reflect and confirm the balance between *erosima* and *thanima* influences in the individual male psyche. The impact of this on the individual boy or man may well be modified by his capacity to access something archetypally *phallic* in the unconscious, irrespective of how deadened *thanima*'s presence in the early mother–son dyad might have been, or how absent or present (literally or psychologically) father may have been.

This element in the equation has a mysterious feel to it – like the magic beans in *Jack and the Beanstalk*, but without it one could say there is little hope of any kind of psychic redemption for the boy or man gripped by the presence of *thanima*.

An important aspect of male 'territory' in the relational context, then, is a tension between needing to hold onto the magic beans of *phallos* (energising and differentiating) while at the same time looking for balm for those early wounds. The constancy of the *erosima* bond to a partner is a source for this balm, one which requires a willingness and capacity to risk dependence on the other in order to access this.

The tension between these two influences reflects the delineations indicated already in archetypally nuanced gender relations: transcendent versus immanent, perfecting versus completing, and perhaps we could add here differentiating versus depending. Men, I suggest, have to face these challenging polarities when they enter, and work to sustain, relationships. The central question arising from these polarities is something like: 'How do I find, and use, the magic beans while allowing for my dependency on others and their dependency on me?'

Chapter 5

Thanimus

But his mother was very angry that Milky White had been sold for a handful of beans. She sent Jack to bed and threw the beans out of the window.

I proposed in the previous chapter that the basics of male development are predicated on the struggle to live with a 'fissure' in the psyche: a splitting away from the 'earth' of mother, which establishes the terms of the struggle between *erosima* and *thanima*. I want to start this chapter from the premise that healthy female development depends on how solid the layers of relational ground established in the original mother–daughter bond are.

These layers are fundamental influences on the girl's trajectory through life, nuanced by personal and archetypal experiences of mother. As with the boy these influences establish relational dynamics, which can also generate complexes; Mother as begetter, carer, imagined lover, and so on. I see these parallel interpersonal and intrapsychic experiences, for example mother's physical touch on the infant's arm being experienced as feeling/sensation/ image within, as being moments-out-of-time which go on to retain a 'time-less' quality in the unconscious while the child proceeds (in-time) towards adulthood.

There are two necessary (and maybe welcome!) riders to set against this 'fundamentalism' about our initial experiences of mother. The first is the recognition, alongside the ongoing presence of these shared 'moments', of the unpredictable, broad and deep range of influences shaping who a child (boy or girl) 'is'. These range from environmental – e.g. where and how a child grows up – and relational – especially the quality and consistency of father's presence, and the availability of *phallos* – through to the influences bequeathed by family genetics and neurobiological variables, which can skip generations or throw up unexpected talents, personality traits or disabilities.

The second rider is to emphasise that there is no suggestion the journey from early childhood through to puberty and beyond is somehow 'easier' for the girl or for the boy. Each will be equally fraught with dangers such as splitting within the psyche, and profound challenges in establishing individual and gendered identity. My focus is more concerned with how these processes and challenges *may differ*, and how this could impact on crucial male–female 'territorial relations' around power, identity and quality of relationship, and life experience as adults.

In this chapter I will explore how the experiencing of women and girls can be described and understood. I will also draw on some of the themes which emerged from the previous chapter on men, in order to provide some comparative discussion. I am doing this as a man, and thereby lay myself open to the risks inherent in speaking for, or about, the 'gendered other'. As I suggested in the introduction, this may render my writing about women misinformed, biased, guarded and/or self-conscious.

I have learned from previous professional, social and personal engagement with women how being too careful to say the right thing and becoming beholden to a deferential sensitivity towards them as 'the historically injured gender' tends to take the life (*erosima*) out of things. Respect and alertness to the legacy of male ignorance, carelessness, violence and abuse is one thing; fearfulness and avoidance is another.

However, as with a previous health warning I felt the need to give when writing about *animus* (Goss, 2008: 146), I want to reiterate the importance for each of us to take responsibility for our responses to how Jung or anybody else refers to *animus*. This point is worth restating because there can be a sense in Jungian circles that it is perhaps unsafe to open up this area because of what it exposes about the attitudes of the founder of analytical psychology, and the 'embarrassing' and beyond-the-pale quality of some of his very nineteenth-century views on what makes women tick – as if we will be tarred with the same brush. This, I would argue, is precisely what *thanimus*, with its shady, complex-like wish to close down reflection and discussion on the possibility of definable gender differences, wants us to think and do.

I will draw on clinical experiences of *animus*, and presentations of *thanimus* in particular, utilising disguised examples from my own practice as a man working with female analysands, but also referring to relevant literature which suggests what the dyad of woman analyst–woman analysand can constellate.

Theoretically, I will explore the significance of Jung's idea of *animus* in woman as the contrasexual *other*, and my further delineation between *erosimus* and *thanimus*. I will also apply some of Jung's archetypal thinking on feminine figures (e.g. *puella, wise woman*) and his focus on the counterpointing archetypal influences (Jung, 1952/1969: para. 627) of 'completing' (feminine) versus 'perfecting' (masculine) – the former, I suggest, being a subtly pervasive influence in the female psyche (though I hold this gendered counterpoint lightly so as not to reify, or overgeneralise, it). I will develop a line of thinking on how this 'completing–perfecting' dynamic seems to mirror in some ways the workings of the self–ego axis, and consider whether this helps in understanding how women may experience relationships with men and the expectations they can have of them (and vice versa).

While the male psyche may attempt to transcend difficulty and get caught up in a kind of 'solving'/'perfecting' tendency (as a way of trying to reconcile the psychic trauma of splitting, or attempting to split, from mother), the female counterpoint may focus more on experiencing a feeling of 'completion'. The little girl, via *erosimus*, experiences a grounded sense of relational 'completing' in the mother–daughter bond – with its psychosexual, bodily underpinning, as suggested by Kristeva (2004). Or, *thanimus* may disrupt this potential through a more faulty bonding. In both cases the archetype of *completion* provides a subtle, idealised, problematic behind the relational, bearing in mind we can never be truly 'complete'.

Animus

My intuition remains strong that *animus* as a concept, and as an archetypal figure in the psyche, has much to offer us in our attempts to understand and work with gender (as a reality *or* an illusion). To reiterate, Jung meant by *animus* the image of man and the masculine principle found in the woman's psyche (Jung, 1953/1966). The task of envisaging *animus* is not helped by the context in which it was born, as the less attractive of the *anima–animus* dyad, the ugly twin brother to the alluring soul quality of *anima*.

Its shadow quality arises from the personal shadow of analytical psychology's founder, as well as from the collective shadow of western patriarchy, which tends to leave it lurking somewhere in the background of our musings about the place of the gendered *other*. Jung thought nothing, within the norms of nineteenth-century Swiss society, of following Freud's lead in assuming women lacked something important men had and envied them for it (Freud, 1920/1991), though for Jung this was not the penis, but instead full consciousness.

Man supposedly had to do woman's thinking for her; the explicit implication of Jung's formula for *negative animus* proposed that women think in a presumptive and emotive way – quick to make judgements based on simplistic views drawn from the collective (represented in dreams by groups of men) 'out there', beyond their narrow world of home and family. This formula can be applied to stories where the 'hero' is female – like Dorothy in *The Wizard of Oz* (Baum, 1900/1993), who encounters inadequate masculine figures (scarecrow, tin man, lion and even the wizard) before learning to confront and destroy the 'witch'. Where a woman got hold of her *positive animus* like this she could think and act in a more effective and 'logical' way; but for Jung this was reserved for activities and interactions within the confines of a limited world view – on the Kansas farmstead rather than in Oz.

This awkward cultural throwback tarnishes what is otherwise an original and valuable concept, one which could offer pointers to a more satisfactory developmental process in Jung's model. Here, *animus* could offer a generalised equivalence to Freud's phallic stage and Lacan's Symbolic Order (Lemaire, 1977), as a move on from a state of *anima* possession at birth (Casement, A., personal communication, 2006), something I incorporated into my developmental model (Chapter 3). It also offers the possibility of better understanding how women experience their erotic, aggressive and other influences, and how 'animosity' between women and men may arise.

In Chapter 2, when setting out my model for understanding archetypal and cultural influences on 'gendered territories', I suggested how the yoked *anima–animus* syzygy could shed light on these. So while *anima* influences may determine the quality of relationship around feeling states (*erosima* as bringing life to relationship and *thanima* bringing deadness), *animus* on this shared level is about often widely held attitudes and ways of perceiving the gendered 'other'. Here, *erosimus* values and enjoys gendered difference. *Thanimus*, meanwhile, is hallmarked by certitude, judgement, even disgust in our perceptions and attitudes towards 'him' or 'her'.

These influences can and do affect what happens in friendships, familial (e.g. sibling) relations and intimate relationships. In my experience this also impacts on clinical work – i.e. on how a woman analysand is influenced by her general attitudes about men in working with me, and also how my approach with her will be influenced by my attitudes about women. This will come through in some of the clinical examples I provide in this chapter.

As suggested in Chapter 2, Jung's ideas on *animus* in a woman as conveying a kind of inferior, not to mention aggravating (for the man), form of expressing thoughts and views, challenges us – once we get beyond the feelings of awkwardness, embarrassment, outrage, and inclinations to dismiss such ideas as laughable and embarrassing – to look at where those feelings and inclinations might come from in us.

We can take this idea a stage further by considering whether this might be seen as reflecting our *shadow* projections onto Jung; in other words how, his strikingly judging, unrelated, even crude, assertions, can catalyse our 'use' of him as an object to deposit all our tendencies to make lazy assertions about the opposite gender. We may find ourselves reacting from our own tendency to channel collective *animus* against men (if I am a woman) or against women (if I am a man). Despite the evident problem of Jung's views – e.g. when he writes of how a woman's world 'outside her husband, terminates in a sort of cosmic mist' (Jung, 1953/1966: para. 338) – it is worth noticing our own responses to this sort of statement. I invite you to do the same, and reflect on what this brings up for you about your gender identity, your attitudes to the other gender, and your perceptions about how women and men experience and view one another.

My fundamental suggestion about the hostile responses which can be triggered by Jung's references to women is: there is a place for *animus* in informing how able or not we are to really 'see' the gendered *other* (Goss, 2008). Blinkered attitudes by women towards men, are, I suggest, where *thanimus* can take hold of the female psyche, in the same way *thanima* can infect a man's attitude towards women. On the other hand, the predominance of *erosimus* or *erosima* enables us to see the 'whole picture' – what makes 'I' as a man similar to 'you' as woman (and vice versa) as well as what may be distinctive. Similarities and differences can be valued, rather than disparaged or used for point scoring.

The roots of female 'territory'

The developmental premise I am working from in this chapter is that female 'territory' has its roots in the daughter's initial bond with mother from the early stages of postnatal life onwards, and in the full, intermittent or faulty experience of relational 'completeness' with her. This experience is identificatory in nature and acts as a template for what a girl unconsciously seeks out in life as she grows to adulthood.

What I am *not* proposing is a stereotyped notion that 'all girls want to be their mother when they grow up'. Rather, I am describing an approach to life – a 'way of being' to borrow Rogers' (1961) phrase again – informed by a 'completing' tendency, a wish to ground lived experience beneath the striving for improvement or achievement. In this sense, Jack's mother's wish to have her son back in one piece, complete, is more important to her than him recovering more treasure from the giant.

As described, gendered territories are not fixed but describe arenas of being which overlap in lots of ways, although they reflect ways in which certain tendencies are more prevalent in one territory than the other. So, when I write of 'completing' being more of an unconscious purpose for women than 'solving' (more a feature of 'male territory'), I am acknowledging that there will be a lot of women who feel the need to solve/perfect and a lot of men who likewise are drawn towards 'completing'. My focus is on where the underlying emphasis lies in 'female' territory: based on the template of mother–daughter bonding at the beginning of life, the seeking out of relational, familial, 'completing' is not by any means the only emphasis, but is a fundamental one.

This is not, I want to emphasise, a paean for the perpetuation of a conservative familial or parenting model. Family and parenting can take all kinds of forms – one parent, two parent, same-sex and so on. To healthily seek out the completing experience of a long-term relationship or family (or professional or creative life project) is not about conserving rigid forms of relating, but it *is* about seeking a feeling of completion, and this, I am suggesting, is more a hallmark of 'female territory'. Its male counterpart is less likely to generate a feeling of 'completion' while the other more 'per-fecting' (or 'solving') tendency is around, with its inherent risk of 'discontinuity' when the perfecting goes askew. These tendencies can show themselves in *styles* of relating and being.

In this context there is something worth elucidating around the relationship between *ego* and self. In Jung's (1951/1968) model, *self* is seen as the underlying, purposive, centre and wholeness of the psyche, subtly directing *ego* (if it will listen) to encounter and deal with individuation tasks to enable the person to become more themselves. *Ego* on the other hand is the centre of the conscious mind, charged with responsibility for overseeing the business of day-to-day life, and with listening to deeper promptings of the self.

I want to play with the idea of male–female relations as, in a generalised way, a mirror to this dynamic. So *ego* tries, ultimately unsuccessfully, to uncover its own perfectibility (male territory) and 'arrive' somewhere which reflects this, sometimes by mistakenly identifying with *self* (female territory) – imagining the process of completing is actually about perfecting or solving something definitively, which of course it is not. It is, rather, ongoing and never in this life fully 'completed' – just like Jung's formula for individuation.

Likewise, *self* (female) may look to *ego* (male) to help in its 'completing' tasks, but instead *ego* may forget about the 'completing' aspect of the partnership and get caught up in perfecting, so rendering *self* as vulnerable to discontinuity as *ego*. Or, to translate this another way regarding women, their identification with *completing* may get confused, via, for example, an over-identification with what father symbolises, off the back of a muddled or unsatisfying experience of *completing* with mother. So instead of being a *completing self* in relationship (to a man or to a woman) they identify with 'perfection' and get caught in the difficulties such an identification can bring – for example somatising *ego* judgement of themselves through extreme dieting to get 'the perfect body'. I will draw on Woodman's (1982) thinking on women and perfection when I return to look at this *self–ego* parallel in the following chapter. Suffice it to say, these potential confusions between 'completing' and 'perfecting' may have important implications for how we make sense of male–female heterosexual relations.

Thanimus and relational discontinuity

The significant consideration arising from this formulation for the experiencing of self, other, and the world for women (again taking care to acknowledge the dangers of generalisation) is how Jung's archetypal notion of the *self* – as a symbol of, and in an ongoing process of, 'completing' – could be worked with as one symbol for 'female territory'. In this respect, the *puella* problem for a woman (like *puer*, we are thinking here of a deep-rooted wish not to grow up and to 'fly away' from grounded reality) is more to do with the unavailability of this 'completing' energy than with a loss of connection with the *wise old woman* archetype. I am therefore arguing in this regard that it does *not* parallel the *puer* problem for the man who seeks out the 'perfected-by-*senex*' straight road/railway track/illusory beanstalk.

A disguised example of this *puella–self* dynamic from my clinical practice is of a woman who was in her thirties and arrived for analysis with a wish to 'find myself before I settle down'. She was in a long-term relationship with a man, but was resisting living together or getting married, even though she said part of her 'really wants this'. Instead, there was a sense of part of her not being missing 'but straggling behind the rest of me'.

Her 'eternal child' (*puella*) wanted away from the choice she faced in the present because of an uncomfortable truth which seemed to be hanging around in the background, something which had its roots in the past. She brought a dream about a bear which sat at the end of a long path waving at her – whenever she moved towards it, it seemed to shrink further away. She offered associations to her most beloved teddy as a child, as well as to her partner, who she referred to as 'my grizzly bear' because of how she experienced him when he got angry or miserable. This was happening more and more because he was frustrated about her unwillingness to take the relationship to another stage.

Something was stopping her from taking such a step and the animal in the dream seemed to point to something instinctual which would not let her get close. The tendency towards completion seemed to be in reverse gear, because the earlier, or *earliest*, template of 'completing' – the deep relational bond to mother – had perhaps not taken hold. I felt something in my countertransference which seemed to echo this – moments where she and I seemed rather distant from one another (like I was the bear and we were just waving at each other). In these moments I was mother, who was there, but only waved from a distance rather than embracing and truly 'holding' her daughter. Or maybe instead of this – or even as well as – I was a version of father (*phallos?*) who was equally unavailable. *Or*, maybe the bear was psyche calling her to attend to something *individual* in herself which meant her relationship should be ended or put on hold. Each version seemed possible, but either way something important had not been experienced.

Her (narcissistic?) expressions such as 'I am quite alone in the world', despite her boyfriend's care towards her, indicated how caught her psyche was in a yearning for the relational imprinting she had not experienced as an infant. *Erosimus* had not been validated, leaving *thanimus* to take hold and slowly precipitate the breakdown of her long-term relationship. This in turn was to lead to an inner crisis which, within the crucible of our analytic work, enabled her to get in touch with the deep wound inflicted on *erosimus*, and allow her to more consciously create the potential for relationship, which could in turn promote her own 'completing' inner dynamic.

This kind of detachment from relationship (which could be characterised as a kind of *puella* flight) can happen because of a distortion or gap in the original mirroring, identificatory, bond with mother (which may get further complicated by the relationship with father). Here narcissism takes hold of the girl or woman to try to convince her she is already complete, to compensate for the nagging sense of incompleteness her psyche is wrestling with or repressing.

Here, we can see a female embodiment of *thanimus discontinuity*, where *thanimus* has apparently unhitched the psyche of the girl from the archetypal and neurologically anticipated pattern of relational development. The lack of a proper experience of relational completing, through a full, deep identification with mother in the first stages of infancy, has left psyche *waiting*. Here, unlike the male 'waiting' I described in the previous chapter, the emphasis is on 'relational' rather than 'erotic', hence her need to experience what she has missed in terms of relational 'completing' before she feels ready to move into a state of 'completed' relationship – with her partner, or with/by herself. *Puella* avoidance and narcissistic attitudes defend her from being pulled into 'completing' although she feels deeply 'incomplete'.

Another example from my practice illustrates this dynamic. It also conveys the influence in the clinical setting of collective *animus* attitudes and perceptions – i.e. men's tendency to hold attitudes and perceptions regarding women, and for women to do the same towards men, and how these can become rigidified. This dimension, as suggested, can help us understand what may generate difficulties and misapprehensions in relationships between men and women.

Working as a man with female antipathy towards male territory

A woman analysand I worked with brought a strong antipathy towards her father. He had been a politician involved in trade union and other activity which had kept him away from the family for significant periods of time – or, as she put it, with a bitter edge in her voice, 'he liked to pretend he had no choice, but he did'. This analysand was convinced, it seemed with good reason, that her father had decided his real 'family' was the 'brotherhood' of workers he often spoke to in different parts of the country or overseas rather than the family she, her brother, sister and mother were part of.

He seemed uninterested in his part in 'completing' his immediate family, but devoted to 'perfecting' the rights of his adoptive family out there. Mother, she said, had become depressed about this 'a long time ago' (pointing towards the *thanimus* flatness in their mother–daughter bond). The impact on her life appeared pervasive – she had had a number of unfulfilling, often short-lived relationships with men, and it was no surprise to find that these men tended to operate in a very similar way to her father: an initial burst of passion and commitment, followed by periods of unavailability, or outright abandonment – such as the man who had fathered her child and then left her while she was pregnant. She was now caught in a cycle of resentment towards life, and men, and with a feeling of incompleteness for herself and her little daughter, on whom she also seemed to be projecting her feelings of abandonment by father. A wish to 'damn the lot of them' (*thanimus*), 'take flight' (*puella*) and never get into a relationship with a man again was taking hold, though there was enough relational energy to bring her into analysis. There was also a narcissistic tone, in a 'men never understand me, I will just rely on myself' kind of way. There was sadness to her presence in the room as well as the razor-sharp bitterness alluded to above.

Inevitably the anger constellated itself strongly towards me. I would argue that I 'caught it' more overtly as a male analyst, though it's quite possible that if I were a woman I would have 'got it in the neck' in more subtle ways. The first time I told her I would need to take a holiday break soon, she smirked and shook her head, as if this was all that could be expected of me. I reflected back to her that I had noticed this and she said, 'I knew this was coming . . . it's the same old story.' I asked her if she could say more. She responded, 'In the end men make their choice and it is always to take the easy way out.'

This exchange clearly gave us much to work with – not least the angry, almost outraged feeling which arose in me. This is the power of a *thanimus* (negative animus) expression or attitude. It can catalyse reactive or even explosive responses in those on the receiving end when the assertions made are sweeping and apparently damning – not to mention the little touches which rub these in, such as the little smirk she offered to me while shaking her head. I remember noticing the strength of my reaction as well as being concerned by how successfully she had 'pressed my buttons'. Unconsciously she had clearly realised this might be the way to get to me, in a way her father had seemed impervious to. This is where *animus* brings with it the possibility of facilitating feelings of emasculation in the opposite gender, and all the power relations which go with this possibility.

I took this material back into my own analysis as well as supervision. I had been aware of how female anger and disappointment about men and the masculine had long been part of my world, not least in how males in the westernised cultural milieu of the late twentieth century (when I had passed into adulthood) were often described as unreliable and flighty when it came to commitment to relationship and family.

What I had not fully got hold of was the hurt and resentment this assertion could stir up in me, which was a measure of my 'gendered sensitivity' as an adult as well as a strong re-constellation of how emasculated I had felt at times growing up as the only male in an all-female household.

This reaction could also be seen as a countertransference experience of the raging depths of this woman's fury towards her father, a rage superseding any possibility of a compensatory relational 'balm' in her connection to mother.

Her anger and aggression were also overwhelming expressions of repressed feelings about herself, and this would come out in more 'passive-aggressive' ways in our work – e.g. a refusal to make eye contact apart from the occasional moment of her choosing, or delays in paying for sessions. She also might drop in the occasional comment about my apparel – e.g. noticing if my shoe laces were undone, or asking me if I had combed my hair that morning. Again, I had to acknowledge my own difficulty with feeling belittled and work hard not to enact my own response to this, but rather check with her who I was for her in the moments she picked up on these observations. On reflection she reckoned I became her 'baby' brother, who had been born when she was fifteen and who, she came to recognise as our work deepened, had caught something of her rage towards father when she picked up on any 'defects' she might detect in his appearance. She also linked this to the way her mother had done the same with her father, seeing the moments when mother would point out a hair out of place on her husband's head (which would invariably annoy him) before he disappeared out the door – one way Mum could make an impact on Dad.

This can be described as an example of an embedded exchange between women and men in long-term (traditional/patriarchal) relationships which reflects a cycle of inter-gender emasculation. So, in this case, father pursues his attempt to 'perfect' ('transcend') what is out there in the world (the entitlements of workers) while mother stays with the here and now ('immanent') hoping for 'completion' in the family context. He emasculates her 'completing' impulses by constantly absenting himself, and she emasculates his 'perfecting' impulse as best she can in the circumstances by pointing out imperfections in his appearance. While this emasculation can happen the other way around, I suggest the still influential patterns of patriarchal heterosexuality tend to set up this kind of cycle, at least until both parties become aware of it and feel ready to do something about it.

The clash between the unconscious 'perfecting' drive of her father and the perhaps more conscious but confused wishes for 'completing' by mother had driven her to distraction – in the sense of not really being able to focus upon her own needs and aspirations properly. This was an internal conflict in which less than fully conscious, gendered tendencies – a clash of *male* and *female* territories – had been acted out in her psyche; a gendered battle between unspoken preoccupations and ideals which the daughter's *thanimus* channelled into the immanent experiencing of her psychic life.

This sorry dance spoke to the sadness which this woman brought into the analysis, as if *she* had been emasculated twice over. As the work progressed, she became more aware of what she, as oldest child, carried of this cycle and I began to experience a lessened sense of being emasculated myself. By the time we stopped working she was more at peace with herself because she had found her own internal space, in which she got closer to a calibration between 'completing' and 'perfecting', reflecting who she is. Her *puella* and narcissistically toned assertions of feeling misunderstood and 'best left alone' also faded as she declared herself ready to head back towards the world of relating once more. I had noticed more of an erotic quality to our work as it had concluded – she found it easier to joke and smile, and this brought a more attractive, appealing side of her nature into the work.

Women and aggression

The aggressive flavour of some of my analysand's verbal and non-verbal responses to me also translated into something more playful but assertive. I want to quote Andrew Samuels here on aggression, particularly in relation to women:

> From the point of view of gender psychology, aggression and especially aggressive fantasy can be an individuation path, especially for women: an imaginary way to be thrusting, penetrative and seminal, to break out of the coils of Eros where the woman is only responsive to the needs of others in a reproduction of mothering.
>
> (Samuels, 2009: 8)

Samuels makes an important point here which feeds into my discussion in two ways. First, 'completing' as I describe it in terms where this is more associated with 'female' territory than 'male' does *not* equal the perpetuation of increasingly outdated ideas concerning mothering as being the only, or primary, route towards experiencing 'completing' for a woman. There are so many other ways a woman can choose to access her own 'completing' energies – professionally or creatively, through relationship or by herself. Second, aggressive fantasy for the woman enables her to break out of constricting definitions of 'completing'. In the case described here, the woman analysand used me as a 'safe-enough' receptacle for her aggression, and shared on one occasion a fantasy she had of tying together my loose shoelaces when I was not looking and watching me fall and bang my head as I stood up at the end of a session. Needless to say she laughed, quietly and long, while telling me this.

While this felt a little eerie to me at the time, I also saw how empowering this idea was for her. Slowly but surely, via exploration and experimentation with self, her aggressive (and erotic) energies were being released. Though *thanimus* may have thought this fantasy was about 'him', in a *trickster*-like expression of aggression and attack-on-the-father, it was in fact *erosimus* who was getting the last laugh, as these kinds of subversive but safe fantasies were allowing 'him' to gradually release himself – while in truth *thanimus* was tripping 'himself' up.

An observation at this point about my own process in writing this chapter: I notice how I have tended to extrapolate from my experience and ideas about women and how they relate in the clinical setting into writing about *relationship*. This contrasts with how I wrote about men in the previous chapter, which seemed to focus more on the deadening, isolating capacities of *thanima* on the individual man.

This observation could imply something about my own experiencing of women – or my 'construction' of them under social influence – as often offering an overtly relational 'way of being', and therefore a projected source of my own capacity to relate as a man. It could also suggest that the relational dimension sits more in female than in male territory, arising from a predominance of archetypal (including neurobiological) and socio-historical influences. Or, again more likely, it is a composite of both. Whichever way, as I construct this chapter, I notice how *I* am constructed as a man writing about women – drawing on their experiencing and relatedness in order to make sense of our 'otherness' and 'sameness'.

Discovering the benevolent mother

With the final disguised example from my practice I make explicit use of the narrative reference point for this book. The giant's wife in *Jack and the Beanstalk* plays what seems like a 'bit part' at first glance, protecting Jack from her husband and providing him with sustenance (a hearty breakfast here and there). But she also represents another version of mother and thereby throws up different possibilities for relationship, providing a useful motif for the situation of the woman I am about to describe.

She was an older woman who had experienced some seismic shifts in her way of life, not least in her sexuality. She had been married for almost thirty years when her husband died suddenly. They had been close though drifting further from each other once their only child had left home over a decade before and in the intervening period before her husband's death she had come to question the 'straightforwardness' (as she put it) of her sexuality, and gradually she had formed an intense attachment with a woman she had known for some time, who had lost her husband. When my analysand's husband died she had been preparing to let him know she wanted to move in with her lesbian partner, and was with her when he collapsed with a fatal heart attack at home.

Knowing her husband had died alone while she was with her beloved new partner, unsurprisingly, evoked guilt. There was also a sense of her fearing I would judge her out of some gendered 'fellow feeling' with him. This linked to a real experience: her son was still furious with her for going into this new relationship (especially 'with another woman!') around the time his father's life was ending. Here again, *animus* as a shared, collective, gendered, reaction to the 'ways' of the opposite gender was rearing its head.

In relation to me, her anxious evocation of *thanimus* was a fear of what I as a man might 'judge' her as having done. Although she felt contained by her new partnership, where *erosimus* was finding new and rich expression, she felt threatened by what was 'out there'. Her husband was dead, her son seemed to hate her, many (though not all) of her old friends had disowned her, and the world, she said, was 'furious with me'.

This opprobrium of friends and family towards her (apparently) changing her sexuality at the point where her husband had passed away was double edged. On the one hand, the natural loyalty to the now deceased partner seems understandable and protective of something valuable; something, now tarnished, which had seemed to represent a version of 'completing' – a stable, happy marriage and family.

On the other hand, the reactions this woman experienced also seem to reflect a pervasive difficulty in our culture in adjusting to the reality of how fluid individual sexuality can be. Accepting this in relation to women takes some further adjustment within patriarchal frames of reference which may still nod towards a 'perfecting' viewpoint whereby women provide a loyal, exclusively heterosexual allegiance to partner, family and the wider social nexus. The perfecting, heterosexual masculine at its most rigid and idealising of 'how things should be' wishes it thus. However, as Maguire (1995: 77) points out, 'sexual identity is convoluted, tenuous and fragmented. We need theories which show how women simultaneously resist and embrace gender stereotypes.' This point is pertinent for this woman as she was moving, in the eyes of some at least, from one 'stereotype' (loyal wife and mother) to another (betraying gay woman).

Maguire goes on to argue: 'We need to understand more about the nature and origins of female sexuality, recognising that although it is shaped within culture it is mediated through the body' (ibid.). Bodily expressed sexuality and desire thus becomes an impetus for a kind of 'completing'.

In terms of how this possible duality with 'male perfecting' may play out in heterosexual relations, the *perfecting* drive in a man tends towards a linear path – 'straight' towards sexual fulfilment via coitus or some other way of arriving at penile ejaculation and orgasm. Intimacy with the woman is a prerequisite for this but not the overarching fulfiller of desire. For the woman, *completing* sexually may be more important – through sexual stimulation and orgasm within the frame of an embodied, relational experience of intimacy.

This area of possible difference once again needs to be bracketed with a recognition that there will be all sorts of nuances and variations associated with these 'positions' of desire and sexual fulfilment (like the multiple 'positions' associated with sexual acts) and that I am simply setting out a generalised portrayal of how these 'completing' versus 'perfecting' tendencies act like subtle magnetic fields most of the time in female as against male 'territories'. One could say that, for this woman, her 'completing' wishes and desires regarding her sexuality were shifting towards forms of expression which were more overtly 'relational'. This wish was superceding the previous, more submissive route of following the male 'perfecting' drive down the straight road to orthodox sexual intercourse and satisfactory orgasm for the man, with occasional attending by him to her wish for a longer, more circuitous route which would take in her desire, too.

So, although she knew she would sorely miss the affectionate embrace and companionship of her husband, she noticed that feelings of completing with him had (long) gone, and when she fell for her new partner it felt clear this was where a new completing cycle could be experienced and fulfilled. The flip side of this was the sense of her 'killing' something – she was planning to end a long marriage, in almost the blink of an eye. Also, her own feelings from childhood towards her father when he had left the family home weighed heavily on her. She had fantasised then, in her hurt and rage, of literally killing him.

So, when she came home, intending to tell her husband she planned to leave him, and found an ambulance outside the house (called by a neighbour who had seen him, through the window, lying on the kitchen floor) there was an almost unbearable storm of conflicting feelings to cope with. When she came to see me a couple of months later we had to stay with the storm until the winds and waves of feeling began to subside and her attempt at beginning a new life came into the foreground.

In the language of *Jack and the Beanstalk*, she had planned to solve the 'problem' of her dead marriage by climbing the beanstalk into a new phase of 'completing' with her new lover, and then cut the beanstalk to her old life, and let it fall. The unexpected death of her husband threw up all sorts of conflicting thoughts and feelings: on the one hand she had wanted him 'out of the way' so she could free herself – but not like this! And worse, she had again to encounter deep and bitter feelings on top of the shock and grief of losing her husband, as this all reconstellated the powerful feelings of anger and disappointment associated with her father leaving the family when she was a child. In this sense she felt a terrific confusion about whether her husband was the 'good father' murdered by the giant, or the tyrannical, uncaring giant who had taken her happiness away. In fact there were moments where *she* felt like the murderous giant in the sky (with her intentions to 'kill' their marriage and her fantasised attacks on father as a child).

The conflict this evoked in her was so powerful that she would sometimes sit for long stretches in a session saying nothing, but looking at me from time to time – sometimes rage was in her eyes as I became the murderous father, and sometimes there was a sad but warm glow as I became the 'good but lost' father.

This is where an equivalent of the 'giant's wife' seemed to get constellated in the work. In the story she is another version of mother who has more power than Jack's real mother. The giant's wife is able to mitigate the unchecked violence and rapaciousness of her husband by supplying Jack with something to eat and somewhere to hide when the giant returns. By doing this she indirectly enables Jack to retrieve his father's treasure and then kill the tyrannical one.

Referring back to the discussion on *phallos* in the previous chapter, the giant's mother wrestled her husband's phallic power away from him by helping Jack subvert his power base – a version of 'phallic mother' which speaks to the struggle of this analysand to find her own power, her own voice.

This returns Jack to his mother, safe on the ground and holding positive father energy in the form of his rightful inheritance of his dead father's treasure. This seems to me a neat metaphor for this analysand's search for a home where her 'treasure' or libido could be held and cherished. The giant's wife is able to mediate between two versions of father and frees her up to pursue her new *completing* impulses. Behind the new lesbian relationship, this dynamic seemed to be waiting to unfold a version of the early mother–daughter relational container, however imperfect this may or may not have been.

In this respect, my place in the analysis seemed to be to 'wait' for these connections to form, holding the 'transcendent function' for her as the two versions of father (uncaring/loving) wrestled to give birth to the 'giant' mother (like a version of a 'great mother' who is more all-encompassing than all the fathers in the world). As she came to trust and relate to me as holding the possibility of mother as well as father (and her permission to herself to be gay as well as straight) she began to allow herself to slip into the new 'completing' pattern she found herself in with her new relationship. Using the metaphor of the giant's wife as mediator between positive and negative fathers, as well as holder of the transcendent function, for this analysand, the way was opened for her to allow herself to embrace her new life and relationship, and 'reclaim her treasure'(erotic and relational).

I have implied throughout how the transcendent gravitates more to 'male' territory while the 'immanent' drifts towards female territory – neither 'belonging' exclusively to one or the other, but a subtly pervasive distinction in trends in thinking and doing – i.e. men *may tend* to look for ways of building on or superseding what 'is', while women *may tend* to stay with what 'is' and transform it from the inside out.

Although I note a feeling of concern about having generalised too much, I want to hold this distinction in mind to see where these might helpfully take us. This distinction does not benefit from being pinned down too particularly, but does enable a freeing up of the *possibility* of difference, rather than closing this down for fear of 'stereotyping' and so on. This feels relevant to this discussion in terms of how the woman analysand described found a more *immanent* and *relational* 'solution' to her predicament than the men I described in the previous chapter, who tended to be looking beyond the present into imagined futures for this.

This woman found a new way of 'completing' herself via an acceptance of a new depth to her sexuality. This refers back to the importance of the first potential 'completing' moment in a little girl's life when she bonds with mother in a predominantly *relational* way (with erotic and other components supporting this). Boys, meanwhile, bond with the 'gender electrics' of erotic energy which are generally more pronounced and therefore liable to spark off in unpredictable directions.

It is the use of the *immanent function*, which facilitates this alongside the *transcendent* version, that enables change to be grounded properly rather than occurring 'ahead of itself'. The *immanent function*, as I have proposed it, has something to do with the capacity of the psyche to 'stay put' even when things do not feel quite right and part of us feels a powerful urge to run from, or somehow transform ('solve'), a problem. It can also refer to a capacity to 'be still' within, like a kind of steady meditative state, though it is not 'empty' of mind as such, but rather watchful of what is happening inside rather than reactive to, or with, it.

The woman in the clinical example had stayed with the *immanence* of her fading feeling and desire in her long marriage and had learnt much from doing so – as she reported it, a kind of wisdom 'in just noticing the muddle in myself . . . and the dying love fading away like a bird flying off in the distance.' She could have acted earlier but she did not – and some of this was, for sure, about familial constraints and social pressure – but as she described it this did seem to be more about checking with herself that this was the right thing to do as well as mourning the passing of a relationship 'in the right way'.

I could feel the sadness as well as a deep feeling of wisdom in her 'waiting' which I experienced as bigger than the work we were doing. On reflection, these feelings seem to speak of the *enantiodromia* of the process – in other words, of her having stayed with the *immanence* of the (on the surface) stuck situation she felt herself to be in, while the contrary emergence of a *transcendent* tendency reflected a change in her life situation. The outer manifestation of the inner process – her new partnership – was the relational embodiment of the searched for 'completing' experience. This carried hallmarks of the template from infancy of being with mother as well as a new awakening of *erosimus* in the experience of her new relationship.

Women working with women analysts

To augment my reflections on clinical work with women, I will now draw on work done by women analysts with women, to further elucidate the themes emerging. Here, analysts are writing from the same 'territory' (i.e.

female) as their analysands. In line with this thought, Jane Haynes indicates what she feels is important about the 'embodied gender' of the analyst in relation to the gender of the person they are working with:

> Whilst I agree that both male and female figures can be projected on to an analyst of either sex, I do think that there are differences which exist independently of transference projections. I am convinced that some of my patients would have had significantly different analyses if they had not taken place with an analyst of the opposite sex.
>
> (Haynes, 2007: 95)

I am in broad agreement with this observation, not least at a *phenomeno-logical* level. In my experience, working with a woman as opposed to a man, or vice versa, simply *feels* different. For example, with a man I usually feel in my body more 'upright' as I shake him by the hand on first meeting (something about 'performing' my shared maleness with him perhaps?), while with a woman my hand might be offered more loosely – as if wanting to give the message it is for her to take (or not) in the way she is comfortable. This seems to be to do with my way of working with the potential heterosexual erotic transference, as well as a consciousness of how sensitive (and fraught with difficulty) the male analyst–female analysand power relation can be.

This is not consciously planned; something in me seems to prepare me for the differences in working with a woman or with a man. A lifetime of cultural conditioning perhaps – or maybe (or also) an intuitive responding to the subtle but important differences which operate in working with female as opposed to male territory. The example refers to the first meeting. Generally, in my experience, these distinctions can become less important as an analysis develops and the gender 'niceties' inform the work less, at least at an overt level.

However, in my view, the embodied gender of the analyst, and of the analysand, continues to matter regarding the underlying direction and feel of the work. An example, comparing Haynes' observations with my own clinical experience, relates to her further point on the erotic transference and how she has experienced this, as a heterosexual woman analyst with heterosexual women analysands. This has enabled them to 'surrender their defences' against the frustrated hopes and desires blocked by parents, metaphorically allowing them to lead 'me by the hand to the heart's ease of their wounds' (Haynes, 2007: 96).

When I set this alongside my experience of working with women I notice a subtle but important difference in terms of how analytic work with women tends to 'open up', or not. The presence of the erotic can hover in the space from the start but will usually only spring to life symbolically if we both feel it is 'safe enough' to be unsafe' – i.e. it is okay to own feelings of attraction or desire and allow them to be present, without acting on them. This can mean that sometimes the analysand's readiness to lead me to their wounds never comes to pass and we remain stuck at the gateway of the path to them – perhaps another reading of the 'bear at the end of the road' from the dream in the first analysis I described? (see p. 125).

With one long-term analysand, we both got caught in a feeling it was 'unsafe to be unsafe' within the presence of *erosimus–erosima* and so the fact that I was a male analyst and she a female analysand was a stumbling block to therapeutic development, though bringing this block to consciousness did provide for some 'fertile' work to occur before it came to an end. At other times, the male–female combination seemed to symbolically, and transferentially, open up blocks in the erotic experiencing of self and others for the analysand. My point is that male–female, female–male, male–male and female–female combinations in the consulting room *are* different and can, and do, make a difference to the process.

Applying this point to literature on woman-to-woman analytic work provides some interesting slants on the general discussion about female territory, completing and immanence. Sherly Williams, for example, writes of the way in which the 'intense reciprocity' (Williams, 2006: 151) experienced by the daughter as an infant while the elemental phase of mirroring (face to face) goes on with mother needs to include 'erotic playback' so the baby experiences her bodily, autoerotic sensations as fused with mother – as a foundation for her own sexuality.

As she points out, healthy development for the little girl in this situation (as for the boy, though in a differently nuanced way) needs to incorporate the emergence of a 'satisfying image of . . . [her] . . . sexual identity' (ibid.) as recognised in the responding of mother. Williams goes on to describe some clinical work with a woman who had not experienced this. Rather, her mother had not truly 'seen' her sexuality, only acknowledging it by resorting to criticism of her daughter if she decided she was flaunting it inappropriately.

Inevitably, this woman sought this recognition of her sexuality in the analysis. At one point Williams reports how her analysand stretched herself out and a button popped open on her dress, allowing herself to be 'seen' bodily and sexually. This yearning could be seen as a legacy of the quality of the early 'completing' experience with mother. Here, the relational dimension of this does not seem to have been reinforced or 'completed' through the recognition of the sexual identity of the little girl. In this case it seems reasonable to assert that the physical presence of a woman analyst would facilitate a *more fully* experienced psychic reconstellation of the unresolved *erosimus* 'problem' of the woman analysand.

This problem allows *thanimus* to retain the upper hand, and re-establishes the girl's, and then the woman's, splitting off of the possibility of accepting her sexualised self-image. This will have prevailed at the pre-pubescent 'moment' which, as I argued earlier, is where sexual identity through adolescence and beyond may get defined – as an echo of early psychosexual 'definition' – and possibly rigidified.

Relevant to this, Williams (ibid.: 152) proposes, in relation to transference–countertransference in woman-to-woman work, that 'when it gets eroticised, it is important that the patient's erotic wishes be understood and mirrored positively.' This needs to happen, she argues, through acknowledging the analysand's 'whole body' not just the 'oral regressive elements'. This way the *erosimus* 'completing' process started with mother can be brought into the present moment and experienced as alive rather than deadened by *thanimus*.

This kind of legacy from the early mother–daughter encounter can also inform the place of *desire* in the life of a woman and the degree to which she knows and owns her desires. Young-Eisendrath (1997: 72) identifies 'a confusion between being the object and the subject of desire . . . female sexual desire is objectified as "how I need to look" rather than experienced as "how I want to feel."' She is referring to how different influences on being a woman impact on her capacity to be aware of what emanates *from* her and what is imposed or projected *upon* her. This ranges from the expectations around 'female appearance' which the media seem to relentlessly produce, to the way the 'gaze' of (heterosexual) men alights upon them as objects of male desire. Young-Eisendrath characterises this in terms of the way society sets up female beauty as a commodity for men to use without reference to the person who is 'behind' it.

This is turn undermines the subjective experiencing of a woman's own desires, as these are overlaid by being the *object* of other's desires. In relation to where early experience impacts on this, the little girl experiences an overwhelming impact on her from the parents' 'gaze' (meaning how the mother, or father, literally 'looks' at her, or more generally 'views' her), particularly where one or both of the parents have unresolved narcissistic needs around being 'noticed and adored' themselves. These can get projected onto the child, so the little girl experiences a sense of being valued for her beauty, rather than for who she really is.

One way of characterising this is to propose that *thanimus* is able to deaden the inner, living sense of who the little girl is and what her *real* felt and sensed desires are, by generating a 'false self' (Winnicott, 1960a) style of 'being' which the girl and then the woman subscribes to, possibly coming to believe that the desires others may have towards her are also her own. Another way of characterising this would be to borrow humanistic terminology and see this as a powerful condition of worth (Tolan, 2003), i.e. 'I only have genuine worth, and am only loved by you (parents or partner) if I am beautiful.'

When this equation comes into the consulting room the analyst's role is, as Williams implies, to see the person as a whole and offer an empathic stance in which the obscured, subjective, *real* desires of the woman can come into her conscious awareness and she can dwell on their presence and the implications of them being available to her. An example given by Marie Maguire (1995: 107) highlights how hard it can be for women to 'break the cycle of expressing desire through the psychic battles for domination and submission in order to move towards a greater sense of equality in sexual and emotional life' – not least because of the way women can be socialised into associating sex with submission. Maguire also alludes to the way the biology of sexuality does not help in breaking this cycle as, in contrast to the more externalised nature of male sexuality (symbolised by the thrusting penis), the sexuality of the woman has a more internal and 'whole body' dimension. The challenge lies in fully recognising how her desires really do emanate from within her (ibid.: 108).

There are parallels here with some of the material discussed in the previous chapter and the men I described as presenting with a kind of 'deadness', often experiencing this lack of *eros* in their sex life; for these men *thanima* had intervened to render desire problematic and even per-secutory. In this respect we can see how *desire* can become a problem for both women and men. The difference between how this constellates in men and in women seems to be that though men experiencing the kinds of difficulties identified above have lost some ownership of the *expression* of their desires, they are still experienced as belonging *to* them.

When women experience difficulty with desire, it seems generally to be more about not being able to feel ownership of it in the first place. For men, *thanima* intervenes and makes the experiencing and expression of their desire 'discontinuous' in time and space, while for women *thanimus* blocks access, or breaks the 'beanstalk' to, the seat of their desire before they can experience it as theirs.

The example Maguire gives concerns a woman who brought fantasies of being 'taken' by a man sexually in a rough and deeply penetrative way; using this fantasy was the only way she could come to orgasm. The only way to access her own subjective desire appeared to be via being the object of a man's full-on desire. This fantasy obviously acts as a powerful meta-phor for the points made about submission, and the objectification of a woman's desire.

The parental dynamic of a father who seemed disinterested and uncertain in his dealings with her, and a mother who she experienced as possessive and controlling, contributed to the uncertainty about what was 'okay' for her to feel and desire, and she brought this uncertainty into the analysis. Having a woman analyst presented her with a fuller opportunity to re-experience the oppressive aspects of mother, through the physical presence of another woman as analyst/mother.

The difficulty with accessing aggressive energies comes because she may identify these with the masculine – so the passive template provided by

father in relation to this could also be revisited in the shadow of the dominating mother-presence. This in turn renders it possible for a key constellation to emerge in the transference–countertransference. As Maguire
puts it: 'We need to recognise both the "holding" mother and the "exciting"
father as elements which make up desire' (ibid.: 127). The role of father as
'exciting' and able to securely allow the daughter to be 'unsafe' with her
sexuality, reflects the earlier point about my clinical experience of being a
male analyst working with women. It also reflects important points made by
Samuels (1989) about how father is pivotal to the daughter getting hold of
her sexuality via the incest-tinged 'play' between them, as long as this 'play'
does not become inappropriate sexual contact. For the girl this should be a
healthy opportunity to be seen as an attractive 'woman to be'; although this
opening up of her sexuality can be hampered or even blocked off by the
father mocking, over-restricting or overlooking her. As Samuels (ibid.: 82)
puts it: 'The father who cannot attain an optimally erotic relation with his
daughter is damaging her in a way that deserves therapeutic attention.'

For the woman described by Maguire, this had clearly not been available
to her and so the initial interference by *thanimus* in her first experience of
relational, plus erotic, connection with mother (through mother's apparent
difficulty in truly valuing her infant daughter for who she was) was
reinforced by the deadened *thanimus* experience of father, particularly as
she moved through puberty. In this case the split in her *animus* at the 'pre-
pubescent' moment of 'it/him' coming back to life, was reinforced by the
lack of erotic feedback (*erosimus*) in her relationship with father during her
teenage years and beyond.

Aggression and oppression

To conclude these clinical vignettes I want to address the nature and place
of aggression in the struggles of a woman to free herself from oppressive
patterns of being and relating, whether this refers to role, image and
sexuality or the patterning of lifelong strategies for dealing repressively with
strong feelings such as anger or misery.

First a few remarks on the extent of externally expressed female aggression. These are made to acknowledge the double bind women can find
themselves in when feeling like acting aggressively. Within our cultural
milieu – though this may be shifting – on the one hand, if a woman does
not respond to provocation she can be assumed to be passive, submissive,
weak. On the other, if she instead becomes 'aggressive' in a verbal or
physical way (whether overtly or threatening to be) then she can be labelled
as out of control and not 'womanly' (whatever that means).

This double bind can be seen as part of the constraining nexus of spoken
and unspoken rules which have traditionally governed the limits on female
actions and attitudes. This is changing, in some ways more explosively than

might have been anticipated – alongside the freeing up of a woman's capacity to assert herself and steer her own course through life, there is also what Kirsta (1994: 11) has labelled 'the rise of machisma'; (i.e. aggressive and violent behaviour by women). She regards this as an inevitable consequence of the pressures women as mothers, lovers and workers are put under, and challenges the rose-tinted notion that many of the more serious expressions of aggression and violence are the 'preserve' of men.

There has always been female aggression and violence. It seems to me to be patronising to suggest otherwise – and yet part of the patriarchal, Christian, myth in the west is that in their *immanent* territory, women only 'care', and when there is aggression around they 'mediate' or 'appease'. Kirsta (ibid.: 68–9) refers to a number of research studies into indigenous cultural practices where it is the women who lead and defend their societies. This indicates that innate aggression in girls and women is constrained in westernised culture, not by biological imperatives but by the overlays of social conditioning about who is 'allowed' (males) to express their aggression overtly and who is not (females).

On the one hand, the growing recognition of the place of female aggression in family and wider community life seems a healthy acknowledgement of a woman's capacity and entitlement to find ways of expressing herself aggressively (within, as applies to men, legal and ethical boundaries). This in turn reflects the importance for women of the ability to fantasise about their aggressive potential, in order to get hold of their entitlement to a fully fledged individuation struggle, and a place in the world which reflects who they are.

There is a parallel here with the problem of desire for women; an uncertainty about whether the aggressive feelings – or any lack of them – which they experience actually *belong* to them or not. There can be a confusion over whether, for example, a woman is feeling the need to remain watchful and inactive (rather than expressive and active) in response to some challenge from another person or situation, because this is an authentic response emanating from her *subjective* core, or whether she has imbibed a message about aggression and what women 'should do' which means she is automatically 'switching off' her capacity to express her real anger, or challenge/defend as needed.

This kind of possible disconnect, like the one concerning desire, is not exclusive to women. There may also be something similar which can happen for men around expressing intimate feelings and the capacity to want to care and nurture – i.e. is the choice to express self or not made on the basis of a man's *subjective* wish, or is the decision made for him (in a sense) by the internalised voice from wider society about 'how a man should be'?

What has happened to woman's aggression while society has censored and circumscribed its outer expression? This raises a further question: what happens to repressed aggression in relation to mother, because of her central place in shaping the psychic life of both boys and girls?

In the *Beanstalk* story, Jack's mother expresses her anger at one point very strongly. Jack has traded the only thing of economic value belonging to the family – the cow – for a bunch of apparently useless beans. She shouts angrily at Jack when he returns with the beans, sends him to his room without any supper and then throws the beans out of the window, regarding them (and Jack) as worse than useless. In this moment all her bottled-up rage and grief at losing her husband as well as all of the family's worldly goods bursts out. She has lost these immeasurably precious things – especially her husband, who, in the patriarchal society of later Middle Ages England, would probably have been the bedrock for her present and future: a fundamental resource for her emotional and practical stability.

What is more, she has lost him to a bigger and more aggressive version of the masculine – the giant who has murdered and possibly eaten him. The masculine she had relied on has been consumed by a huge and nasty version of it and the only version she has left is an apparently weak and under-developed form of it – her son, well meaning but dreamy and 'useless'. What is fascinating about this moment is how Jack's mother's fury actually releases the energy locked up in the magic beans (the apparently unavail-able potency of the boy) when she throws them out of the window – allowing them to be fertilised in the soil and then grow up to the sky. It is a chthonic moment where the hurt inflicted on Jack by her bitter denouncing of his naive and foolish actions is one side of a double-edged sword, the other side being the way this facilitates the release of the energy previously unavailable to the depressed mother – and to the boy. The established psychological axiom of depression being an expression of repressed anger is most relevant here, but gets further extrapolated into something about the mother–son dyad; one of them needs to express the rage behind the depression in order for something to change. This, preferably, will happen in a healthy way without someone getting hurt, but there is always a risk of psychological damage or even physical pain being inflicted in such uncon-tained moments. This is true, too, when the whole thing stays dammed up – deep psychological suffering which can also get somatised.

Here, the mother has clearly pushed her aggression away and down into herself and she relies on a son who is not ready to take on the mantle of adult bartering to do just that with their only asset, rather than doing it herself. The difficult, dark side of this, relevant to our clinical discussion, concerns what mothers 'do' with their repressed aggression. It has to come out somewhere and I want to suggest that there are two main forms in which it can do so.

First, her aggression may show through an over-appropriation of the only 'territory' left to her – the close mothering of her children, and the domestic sphere more generally. A kind of possessiveness and certitude may come into play here – i.e. an 'I know best' attitude when it comes to looking after children and the physical space of the home, as a way of compensating for not feeling able to express or put 'out there' her capacity for using her aggression in more creative and satisfying ways. Power – whether one describes it in terms of grabbing the *phallus*, or as a way of experiencing a kind of feminine authority which is aiming to subjugate it – arises from having possession of the *territory* of home and family. Here a kind of archetypally oppressive version of mother can get constellated which is rooted in an identification between mother-home-family. This is something I will look at with respect to potential difficulties in male–female relations in the final chapter, where I ponder 'the problem of home'.

The other form in which I am suggesting this repressed aggression can manifest is potentially more significant for the forming and sustaining of *thanimus* domination of the psyche in girls and women. If a woman has internalised in a fundamental way the splitting message about aggression belonging to what is 'out there' rather than 'in here' (and it may be reasonable to assert that if this is happening with aggressive energies then this will probably also be the case with her erotic and relational *desires*), this will impact beyond, as well as in, her daughter's early experiencing of the infant–mother dyad, and the struggle between *erosimus* and *thanimus* within this phase, as well as during later (psychosexual and relational) stages of development.

For women there is an implication about how the early experience of the 'completing–relational' in their psychosexual bonding with mother is impacted. Here, *thanimus* may well also make its presence felt through a similar feeling of danger or threat in relation to using aggression to express self, a threat hovering behind the deadening, depressed atmosphere surrounding the mirroring connection with mother. This, I suggest, will be further emphasised by the identificatory nature of the daughter–mother relationship. The messages around holding back on outwardly expressing aggressive energies from within will be reinforcing in this sense; part of an inhibiting, self-sacrificial style of the reproduction of mothering.

In classical Jungian language this problem with aggression is prime *animus* territory for a woman, and often seems to get focused on father – perhaps because the unhappy parental dynamic of father becoming unboundaried in his aggression, and even violence, while mother gets swallowed up in her patterned, internalised passive-aggression is all too common. As Woodman (1990) puts it when describing a piece of clinical work with a female analysand, *animus* can become dangerously split where the energy of its darker side remains trapped and less than conscious. In this case 'Kate', her analysand, was caught up in her anger towards her father, whose drunken rages used to menace and terrify her. Her dreams were haunted by Luciferean figures which alternated between rebel and criminal images, the obvious danger for Kate being how 'the energy . . . can move from rebel to criminal very fast' (ibid.: 153), and that therefore she might find herself acting out her rage.

As implied, this negative father complex was charged more strongly with hostile *thanimus* energy because there was a complementary negative *mother* complex at work; in this case the 'giant' (which is what a complex is like – it becomes 'bigger than us' and, as Jung puts it, possesses us with the power and strength of its constellated energy) was not compensated by a relationally aware 'giant's wife' who could give Kate a way out of her predicament. Woodman (ibid.: 154) describes how, rather, Kate felt very keenly the lack of bonding with mother, which she could trace back to early life. This rendered her situation doubly difficult. Though she could find positive traits in each parent that she could identify with (father's creativity and mother's single-mindedness) there was almost nothing to anchor her deeper feelings about them. In this sense the internalised 'giant parental couple' of her drunken, violent, father, with his sense of discontinuity between a perfecting ideal of being a published poet and a reality of being stuck with his ego weakness, and a mother who experienced her own sense of 'incompleteness' (implied by the 'incomplete' relational bond with her daughter) were lumbering around her psyche, wreaking havoc.

Woodman captures well the way *thanimus* takes its power in relation to parental complexes: 'In women, where the primary betrayal was in the relationship with the mother, the loss may be so deep that it does not even appear in dreams until the dreamer has worked on the father complex for years' (ibid.: 155).

This is the contrasexual principle which can keep a woman away from resolving deep wounds. It is interesting to speculate whether, in this case, by working analytically in the embodied presence of another woman, Kate gave herself more of a chance to find her way back to the embodied, incomplete experience she had initially had with her mother. The formula for getting to that point seems to involve *thanimus* insisting 'he' is dealt with first, as his masculine dream appearances suggest, before the deeper relational wound is uncovered, where *erosimus* lies bound and gagged, and can hopefully be released.

Inevitably, this problem means that for someone like Kate, when she moves through her 'pre-pubescent moment' after latency, *erosimus* will remain kidnapped and locked away, and relations with men in particular during adolescence and then adulthood will probably get hallmarked by instability, hostility and disappointment. By making her rage and disappointment conscious, and working with it in the therapeutic setting and elsewhere in her life, Woodman (ibid.) reports, Kate became more able to channel her aggression into the 'single-minded creativity' she did pick up as a useful characteristic of the parental dyad.

The formula of 'father complex' first, 'mother complex' second is not cast in stone but it does suggest, again being careful to acknowledge the shifting possibilities of gendered experiencing, how the contrasexual principle in the psyche may generate subtle differences in the way women project compared with men – something about *thanimus or erosimus* ways of projecting (women onto men) as against *thanima or erosima* ways/styles (men onto women).

In both cases there is a need to search for the aggressive and erotic presence of the other (which will also be a projection of their own). For a woman this search refers back to the same way these two elements will have been experienced *as relational* factors in the original mother–daughter dyad. For the man it can often be the search for the relational connection which is more elusive than the aggressive and erotic ones.

Concluding comments

I will further consider these subtle differences in how women project onto men, and how men project onto women in Chapter 7. To conclude this chapter, I want to make a few comments about power, and time and space. The ways in which a woman's power can be emasculated are implied clearly from some of the themes explored in this chapter. The collective influences on self-image and expression of feeling can get reproduced all too easily via their unconscious and conscious transmission from mother to daughter. Father can also too easily generate or reinforce these messages (the father of a woman I worked with either overlooked her emerging womanhood or commented coldly about her 'weight problem' during adolescence, a subtly lethal injection of *thanimus*, bound to deaden her somatised sense of erotic expression and potential).

This emasculation of a woman's erotic and relational expression comes hand in hand with a consonant disallowing of her aggressive energies and how these might be used to articulate her sense of self. This is a familiar template for how men have found ways to restrict, and sometimes oppress and persecute, women within domestic as well as wider social and political contexts, disallowing relational – including playful – erotic expression. This in part at least may be because some men may fear this as a re-constellation of oedipal 'moments' where the little boy has sensed the presence of father as being more alluring to mother than his own. It is also to do with social influence on male perceptions of 'how things should be'.

Within the wider socio-political arena, this has been historically framed by the patriarchal Judeo-Christian settlement which has underpinned the workings of western civilisation for a couple of millennia at least: i.e. women are only 'allowed' to operate within an *immanent* position of home and family. The radical breaking out of women from this position in the last hundred years only goes to demonstrate how much locked-in but healthy erotic and aggressive energy (*erosimus*) has been held within the confines of this settlement. This settlement could be characterised as an expression of man's collective 'giant' *thanima* energy emanating from an unhealthy 'perfecting transcendence' and coming down heavily on women's *immanent erosimus* potential, keeping it trapped, pinned to the ground by the giant's huge hand.

On a more individual scale, the experiencing of self in relation to others, as well as in relation to time and space, *may*, in a general way, have subtle differences for women compared with men. A key factor here refers to my arguments about continuity and discontinuity. The male psyche seems to inhabit a space in which linear time can act as an anchor to his sense of self-in-time, with an underlying emphasis on 'becoming'. This may get underlined by the pressure for a clearly defined frame of reference, such as a need to 'provide solutions', in order to counter the fuzzier boundaries around defining when a boy becomes a man.

This makes him more vulnerable to a state of 'discontinuity' where this becoming/solving/perfecting trend is disrupted. For some men, perhaps more vulnerable to the neurobiological vagaries of the male brain, this can link unhelpfully to their relationship to space as well as time – struggling in inhibited or clumsy ways in relation to their environment whenever the 'straight road' or 'railtrack' into the future gets obscured.

For women, the presence of a more reliably 'continuous' psyche is based on the broader, deeper relational base to their beginning in life, which does not rely so much on successfully managing an *erosima* healthily discontinuous rupture from mother (and then overcoming other less healthy versions of discontinuity). Time and space within the healthy unfolding of this scenario offers a secure flexibility in terms of the 'completing' movements of a girl's and then a woman's life. The reveries of mirroring and identifying in relational and psychosexual ways with mother will have established this.

However, girls and women seem to be vulnerable in other ways. While there is generally a feeling of continuity (a sense of 'I-am-reliably-located-in-time-and-space'), this does not guarantee an alive, *erosimus* feeling of 'completing'. Instead, if the girl has encountered an incomplete experience of relational bonding with mother at the beginning of life, then relations generally seem to get infected with this sense. Father may compensate for this if he is able to help her locate her *erosimus* in his attending to her blossoming womanhood in puberty, but it seems more likely that her closed-down or skewed erotic energies, as well as the implied imbalances in the parental relationship and how this may be expressed by father (lack of eros and/or hostile *thanimus*), will not make her *erosimus* energies available to her in a free-flowing or satisfying way.

In this respect the passing of time for some women may be all too easy to experience. Rather than experiencing time as 'standing still', she may take pleasure in being reminded of what she is not completing – for herself or with others – whether that be becoming a mother, achieving a career goal, or just having a sense of who she really is, expressed in what she does and how others experience her. Such are the burdens inflicted on girls and women by *thanimus* – as portrayed by the clinical material and wider discussion in this chapter – as it sabotages their aggressive and erotic energies and requires the female psyche to mark time, not live it out.

Chapter 6

Climbing the beanstalk: Personal and collective adolescence

> Jack decided to climb the beanstalk and with that he stepped out of the window onto the beanstalk and began to climb upwards.

Two questions to begin this chapter with: How grown up are we? How far up the beanstalk is the human race, or at least the westernised parts of it? These are 'big' questions to play with, to fall into reverie about, to begin this chapter with – inane, maybe pretentious questions in some ways (considering they imply there is something we should be 'aiming' for, in a 'masculine', perfecting/transcending way). But, they are ones which seem a good place to start as they replicate a *cri de coeur* of the adolescent young woman or man as they stand in front of the mirror, watching their body change almost before their eyes, wondering: 'How grown up am I?'; 'Am I an adult yet?'

More pertinent to our discussion, this latter question usually gets reframed in the mind of the teenager according to the gender they have been ascribed by their genetic inheritance, early attachment experiences and socialisation: 'Am I a man yet?' or 'Am I a woman yet?' The discussion in this chapter will examine how the transformations of adolescent years impact on male and female teenagers and how this can set the scene for adult relating.

The context here is developmental and I want to bring the schema in Chapter 3 (see pp. 68–9) up to adulthood and in particular examine what happens during puberty and adolescence to lay the foundations for adult male–female relating, particularly with respect to the profoundly powerful re-constellations of identity during this life stage. To inform this, I will look at the emerging research and theoretical formulations on male–female differences arising from neurobiological studies.

To complement this there will also be some reflection on the development of male and female consciousness on the wider collective stage, and how 'adult' or 'adolescent' this might be. This frame of reference which I begin with considers the relationship between 'archetypal gender' (masculine and feminine) influences in the individual psyche, and the experience of being female or being male. This will include considering how one maps onto the other – e.g. in what ways might 'the feminine' correspond to being female, and how far is it reasonable to assert that female territory 'holds' the feminine more than male territory? I have constructed a generalised historical schema – based loosely on Jung's approach to the development of religious consciousness in humanity – to try and tease out what may have evolved in our way of articulating the polarities of masculine–feminine and male–female, at least in western consciousness. This schema loosely parallels (as does Jung's) the individual journey from birth through to the cusp of adulthood.

Human 'ale' and Giant '(w)ine'

Beginning with the question of the relationship between *masculine and feminine* and *male and female*, it sometimes seems as if our confusions about gender revolve around this very issue: i.e. to what degree does male = masculine and female = feminine, an essentialist position? Or, to what degree is this an infinitely variable relationship, so male (or female) can = masculine *or* feminine *or* a combination of both, at any one time? This is a more socially constructivist position, although it appears to admit the presence, at least at a conceptual level, of the feminine and the masculine as archetypal influences. To put it another way, to what degree does the 'ale' (m and f) blend well with the (w)'ine' (m and f), or, like mixing up a pint of old English bitter ale with the wine of the gods, does this result in no more than a sickly palate and a grim hangover the next morning?

To start with the nectar of the gods, when Jung writes about masculine and feminine, the emphasis is on their archetypal pairing within the psyche; the 'bisexual primordial' (Jung, 1940/1968) nature of their bound-together source in the shape of ancient gods. He explored impacts of 'moments of meeting' between the two faces of this bisexual form of origin on the human level of experiencing self and other. A crucial implication he derived from this bisexual root of each of us is that:

> Just as every individual derives from masculine and feminine genes, and the sex is determined by the predominance of the corresponding genes, so in the psyche it is only the conscious mind, in a man, that has the masculine sign, while the unconscious is by nature feminine. The reverse is true in the case of a woman.
>
> (Jung, 1940: para. 294)

Here, Jung seems to suggest how the archetypal masculine and feminine come through into lived experience – through a principle of *predominance*, a predominating *style of consciousness (and unconsciousness)* which presents in a subtle but pervasive difference between women and men. This means there are ways in which one or the other can predominate in aspects of being human; in this case male consciousness has a predominance of a 'masculine' capacity for *logical thinking* associated with it, while the predominating 'feminine' capacity for *relational feeling* characterises the consciousness of women. The flip-side of this equation is a kind of unconscious ('inferior' as it is less within a woman's command) capacity for logical thinking (*logos*) in women and a consonant 'inferior', unconscious capacity for relational feeling (*eros*) in men.

This approach helps to explain how he ended up describing women as having a kind of 'problem with being fully conscious', as *logos* is not fully available to help them 'be conscious', and instead has a subversive capacity to over-simplify the complexities of life, or get confused. He strongly implies this in his ascribing of *animus* as being limited in its capacity to 'think straight' about things.

It is a surprisingly simplistic way of equating 'feminine unconscious *logos*' with 'females'. He seems to be saying 'feminine = unconscious *logos*'; females are predominantly feminine, therefore, generally speaking, 'female = limited capacity for consciousness'. There is a further implication here because Jung seems to be implying a kind of equation between levels of consciousness and the capacity to rationalise cogently (though he is *not* saying this is the only component to 'being conscious'). He seems to have confused the ale for wine. His formula seems to be:

1   Females are predominantly feminine.
2   The predominant feminine accrues *logos* unconsciousness.
3   *Therefore* females have a more limited level of consciousness than men.
4   Levels of *logos* consciousness impact on levels of capacity to be rational.
5   *Therefore* females are less rational than males.

This is striking in the light of the point I made in the introduction about people with severe learning difficulties. Research has shown that two in three people who experience these are male (Male, 1996) and that the basis of these difficulties are often genetic. Somehow the masculine emphasis on 'being more conscious' and being able to draw on intellectual (including cogently rationalising) capacities is sabotaged and reversed here, at least in its neurophysiological foundations in males. There is a link here also with the point about the 'male brain' and autism, discussed earlier in Chapter 4, and its apparently greater vulnerability to being afflicted with limitations to how conscious it can sometimes be. Finally there is also a paradox arising from research on 'brain-sex' (which I will look at later in this chapter). This suggests that adolescent and adult males are more prone to some forms of 'driven' and less thought-through activity than females (some impetuous or aggressive activities etc.) which can render them more vulnerable to accidents, violent injury and suicide. All in all, Jung's implied formulation can be evidenced as flawed and unhelpful.

The fragility of how men are (while recognising men predominantly have greater physical strength), as against how 'tough' they have been portrayed to be in our culture, needs to be factored into 'male territory'. I suggest that this is to do with the predominant (*not* ubiquitous) draw towards *perfecting/ solving/transcending* in the male psyche. The myth of male toughness acts as a reflection of a man's wish to be 'the best', but then becomes the straight, inflexible, road towards 'a solution' which can so easily snap in two when its upward trajectory aims exclusively for this.

In this respect male territory can seem to be closer to the shady territory of the dead: pursue the straight road when it is not the right one and this is where one can end. This is the territory of the avidly fixated adventurous sportsperson (*predominantly* male) – where climbing a mountain or trying to beat a speed record in a machine of some description can result in death. Less dramatically, there are driven attitudes and behaviours which result in professional failure, relationship breakdown, or health problems. Meanwhile, female territory is *predominantly* (again, I want to stress, *not* ubiquitously) characterised by a more *immanent, completing* embrace of the 'here and now', and possibly more *embodied*. The pull towards the hinterlands between life and death, between the secure and the risky, is less prevalent.

To return to the erroneous aspects of Jung's formula about contrasexuality and women, I suggest his equating of 'female' with lower levels of consciousness (a kind of *animus* flawed *logos*) about the world around them is a category error, as he implies contrasexual influence in the psyche is about *levels* not *styles*. I want to argue that men's consciousness is, in some ways, predominantly different to women's consciousness *stylistically* – and vice versa. My guess is that because of the cultural atmosphere in which Jung lived and worked, where women were kept out of key social and political institutions and processes, it was easy to slip into implying that women's capacity for honed thinking operated at a *lesser level* than in men.

So, Jung's elucidation of how the 'feminine generates females' and the impact this has on a woman's capacity to utilise her masculine psychic aspects, does not allow for the flexibility inherent in the term 'predominance'. It that seems wine ('up there' archetypal gender) and ale ('down here' male–female relations) simply do not mix well. Rather, they *complement* each other when positioned carefully, like a *maitre de* getting the right lager to accompany the starter, and a spot-on claret to go with the main course. However, I am following Jung's (op. cit.) use of the term 'predominance'; in my case, it is useful for describing possible gendered tendencies and for informing my descriptions of 'male' and 'female' territories.

'Predominance' implies that there is a kind of tipping point between male and female 'ways of being', beyond which there are predominantly differing 'styles' of consciousness. From a psychoanalytic viewpoint, this 'tipping point' may also have something to do with the need for men to distinguish themselves from women (and vice versa), as a way of maintaining the incest taboo (see Chapter 8). Whatever all the components are for the dynamics of gender differentiation, I contend that important *stylistic* differences do result, which I will elucidate further in Chapter 7.

I see contrasexual *capacities* as coming into play in relation to what of the feminine actually, subjectively and (hopefully) consciously *belongs* to me and is in my power to *stylistically* use, rather than *anima* being an elusive, autonomous figure in my psyche that I need to wrestle with to get those attributes *back*. For example, my *erosima*-influenced capacity to nurture my children is something I consciously noticed when my first child was born, and this gets articulated through my *style* of fathering, and in how I tend to the emotional needs of my children. I suggest that a similar process happens in a woman's accessing of *erosimus*. In both cases positive contrasexual energies are available to the conscious mind and get articulated through the unique individual style of the person concerned.

There is a distinction here between, on the one hand, the unconscious power of *eros–thanima* or *eros–thanimus* to drive or curtail our deeper erotic, aggressive and relational needs and responses, and on the other, our *conscious* capacity to draw on feminine and masculine aspects of what lives within our fields of awareness. So, contrasexual influence operates in a conscious way where we choose to operate out of the life-enhancing presence of *erosima* or *erosimus*, and less so where *thanima* or *thanimus* draws us into hostile, deadened or fractured ways of being in relating to others, as well as in having trouble being able to use *positive* contrasexual attributes. We do have choices when we attack, or withdraw from, other people – but *thanima/us* renders the alternative *eros* responses (to negotiate etc.) less available within our conscious repertoire of responses.

This links to how contrasexuality in the psyche acts as a gatekeeper to the collective unconscious (Jung, 1959: 40), letting in deep influences – either welcome ones in *eros* guise, or slipping into conscious activity in a less welcome *thanatos* way. An obvious example of this would be how, in an insidious way, *thanima* might impact on my capacity as a man to actively get hold of more archetypal 'feminine' attributes (e.g. nurturing, relating); the same could happen in reverse for a woman, where archetypal 'masculine' traits of her personality (e.g. analysing, defending herself) can be rendered less available by the deep influence of *thanimus* in her psyche.

The distinction I make here is important, as it suggests there has been, over time, an evolving bifurcation between contrasexual unconscious presences (*anima–animus*) in the psyche, and a developing *conscious awareness* of 'what of me is feminine and what is masculine' and 'how I can use this awareness actively in the present'. I will hold onto this proposition as we explore the evolving relationship between the archetypal level of gender and the human one. I will draw on the distinctions Jung made between different 'stages' of humanity's religious development – describing primitive, ancient and modern stages (Jung, 1918/1970; 1938/1969). These were refined further by Robert Segal (1992) when he added the 'contemporary' stage. I will apply these to a 'history of gender'.

As implied by any evolutionary process where the nature and style of (in this case, human) operation becomes more complex over time (as consciousness, and the neurological capacities of the brain, evolve more nuanced responses to experience and the environment), there is an underlying assumption here of our relationship to the nature and presence of gender becoming more complex.

This does not, though, necessarily equate with people becoming more 'gender aware' over time (in a linear, *perfecting* way). Societies throughout history have had to make decisions about what we might term 'gender' (for example about the ascribed roles of men and women in relation to work, family and social hierarchy) and it seems evident that where points of crisis are reached about how men perceive or treat women (or vice versa), there will be a more heightened level of consciousness about 'gender' (or however it is termed within a particular culture or era).

At other times, where society seems to be 'ticking over' fairly happily, or where 'the rules' governing gendered roles and relations are determined by religious/political authority (which is acquiesced with), then the question of gender will be less pressing. This can also apply where a society is embattled and there is a united goal around survival. The Second World War is a good example of this, where men and women focused on defeating Hitler. But when this goal was achieved, the 'settlement' between men and women eventually became very much a living issue.

So, the evolving development in western consciousness around gender cannot be accurately described in a linear way, though the underlying shifts in consciousness, I would argue, do carry some hallmarks of a prospective aspect in terms of some kind of attempt to resolve, or at least make more workable, the relationship between men and women.

A brief psychological history of gender – archetypal and personal

This portrayal is offered within the binary dynamics of the feminine–masculine and male–female polarities, and is focused on the *power dynamics* between male and female territory. Jung denotes 'primitives' as representing an initial stage in emerging human consciousness where ego is barely present, and the unconscious is fully projected out onto the environment. This would include a powerful experiencing of a strong presence of bisexual energies in how 'alive' the natural world, in a spiritual sense, was for early societies. Jung's description of these primitive energies was *mana* (Jung 1951/1968b: para. 394, n. 88) – undifferentiated and not taking any form we could characterise as 'feminine', 'masculine' or 'gods'.

The whole environment could become charged with these energies, and a powerful, frightening version of religiosity, rather like living permanently up in the kingdom of the giants, with no beanstalk to bring them back down to earth. I speculate that this is the residual primitive layer of our psyches, where the giants remain and keep their appeal – as remnants of a way of projecting self onto the external world in a primitive way.

The conjoined duality of maleness and femaleness remained (conceptually) undifferentiated in this primitive state. Although, *biologically*, a man's masculine elements and a woman's feminine ones were critical aspects of who they were – translating into a man's predominant 'fight or flight', hunter-gatherer instincts and actions and a woman's predominant 'tend and befriend' familial ones – these were unconscious and instinctual, so one could say they did not *belong* to them; rather, they were 'loaned' to them by the bisexual *mana* source embodied in nature and their physicality. This primitive phase mirrors the earliest phases of infancy, which are hallmarked by undifferentiated 'fusion' and introjected 'giant' versions of parents.

The 'ancients' are ascribed to the next stage, which lasted from the foundations of what can commonly be called the western and arabic civilisation (Segal, 1992a) era up to and beyond the first stirrings of modernity (the Renaissance, the Enlightenment, the Industrial Revolution etc.). Here there was a gradual shift into differentiating the archetypal masculine and feminine and the emergence of gods representative of them.

These gods, or giants of the psyche, could take both feminine and masculine forms – mother as *luna*, or father as *sol* (or vice versa) – or take the form of other living or inanimate entities worshiped to protect a tribe or provide food. However, in the early stages of this differentiation, rather than masculine and feminine gods having wholly separate forms or identities, these were interchangeable in their animation of the natural world and provided an overwhelmingly powerful presence of the bisexual godhead. So although men and women *may* have noticed that they were different in some physical and other respects, the feminine and/or masculine godheads held a person's femininity or masculinity in the palm of their hand.

However, the strengthening personification of gods – masculine and feminine (as in the pantheon of Gods on Olympus) – illustrated how these archetypes could correspond to human forms, and so a correspondence emerged between these, and male and female, as emerging differentiated forms of being human. This formula then became the arena in which personification of the archetypal turned into a struggle for domination which the Judeo-Christian tradition perfected on behalf of the masculine and men, superceding the 'goddess' cultures (Baring and Cashford, 1991) where the feminine, portrayed by gods in the form of female figures, held sway. Jung equates this shift with the emergence of an equation: hero = masculine, and the ego freeing itself from the Great Mother of the unconscious (Jung, 1912/1952).

The figure of Jesus Christ, as 'perfected man' or 'God made man', was (is still for some) the apotheosis of an equation between the divine, archetypally god-like masculine, and the figure of a man. The significance here, in terms of shifting consciousness, is in how archetype is equated with 'sexed' form – i.e. divine man is pictured as a human man, as divine woman has also been equated with the image of a woman. This is where 'gender certainty' seems to have been given a huge shot in the arm, beginning a trend which later rigidified gender roles in the 'modern' period.

So, 'ancient' men are full of archetypal masculinity and women are likewise archetypally feminine. It is also where *Jack and the Beanstalk* finds its ground (and sky) as a later medieval story. The giant couple catch the mood of this period perfectly – the bigness of the masculine–feminine struggle, and the dominance of their coupling together, in the sky, overlaid upon the lives of struggling peasants. Jack's mother embodies, in ancient terms, the passive feminine – lost without her husband, the patriarchal protector. Jack is the archetypal nascent masculine, waiting to be the hero. In the patriarchal equating of feminine = female, women like Jack's mother were thoroughly defined, and constrained, by *thanimus* – squashing and deadening their individual potential beyond clearly defined lines of demarcation (an invisible line drawn often within a day's walk from home).

As Robert Segal (personal communication, 2009) has pointed out to me, there is a different reading possible of Jack's and his mother's situation, which is not focused on gender: Jack's mother's predicament is because she is poor and widowed, not because she is a woman; and Jack is a lazy youth, not a bereft son. This is a valid point, but I see these factors as intertwined in a *gendered* way. First there is mother's dependence, in a patriarchal universe, on male (heroic) pro-action to save the day, and second, Jack (in some versions of the story) has had an indulgent (and lazy) life up to the time of his father's death, because he was the 'crown prince', reaping the benefit of his father's wealth.

The predominating ancient identification between being male and the perfecting/solving/transcending quality of the masculine reflects the Christian myth – especially where this involves 'Imitation of Christ' approaches (À Kempis and Shirley-Price, 1952) to emulating his 'perfection' – as well as the 'up-in-the-sky' quality of *Jack and the Beanstalk*. In contrast, the identification between being female and the completing/immanent nature of the archetypal feminine very much keeps both 'on the ground', in a deferential, even obedient, position towards the male–masculine conjunction.

In both cases, the Ancient period, through its gendered identifications with spiritual figures (e.g. a man with Christ, or a woman with Mary), shifted the numinous masculine and feminine into men and women themselves, although their ego strength remained variable, so they would still project this power 'out there' onto God or gods (usually 'up in the sky'). I also suggest that this ancient phase mirrors aspects of oedipal experiencing where contrasexual images represent drives in the psyche: so women would be as drawn to some masculine god images (as representing the desired father) as they would identify with feminine god images and men likewise would be nourished by feminine goddesses/holy images. As the ancient period came into its own, *erosima* and *erosimus* came to life, before becoming more rigidified into set forms of male and female perceiving and operating – something which continued into the modern era.

The close of the 'modern' period, gender-wise, is when the 'archetypal'–'embodied gender' equation finally comes unstuck. As visualised by Jung, 'the difference between moderns and ancients is that moderns possess a fully independent ego' (Segal, 1992: 14) and this shift brings with it a de-mythologising of the world, enabling us to see it as it is, and each other for who we are – including an emerging clarity about what is different, and similar, about being male or being female.

The seeds for this development can be seen in stories like *Jack and the Beanstalk*, where Jack gradually becomes more conscious after following his unconscious intuition to trade the cow in for the beans. Once he realises what is in the unconscious, up there in the sky, he returns again and again to retrieve it, until there is enough treasure to sustain the conscious life he shares with his mother on the ground for the foreseeable future. This emerging capacity to resource oneself without relying on the 'giants' in the unconscious is a hallmark of the move from 'ancient' to 'modern', as is the capacity to struggle with the *real* gendered 'other' (not with the projected versions 'in the sky'), as Jack and his mother do over his decision to accept the beans as payment for the cow. Man experiencing woman as 'not the same', and vice versa, is clearly a reflection of increased ego strength.

So all the key features of secularisation and industrialisation – e.g. urbanisation, greater mobility and the growing recognition of the importance of woman as economic as well as domestic players – eventually threw the cumbersome, simplistic equation of archetypal gender as being equivalent to the embodied, lived version into relief. The rigidity of 'gender certainty' was at its zenith but, via a blossoming of gendered awareness in women, the many ways the archetypal feminine and masculine cannot be authentically replicated in ordinary ways became clearer. This is where the 'modern' stage replicated the move on from 'latency' via the 'pre-pubescent moment' – sublimated archetypal forces bursting back to life.

Imagined in caricature, it could be said that women had been shouldering the *immanent* weight of this gender illusion, working hard to hold things together (keeping things *'complete'* enough) while men floated in their *transcending, perfecting* – and in many ways, controlling and avoiding – place in the sky. It is important to set alongside this generalised picture the reality that 'gender' might not have been at the forefront of ordinary people's minds when they were struggling simply to *survive* (keeping families fed and safe) rather than having the luxury to notice the difference made to one's life experience if 'I' am a woman or a man.

However, consciousness about felt injustice and role imbalance did spark to life in women, and men were (in a way) put on the back foot collectively as they had not journeyed into gendered awareness in the same way. One consequence was, and maybe still can be, a harsh breakdown of consensus between men and women on what consists of harmonious roles and satisfying relationships.

This in turn gradually gave way to the 'contemporary' or postmodern sensibility – I stress 'gradually' because, as argued, I think we are still somewhat caught between the modern and the postmodern where gender and heterosexual relationships are concerned – hence this stage we are in being comparable to the confusion of adolescence. We struggle with tensions around binaries such as stasis versus deconstruction and equality versus difference, which implies an uncertainty about how at ease we are with our 'consciousing of consciousness' (Hauke, 2000) – our 'meta-awareness' as we watch ourselves deal with gender relations. This is what may lie behind the question of whether we choose new and more fluid forms of constituting and maintaining intimate relationships between men and women, or whether we choose to reaffirm the more apparently straightforward bounds of conventional married and family life which remained the bedrock of many 'modern' forms of long-term heterosexual relationships – or whether we want to do both?

Segal (1992: 17) defines the distinction between moderns and contemporaries as the former being fixed in a one-sided rationalism, while the latter are conscious of their less rational aspects, and in this respect have a psychological bond with the ancients, as both struggle with the balance between ego capacity and valuing the contents of the unconscious. This seems to me to helpfully describe the balance people who seriously think about gender struggle with – trying to consciously understand what it 'is' and how it might impact on them, while at the same time recognising the power of unconscious forces to influence our relationships.

In the ancient and modern phases of gender ascription there was a common perception whereby 'being' a man equalled being masculine and being a woman equalled being feminine, and this was apparently based on patriarchal certitude. As definitions of masculine and feminine inevitably became more nuanced, via pivotal developments such as the flowering of cultural life in the Rennaisance, and the huge stimulus to intellectual thought and critique of conventional religious and social norms generated by the Enlightenment, it became clearer that these overarching forms – masculinity and femininity – would not successfully translate wholesale into the physical forms of man and woman. This trend, alongside the radical change in the perceptions of women about their 'place' and potential in life, brought itself to bear on the destabilising of traditional forms of the heterosexual relationship.

The movement from modern to contemporary forms of relationship was marked by a spectacular collapse in the ubiquity of marriage as the standard 'container' for long-term heterosexual relationships in countries such as the UK – around 14 per cent of married people divorced in 1993, though this figure has declined in recent years to 11.9 per cent in 2007 (ONS, 2009). The volatile patterns here suggest that the archetypal feminine and masculine have burst through the straitjacket that societies imposed on themselves, to declare they cannot be thus contained via being narrowly equated with female and male.

Instead, one could say they have comfortably outrun the efforts of people to box them in, by bringing to conscious awareness the limitations of a one-size-fits-all approach to relationships and family. Other expressions of the erotic and relational – gay, lesbian and transgender – as well as wide variations in how heterosexual desire (e.g. sadomasochistic practices) and lifestyle choice (e.g. cohabitation) manifest themselves, have made irrefutable claims to be accepted as equally valid, rather than remaining repressed individually, or censored collectively.

Over time, the freeing up of expression of gendered identity and gendered sexuality has been made possible by a loosening of the fixed association of male with masculine and female with feminine, though this remains counterpointed by a deeply maintained connection between them in how our societies organise themselves and how our children are inducted into them. As indicated, there has, though, been a tipping point – a collective 'prepubescent moment' where *anima* and *animus* energies have reawakened and moved us into a collective adolescence (in the westernised world at least) in which men and women are renegotiating their identities and relationships. We move between emerging mature forms and regressed defensive/hostile forms which refer back to the modern stage, where things got in some ways rigidified – back and forth like a teenager swinging between 'child' and 'adult'.

When Jung talks about a newborn baby containing a two-million-year-old person (McGuire, 1980: 99) he rightly in my view points to the need to live with all four (primitive, ancient, modern and contemporary) layers of the history of the psyche; each of these is particularly pertinent to our confusions about gender, though those who see themselves as contemporaries might want to argue that they are edging towards a more authentic balance between 'gender certainty' and 'gender uncertainty'.

Certainly, during the 'modern' phase it was as if the archetypal streams of the feminine and the masculine had gone underground, into a 'latent' sleep in term of their capacity to generate new forms of relational expression, while the patriarchal male–female relational equation was wholly dominant. Comparing this with the individualised developmental model I proposed in Chapter 3, there seems to be a parallel.

This mirrors the more fixed, stereotyped positions of boy and girl that one might associate with the latency stage, i.e. primary school age, where children tend to identify much more closely with their same-sex peers and 'gender certainty' becomes important. They are initiated into the *Symbolic Order* (Lemaire, 1977), where fitting into perceived social expectations about 'being a boy' or 'being a girl' usually becomes vividly important in terms of identity formation.

Then there is the 'pre-pubescent moment', which I proposed occurs ahead of the full outbreak of reawakened *anima* or *animus* – a moment which recapitulates 'out-of-time' moments in infancy where the feel and quality of the relationship with mother comes to define whether *erosimus* or *thanimus* (in a girl) or *erosima* or *thanima* (in a boy) will come to dominate psyche. There then follows an outbreak of the dominant (positive or negative) version of *anima* or *animus* as puberty begins, influencing to a degree how adolescence will be experienced by the young man or woman. This moment, energetically, is also one of *enantiodromia* – gender certainty gets so rigidified that the opposite becomes constellated – and profound uncertainty about gender roles, relationships and sexuality.

So, at the risk of appearing fanciful, I propose that perhaps collectively we are at a similar 'moment', one where we have emerged from a latent state of dependence on equating feminine with female and masculine with male, and sticking with limited formulas for how relations between each should be described and contained. It may be, to take this analogy further, that for some time western consciousness was not ready to wake from this less conscious attitudinal state – which at times has provided people with a feeling of contentment and stability, and at others times left them stifled and restless.

While the domination of grand narratives on religion, politics and how we look at ourselves remained – as a version of *transcendent* 'laws' of human being – the more *immanent* nature of human identity as divergent and individualised, especially through sexuality and its interplay with gender, was overlooked. Now this situation has changed (the spirit of *pisces* giving way to *aquarius*). We are crossing into a 'new age' – though not the purely *transcending, perfecting* one sometimes dreamed of by subscribers to that term. In this reading of what is shifting we have entered puberty – a volatile but rich era where *eros* and *thanima* struggle to bring about the best balance they can between *transcending* impulses and more *completing* ones.

It is the *completeness* of the picture around expressions of gendered being – aggressive, erotic and relational aspects all coming into view and more or less available to each of us – which has been lacking, but now there is a messy but real shift towards something like this. This, I suggest, is what the *animus* in the western collective had managed to block for a considerable time during the 'modern' gender era. Naming *animus* as the 'culprit' seems about right, as the masculine contrasexual influence on the female psyche of Jung's original formulation is both *patriarchal* in its view of gender relations as well as *rigid* in its judgemental expression, making it harder to 'see' past. To take this one step further, there is potential for *eros* in women to find fuller expression, through the conversion of *thanimus* oppressive dominance in female psyches into a flowering of *erosimus*.

My reading of the situation for men is not so optimistic – at least not in the short term. Two principles apply here: first a simple one of complementarity, i.e. when one side of an equation or partnership takes or reclaims power or identity, the other has to let go of some of theirs. As the *thanimus* oppressive influences on women from patriarchal forms of governance and relating fade, there seems to be an almost unstoppable recalibration of power relations in society. This applies more to familial, social and educational contexts, as there remains clear evidence of imbalance in pay and opportunities tilted against women in very many sectors of the working world (e.g. United Nations, 2005).

Some men seem better at clinging to the top of the 'beanstalk' than those further down (e.g. in the UK, the House of Commons and financial institutions in the City remain predominantly male bastions). The point here, though, is – taking my analogy of western consciousness, gender-wise, just hitting 'puberty' – that men may be doing this dominated by *thanima* – disoriented, fearful and clinging to the old certainties familiar from the 'latent' patriarchal stage when everything was rigid but safe.

Women, on the other hand, could be envisaged as bursting out of this stage with a zestful flowering of *erosimus*. As they rightly claim their entitlement to equal and free expression of self, men may stumble back into themselves, and this is where the second principle can compound the problem of *thanima* for men. This refers back to the constellation of a 'dead mother' complex for men in individual experiencing (as described in Chapter 4), which may be around on a more collective level, though not with all men by any means.

'Waiting for dead mother to come to life, so *erosima* can return' is like men waiting for permission to rework themselves into forms of being male which work for them, as well as connecting with 'what women want', rather than feeling caught between reacting against, or passively accommodating, this. This leaves an equation that is again resonant with individual developmental principles, which can serve as a working hypothesis to inform the discussion: girls *predominantly* grow up quicker than boys, and young men *predominantly* have a rougher time defining themselves as men.

Boys versus girls: The race up the beanstalk

This discussion will lead us towards a fuller definition of what male and female adult 'territories' may look like. It will include a consideration of what 'brain-sex' factors help understand the movement from childhood to adulthood, and how adolescence refers itself prospectively forwards (including towards death) as well as developmentally speaking, back to early influences.

I will begin where the developmental discussion left off in Chapter 3, with what I termed the 'pre-pubescent moment' and the move towards adolescence as defined by either *erosima* or *thanima* in boys or *erosimus* or *thanimus* in girls. This is the decisive moment when the beans are thrown out of the window by mother. If they are magic beans then the beanstalk will shoot skywards, towards adulthood, and the boy or girl can begin the climb with a certain, unspoken assuredness – 'even if I slip I will find my footing' (with Mum and/or Dad at the bottom to catch me if I do not).

However, if the beans are duds then either the beanstalk will not grow at all and the child is faced with getting horribly stuck on the 'ground' or the child will need to improvise their own version – no easy task. Here, confidence in the journey has to be manufactured and if the young man or woman looks down on their way up they may notice the shakiness of the beanstalk – and be victims of vertigo.

Two brief, disguised clinical examples: A man whose parents split up when he was ten, just when the pre-pubescent moment was pending, struggled to find his nerve in adulthood, having hauled himself up through adolescence while his two hurt parents had their own regression into teenage spats in the family courts; and a woman who had been in and out of an addictions clinic, after being brought up by foster parents from the age of fourteen after long stays in residential schools since, at the age of six, being removed from the family home by social services.

In both cases, the 'beanstalk' was not really there for them and they had to find ways of improvising one – for the woman, addictive behaviours; for the man, a retreat into a world of computer games, books and music. The latter example points towards another possibility – for some young people, however stable their background seems to be, there is a need to 'make their own beanstalk' anyway, outside the standard expectations of the adult world.

This seems to have applied to another female analysand from my practice who had to a large degree shut herself off from the warmth and privileges of her wealthy and stable family set-up, choosing to write in isolation of an evening rather than join the rest of the family or the potential friends of her age. This laid the foundations for a successful career as a writer in adulthood. Her beanstalk sprung from 'magic beans' which had no obvious provenance in her parents' ways (a farmer and a businesswoman). She did discover some writing lineage two generations earlier on her father's side so one could speculate that these were beans from the early twentieth century waiting to re-sprout, though her approach to her writing was fiercely original.

These examples remind us of how precarious and unpredictable the journey through adolescence can be. It is also a phase which can easily get categorised only in developmental terms. While I have proposed a pre-pubescent moment as being a moment out of time which refers back to the earlier acausal 'moment' in very early childhood between mother and infant girl or boy (which configures the dominating side of *anima* or *animus*), it is important to see the adolescent 'climbing up the beanstalk' as a really important 'moment' in itself – a moment where profound, archetypal experiences happen. These can be very isolating as well as overwhelmingly tinged with existential fear or *ennui* in realising parents are fallible, the world can be an unsafe place and death is a part of life.

I accord with Richard Frankel's (1998) approach here. He argues for the use of Jung's emphasis on the teleological, i.e. looking forward and asking where a particular adolescent behaviour or attitude is aiming for in the *future*, as well as the developmental 'looking back' at where this might originate. This point resonates with some of my experiences as a teacher and therapist in schools, and how a young person can attach themselves to a very specific goal which is not attainable in the short term but reflects who they are, or can be.

Believing that one day he or she will be a successful rock musician can sustain a young person through the struggle to get good grades at GCSE or A Level in order to fulfil some societal idea of achievement. On the other hand, especially in the realm of special educational needs, a young person may discern – often accurately – that they do *not* really have a future in socially conventional terms, and so exhibit behaviours which convey a depressed sense about the future (e.g. becoming withdrawn, or perhaps aggressive towards others), irrespective of how loved and well cared for they have been.

Frankel also makes a good case for working with adolescents *phenomeno-logically*, on the basis that we can only understand what is happening for a teenager if we recall how it felt when *we* were there, and interact closely with those who are 'there' now. This is not easy, as Frankel conveys: 'Given that the art of concealment plays such a natural role in adolescence, it is perhaps more formidable to enact this kind of "I–thou" encounter with an adolescent than it is with either children or adults. Patience and forbearance are necessary requirements for sustaining a phenomenologically rich vision' (Frankel, 1998: 3).

Before moving on to the implications for male and female psychic development I will explore the significant neurobiological changes which occur at this stage of life in the adolescent brain and what differences may arise between the female and the male brain.

The adolescent brain

First, it is clear that the adolescent brain enters another period of *plasticity*, which parallels the early stages of life when neural pathways are being laid down – though not quite to the same degree of formative influence. However, there is an important point here, reflecting Frankel – i.e. the 'map' of the adolescent psyche is not complete if one only points back to the pattern set in the first years of life, though influences such as how *anima* or *animus* are 'installed' remain pivotal. Rather, the prospective, subtly purposeful, 'selfing' potential of the adolescent brain influences the processes of change as does the phenomenological experiencing of self, others and environment. Relations in the present matter as well as those internalised (in an object-relations sense) from the beginning of life.

Second, I want to illustrate the paradoxical nature of adolescence. It is a time when the physiological structure and its protective systems become markedly more robust, and a young person on average attains equivalent cognitive skills to an adult by the age of fifteen. However, it is also a time of acute vulnerability: rates of morbidity can rise significantly (Maurer and Smith, 2005: 167), in line with the overall explosion in some young people of an emotional instability and craving for more 'sensational' experiences, which in turn can open them to risky situations and habits (e.g. drugs). Another paradox is the brain's need for longer sleep (especially into late mornings) while the demands placed on adolescents as learners in particular are often acute. Everything can seem to be out of sync – an adolescent *'longeur* out of time' lasting from around aged twelve through to the early twenties. This is strongly influenced by the upsurge and recapitulation of the *erosimus–thanimus* or *erosima–thanima* equation at the 'pre-pubescent moment'.

As far as gender differences are concerned there do seem to be some key ones – depression emerges in twice as many females in adolescence as in males (Moir, 2009: 12) and while this could be linked in some ways to social and familial pressures around expectations of how to 'be' a young woman, research suggests the increased risk for adolescent females appears to be predominantly hormonal.

Another key factor is testosterone. At puberty boys' testosterone levels shoot up to as much as ten to twenty times more prevalent in the blood-stream than in girls (ibid.: 9). As this is linked to mood it can impact on behaviour; if a young man is involved in an exciting or challenging situation, the presence of high levels of testosterone will in turn generate a rise in dopamine levels, and this offers him a kind of natural 'high' which may make the seeking of sensation – by however dangerous means (to himself or others) – more inviting. Men also have lower levels of serotonin than women and this, when linked to high dopamine levels, has been shown to have a significant association with sensation-seeking personality traits.

The strong implication of all of this (Zukerman, 1994) is that risk-taking can be easier to fall into for men, because it can be pleasurable – whether this be in business, sporting or personal contexts. This is not in any way to excuse antisocial, violent, abusive or criminal behaviour by males, in adolescence or after (or before) it; ego capacity to pull back from enticing, risky activity is an essential component of the social and ethical responsibility for any males (or females) considering putting others at risk just because the risk seems delicious to them.

Whether these observations can reliably imply male mood swings are neurologically driven is a moot question. Nevertheless, there clearly is a higher prevalence of violent behaviour in men. For example, antisocial personality disorder is consistently and clearly more common in men than in women (Mind, 2007) and suicide is four times more common in men than in women in the twenty-five to forty-four-year-old age group in the UK (ONS, 2007).

Socialisation will of course play some part in this, and Kirsta (1994: Ch. 2) offers a valuable counterbalance when she points out how, although it appears physical aggression does tend to decline in young women after adolescence, verbal forms (abusive language etc.) are as prevalent in women as in men. She cautions us not to forget how the socialisation of 'self-denial' in women may be as much of an inhibitory factor in limiting forms of female aggression as the brain-based ones. The increasingly regular explosions of 'ladette', often drink-infused, violence on late night streets (in Britain at least) seems to underline this point (Whitehead, 2009).

Again, I hold apparent differences in brain and neurochemical development 'lightly'; not as *defining* what shapes a woman's or a man's sense of identity or relational capacity, but informing it in a subtle but *predominating* way. In between male and female 'territories' is an invisible, but deeply influential fork in the road, which will probably take a young man towards certain styles of being and a young woman towards others. The opaqueness of this movement one way or the other is reinforced by the circularity of the pattern of influence between neurobiological factors, and social and familial expectations.

An example of how *predominance* operates would be the possible difference in male–female brain formation addressed in Chapter 3. An important argument is made here by some researchers (e.g. Moir and Jessel, 1991) from the finding that the female brain is more networked because of its bilateral organisation than the male one: e.g. in terms of verbal language, only one side of a boy/man's brain 'lights up' when scanned if using verbal skills, while both sides do in a woman – hence the much greater difficulties a man can have in relearning verbal skills after a stroke. There is also evidence that the female brain matures three or four years earlier than the male one, leaving women more emotionally 'ready' for adulthood (Moir, 2009).

The argument is that this difference – manifested in the female brain having a larger corpus callosum (which has the job of transmitting information from one side of the brain to the other) – means there is greater communication in girls and women between the two brain hemispheres, so verbalising feelings comes more naturally; the male brain literally 'takes longer' to convert feeling into language.

Also, the 'sexed' formation of the amygdala, which generates feelings and processes emotionally charged memories, is significant. Research suggests the male brain globally processes memories in the right side of the amygdala, while the female brain does so – and in more detail – in the left side (Killgore *et al.*, 2001). This may lead women to remember more details of emotionally significant, 'relational', events and renders men prone to having less control over their impulses as they do not contextualise them so well.

This distinction *may* provide a clue to what Jung intuitively, but sometimes in a horribly clumsy way, was thinking of when referring to the preoccupations he felt *animus* could sometimes disproportionately bring about for women: i.e. a kind of fixation on emotionally significant events, which get repeatedly revisited.

If we combine these observations with two neurochemical factors: significantly higher levels of oestrogen in women from puberty onwards (between five and twenty times more) and of oxytocin (associated with labour and lactation in women), compared with men (Moir, 2009), then neurobiological arguments for why relational sensitivity and skills may be more prevalent in females than males, especially from puberty, appears to hold some water. When linked with a central thesis of this book – how the mother–daughter bond from early life promotes and consolidates a greater 'natural' relationality in females than in males – it appears to provide a credible and formidable blend of influences which come into play during adolescence.

From this, I will speculatively frame the two gendered pathways in adolescence. While a young woman's nascent relational tendency may flower under *erosimus's* influence, or get skewed, or even crushed, by *thanimus*, a young man's tendency towards risk-taking and thrill-seeking may either get channelled positively by *erosima* (including the capacity for relationship to predominantly more relationally effective young women, and to other men) or throw him into *thanima*-led danger and/or relational deadness or awkwardness.

My speculations arising from the brain-based research referred to here are given an extra, living, quality by bringing to bear the two other dimensions advocated by Frankel, i.e. a prospective, *forward-looking* approach to adolescent development as well as the phenomenological experience of self.

James Hillman wrote of adolescence as being, amongst other things, 'the emergence of spirit within the psyche' (Hillman, 1990: 190). The young man or woman, in this sense, is undergoing change which does not just refer *back* to the predominating emphasis in the installation of *anima* or *animus* during the pre-oedipal stage. It is change which also refers to future possibility, to the unfolding of nascent creative potentialities, the setting and testing of ideals, and the uncovering of as yet unlived aspects of self.

Frankel follows Hillman in asserting how something genuinely new comes into being in adolescence, something which 'is hungry for experience and seeks extreme states of being . . . [and which is] . . . unique and originary' (Frankel, 1998: 49–50). This hints at a further dimension to the formation of (gendered) identity. Flowing from a combination of the profound brain-sex developments partially described above, and the renewing contrasexual impact of *erosima/thanima* or *erosimus/thanimus*, a new version of being male or being female gets constellated in adolescence.

These two elemental influences create the conditions in which these hidden potentialities begin to reveal themselves. Neurobiological change and the reawakening of *anima* or *animus* in the period following on from the 'pre-pubescent moment' create a tension together to enable a 'transcending third' of nascent adult potential which can break free from latent, parentally influenced captivity and establish a new identity, filtered through gender.

This way of looking at how adolescent identity, including its gendered presentations, can get reconfigured, and even transformed, conveys the archetypal power of the changes which happen to young people and how they can seem, for a period at least, to be like 'strangers in the house' to their parents. Where Frankel refers to the 'originary' power at work in adolescence, this reflects the complex dynamics at work in 'gendered' formation and development. This can make it hard to see where an attitude or behaviour has originated – because the business of 'originating' is organic and circular between brain, intrapsychic struggle and social/relational influence. At adolescence a powerful outbreak of 'originary' activity surges through this circuit and the 'gender electrics' are reconfigured.

In getting closer to this it is valuable to draw upon the experiential reflections of young people who are going through this time of upheaval, of 'storm and stress'. At times this period can seem like a disintegration, and be all the more alarming for those around a young person. Using post-Jungian terminology, this can also be understood as a time for deep-seated *deintegration* – i.e. the self is fragmenting in order to enable a more expansive *reintegration* of what needs to be experienced and incorporated

(Fordham, 1985). This rocky but necessary process enables the young person to move into new ways of being, including in how they experiment with, and live out, their being 'male' or being 'female'.

I will draw on two more disguised clinical examples from my work with young people to illustrate how they can experience the move from 'boy towards man' and 'girl towards woman'. The disorientations as well as excitements inherent in their former sense of self deintegrating in order to incorporate massive sexual, bodily and psychological change convey how all-consuming the storm can be. In both cases, the young person involved had had a very uncertain start to life, hallmarked by unreliable attachments and some abusive experiences. This almost certainly contributed to the chaotic feel of their adolescence, when these difficult influences revealed themselves once more: the self allowing itself to break up in order to be 'made anew'.

A teenage young man described to me the 'amazing rush' which surged through him almost every time he got into situations of potential conflict. The rather catch-all term of 'reactive attachment disorder' (Chaffin *et al.*, 2006) had been applied by professionals to his way of responding to others – generally defensive and hostile unless things were going his way. He had recently got into a situation with a member of staff at the special school he attended where she had challenged his perceived lack of motivation, saying something to him to the effect that he 'would never get anywhere with that attitude'. This, he said, had made him very angry, and he had 'battered her' – punched and then pushed her to the ground before other staff had got close enough to restrain him and calm him down (fortunately the staff member landed on some soft furniture, and only sustained a bruise to her face – not that the 'only' is meant to imply insignificance).

As well as being dealt with within the school's framework for sanctioning inappropriate or violent behaviours, he had been referred to me to look at this incident, and others where he had 'exploded' in reaction to others' words, or even 'just the way they looked at me', as he put it. In this case it seemed that more had happened than a reactive, testosterone-infused upsurge of rage – which, with the male-brain emphasis on the right hand side of the amygdala, meant he was less likely to be able to stand back from the feeling and contextualise it in the space between him and the staff member. It felt, too, that behind his apparent pattern of reacting to the outstretched arm offering relationship, rather than accepting it, there was an angry *thanima* rejection of warmth or care, as constellated in the early, unreliable attachment with his mother.

When I asked him what he had thought and felt when she said to him he 'would never get anywhere', he told me he saw in his head 'a picture of a massive road and I was bombing down it in a car'. When asked, he said the road 'was going somewhere good'. He also said the idea he could not get anywhere 'made this picture come into my head' and he could not stand those words 'when I just know I can get down that road'. This example reflects how, alongside all the other influences at work, puberty engenders a prospective intuition of life's possibilities, and in a teenage boy this may generate a *puer*-like sense of wanting escape from the present, violently sparked in this case by an adult's challenge.

A young woman described something not dissimilar, though it revealed itself in less overtly explosive circumstances. This is not to say she consistently expressed herself in a passive way – she had a track record of aggressive outbursts against adults and sometimes got into fights with other students. She characterised her life as 'going nowhere' and said she 'never has a choice' in what she does. She also said she 'doesn't care about anyone'. It seemed that her way of expressing this depressed and untrusting sense of self was to oscillate between periods of withdrawing into her room at the residential school she attended or trying to run away. On one occasion, when she had felt particularly low after another girl had told her she had 'no friends', she left her favourite music playing loudly in her room while she slipped out of the building (as staff handed over shifts) and managed to get onto a train at the local town.

She said she had planned to get a ticket for a train back to her home town, but suddenly 'something inside me' told her to try 'somewhere new, somewhere special'. She looked down the timetable and saw a train for Edinburgh, where her favourite band came from. She 'could see the band standing on the platform there, waiting for me'. So, this young woman took a train to Edinburgh, although she 'knew it was just a dream' that they would be waiting for her, but this did not matter. The act of going there by herself *did*. She told me with a smile how she got off the train at the other end and kissed the platform ('though everyone thought I was a weirdo') before waiting for a train back to the town near the school.

Here again is a spontaneous intuition of there being 'something more' than the rather miserable life she was in. Again, an 'adolescent reaction' (here to being reminded of her friendship/attachment difficulties) – a sad, nasty, *thanimus* moment re-constellating formative life experiences. There is also a hallmark of a more 'female' depressed state, an activation of the female-brain left amygdala tendency to really take words to heart ('you have no friends'), including a need to go over them again and again – and maybe compensate by imagining a welcome from her 'friends' in the band she adores.

More than this, though, like the young man, the emotional straitjacket that can feel like it is strangling them, seems to constellate these moments of intuition and possibly visualisation about the future, however fanciful a form this may take. In this case, a distinction between the young woman and the young man is her imagining the future in more relational terms, while the young man pictures it as a linear 'going away/up/forwards' open road, something which may reflect a *predominating* distinction (rather than a rigid distinction which applies to all young women and men).

Adolescence, then, brings gender to life as sexuality surges into lived experience and brain changes confirm distinctions between the more female and male arrangements of the cerebral furniture. It also illustrates the temporal dynamism of gendered identity, with its referral back to formative contrasexual relations (recapitulated by *anima* reawakening in males and *animus* reawakening in females), its powerful expressions in the present, sometimes fed by social conventions, and the important presence of prospective intuitions about future self which may be tinged by a predominance of maleness or femaleness.

Mapping contrasexual influence from puberty to adulthood

Table 6.1 sets out generally how *thanima/thanimus* and *erosima/erosimus* influence the passage from puberty to adulthood; this includes reference to the psychological tensions suggested by Erikson (1950). These, as described above, suggest a bias towards male experience, but still offer a useful generalised set of indicators for themes which may be around during the phases highlighted in the table. In the '28 onwards' column Erikson's opposing influences are combined from the latter two stages of his schema to indicate how these, plus the 'Intimacy versus Isolation' binary from the young adult phase, will all remain across the lifespan.

The way in which puberty impacts differently on girls (predominantly earlier, more defining of identity) compared with boys (later, more ambiguous) is the only clearly delineated point of difference here, but this has a significant impact on what comes later – e.g. in how *thanimus* may promote a woman's stuckness in relating, and how *erosima* can hamper the continuous expression of self for a man.

A collective adolescence?

I have argued that it is useful to think of us, in westernised societies, as collectively being in a kind of movement from the 'pubescent moment' into a state of adolescence. This refers to a developmental parallel in terms of women and men regularly renegotiating their lives and relationships as the 'storm and stress' of social change rages around us and generates further gender electrics. It also relates to the history of *psyche*, and how our notions of *male and female* are just emerging from an entanglement with archetypal notions of *masculine and feminine*. There is some way to go to 'adulthood' in this regard – the point where we can clearly see what it means to be male compared with what it means to be female.

The clouds of collective *animus* are lifting – but slowly.

Table 6.1 Map of gendered development (2): puberty to full adulthood

Puberty and adolescence (11–18)	Late adolescence/early adulthood (18–28)	Full adulthood (28 onwards)
	Young men	
Intermittent initiation via ritual/conflict. Erosima starts to orient towards healthy maturation and adulthood. or	Erosima matures. Identity as man emerges.	Erosima moves man into life of engagement with relational, work and social dimensions
Thanima draws back from healthy male maturation and adulthood	Thanima impedes/stifles development Real identity as man partly/fully hidden	Thanima holds man back from satisfactory engagement with life and self
	Both	
Identity versus Role confusion	Intimacy versus Isolation	Generativity and ego integrity versus Stagnation and despair
	Young women	
Initiation via menses. Erosimus installs sense of 'adult woman' identity. or	Erosimus consolidates strengthened sense of identity as a woman	Erosimus moves woman into life: with relational, work and social dimensions.
Thanimus blocks this installation	Thanimus blocks sense of identity as woman	Thanimus blocks engagement with life and self

Chapter 7

Walking on clouds: Male and female territories

He climbed through the clouds until he reached the top. There he saw a road which went straight towards a big castle in the distance.

In front of him, Jack sees what has been taken away from him because of the murder of his father. The 'new country' in front of him is a reflection of all his positive *anima* energy could make possible for him if only he could reclaim it. This is a vision of *his* territory, and sure enough it is an *erosima* figure – the fairy – who then confirms what belongs to him. Meanwhile, the giant, an exaggerated, tyrannical, parental *senex* figure, has hold of his birthright. This is a father complex (or more fully, a dyadic parental complex: the crazy, murderous giant, and his canny but colluding wife) infused with an oppressive *thanima* quality, haunted by his dead father.

What Jack sees is the challenge we all encounter not to be thoroughly possessed by our parental complexes, but to take back what is ours, and experience our territory as truly our own. This parallels the problem with gender. It is hard to see what our gendered identity truly 'is', to see what is 'female' or 'male' territory, because it has been defined over and again for us by biology, history, social constructs and our parents, *and* it is constantly being questioned by personal experiences and influences. We cannot authentically reclaim these territories with the click of a mouse from which definitive insight tumbles onto the screen, or a flick of a wrist which releases the magic beans of understanding. The electrics of gender relations are too powerful, too charged with archetypal, historical and individual elements, for anything to be so simple. But it is still worth going up the beanstalk to see what might be there.

Adult male and female territories

So, the discussion arrives at, in a way, its most defining stage. Having climbed up the beanstalk, via developmental, clinical and wider theoretical critical analysis of the world of gendered identity and relations, we now stand on the shifting cloudscape of male and female territories as they hang in the air, being blown by the breezes of social and psychological change but, like cloud formations (Pretor-Pinney, 2006), returning to regroup – differently nuanced each time we look at them, but still retaining an elemental, established identity.

Taking *cumulus* metaphorically, with its capacity to pile up in tufts in the sky, *cirrocumulus* (the higher version) could be the male and *altocumulus* (lower) the female formations – reflecting their predominant *transcending* and *immanent* tendencies. The shared male and female territory gets connected at times by the overall presence of *cumulus* and at other times is separate and distinct. Another cloud type to factor into the equation here is *cumulonimbus* – thunderclouds which pile up and generate powerful electric storms – a metaphor for when the calm of *cumulus* in male–female relationships gets overtaken by the 'gender electrics' of conflict and hurt.

This discussion will map out the *predominantly* distinctive qualities of the male and female 'formations', or territories, while recognising the shared features of (*cumulus*) common ground and where it fractures (*cumulonimbus*). I will also reflect on how dynamics within a partner dyad can constellate archetypal and personal tensions and conflicts, as well as deep, real moments of meeting which nourish both individual human psyches.

Female territory: Relational completeness versus individuated separation

With our watchword of 'predominance' held in mind, we will venture into *female territory*, the *altocumulus*, with its shifting shapes but underlying archetypal patterns of being, subtly but predominantly influencing what happens on the ground of here-and-now experiencing for women. On the one hand there is the drive for relational completeness, arising from the original experiencing of the early *erosimus/thanimus* bonding with mother. On the other there is the more conscious, but unconsciously informed – via the purposive workings of *self* (Jung, 1948/1968: para. 114) – seeking out of a more separate sense of identity as a woman. Orbach and Eichenbaum (1994: 169) have characterised this latter state in terms of the duality of 'separated attachments/connected autonomy'. They argue convincingly that we are witnessing a process by which what I term female territory is increasingly hallmarked by a greater capacity for differentiation by a woman from what they describe as 'merged attachments' (ibid.: 53).

While I argue that this places a little girl firmly on the *inside* of the relational space, setting up a pattern which seeks out relational completeness in the future, Orbach and Eichenbaum highlight this as a problematic double bind. The identification works both ways so the mother just as powerfully identifies with the daughter: 'The mother is not separate from her daughter and, as her daughter expresses her needs, the mother experiences them *with* her, almost as though they were her *own*' (ibid.: 53).

A crucial consequence of this situation, they argue, is that a woman's need for individuated selfhood can get repressed out of conscious awareness and a kind of compulsive need to care for others can take its place. Indeed, in an earlier work (Eisenbaum and Orbach, 1982: 29) they suggest there is a complementary way in which 'our culture does not have a positive image of a woman on her own.' While this may have shifted in the quarter of a century since then, and autonomous power now accrues to female cultural icons such as the women characters in *Sex and the City* (Starr, 1998), this 'merging–caring' dynamic remains a powerfully endemic influence on female territory.

An idea I want to introduce here which alludes to how 'gender' may operate as a distorting, sometimes *'cumulonimbus'* disrupting, feature of male–female relationships is how the presence of the gendered 'other' generates psychic opposition. This refers to how for a woman the presence of a man may generate a heightened consciousness about her own identity as *not being* the same as his (and vice versa). The insight provided by Juliet Mitchell is pertinent here, when she points out how 'gender' 'is not the maximal difference between mothers and fathers but the minimal difference of sibling sexual relations, which themselves are only a shade away from a narcissistic economy in which the other is the self' (Mitchell, 2004: 67).

Mitchell suggests that the incest taboo between brothers and sisters is at the root of how 'gender' becomes reified into territorially distinctive 'norms', rather than maleness and femaleness being only expressions of sexual and reproductive difference. She argues that 'gender' has thus been separated from 'sexuality' (i.e. the sexual dimension gets repressed) and this has had a significant impact on how psychoanalysis perceives and conducts itself (Mitchell, 2004). I would argue that the emphasis we may make on our gendered identity can also *heighten* awareness of *hetero*sexuality, but she still makes an important point.

If *sexual taboo* sits at the heart of our need to distinguish ourselves from the other sex, then one can see why the territories I am trying to map out may have such deep foundations. If these sibling taboos then become the template for how we learn to relate to extended family members and then friends of the opposite sex, something gets set up which adds a further differentiating layer to male–female relations. Although Mitchell may be right in suggesting that the erotically deadening impact of latency on boys and girls could be thawing, as it seems that more children may be embracing sexual activity earlier (ibid.: 76), this phase still generally 'de-sexualises' sibling and wider peer relationships.

The tendency to separate gender from sexuality also speaks to a wish for clarity in the face of how hard the slippery but influential presence of 'gender' can be to pin down, as was highlighted in Chapter 2 (e.g. Butler,

1990). The unpredictability of the sexual polymorphism of the pre-oedipal infant lies behind this elusiveness, constantly shifting the deeper layers of psychic sediment beneath it – the sublimated erotic, aggressive and relational chaos we came into the world with. In the face of this it is easier to ascribe fixed gendered attributes when practising and theorising.

The basis on which women respond to the presence of men is predominantly influenced, I would argue, by a psychic tendency towards 'in-ness' a familiar feeling of being *on mother's ground* which gets constellated in early life, and which pulls the girl's heterosexual tendencies towards replicating this ground. The disquieting 'just otherness' of men compounds a woman's feeling of needing to be different; a difference felt as being *within* mother's ground and *home*, rather than without it.

This operates alongside the differences in brain-sex development previously highlighted to *predominantly* (not comprehensively) generate:

- A greater tendency towards 'relational completing' as an expression of self
- A lesser tendency for expressing self violently or in an extremely competitive style
- A greater tendency to release stress through communicative means.

These three possible modalities of gendered expression then feed into the three areas of possible difference I suggested in Chapter 2: continuity through time and space; projection; and power and authority.

Time and space

I want to reassert the possibility that women may, *predominantly*, live more fully in the present (the 'now') and in the localised space ('here') than men. I recognise how sweeping this assertion may appear, and how many women may experience a sense of discontinuity. It is offered, though, as informed generalisation, grounded in the themes emerging from developmental neurobiological, depth psychological, and socially constructive strands. This also stands alongside the less than scientific, but still phenomenologically worthwhile, reflections on how women respond to men (arising from my own experiences, as well as those reported to me by other men). Here, subjectivity comes more boldly into play, and I invite the reader to notice their own intuitions, projections and associations about how the other gender operates.

As argued in the previous chapter, where women's sense of discontinuity arises, this is predominantly in connection with a sense of 'incompleteness' in the present. This can get constellated by the presence of the gendered other. Things 'not being right' (i.e. not complete) are, in my own experience, something I have noticed some women in professional contexts being more pronounced about than their male colleagues.

When I have been in management positions, for example, I have experienced the feeling that my presence as a man has constellated dissatisfactions for some women – a feeling of 'incompletion' (intrapsychically, relationally and/or professionally) – and they have articulated this by suggesting what strategies are 'not working' with pupils (in special school contexts), or what they feel is 'lacking' in how other people operate in an organisation (e.g. in higher education contexts).

In terms of physical *space*, this predominant leaning towards 'completion' can get reflected by a focus on whether the space around a woman is 'right'; whether this be the living space of home, the professional work space or other community spaces. Rather than being a result of social conditioning, the 'grounding' of maternal identification, or neurobiological imprinting it is, as I have argued throughout, a more complex product of all three. What is important is the possible impact of this predominant tendency on female–male relationships.

The presence of the 'gendered other' (men) may exacerbate a woman's experiencing of this impetus ('why can he not see what needs to be done?'), where a man can be experienced as 'unconscious' or at least 'less conscious' of the priority of 'completing' the shared space in which men and women coexist. This may lead to dissatisfaction for a woman that the man is not focused on 'completing' the shared living space in the same, prioritised, way as she is.

This leads us back to the question of contrasexuality and the possibility that *animus* aspects in women get constellated by the presence of men – the *outer* masculine in the room maybe makes some women more conscious of an active 'masculine' archetypal presence in the internal 'room' of the psyche. This then seems to constellate in either an *erosimus* feeling of things being 'as they should be' ('complete') or a *thanimus* sense of things not being where they should be, and this becoming somehow associated with a man's lack of environmental consciousness (whether or not he is really attentive to his surroundings). I find myself drawn to these speculations partly based on my experience of being 'the male in the room'. By 'room' I refer to any physical space, usually indoors or sometimes a garden. On countless occasions I have experienced women pointing out either what looks right in a space or, more commonly, what does not.

When it is 'not right' (incomplete) it may well be that the female 'brain-sex' tendency (Moir, 2009: 13–14) to relieve stress via communicating creates a strong impetus to say something about what does not appear to be right. A woman *may* be more predominantly likely to say something about what they have noticed about a room, the contents of it or even someone standing in it (if not straight away, then saving the observation to share with someone later) than a man, for whom the observation may be less important, or the stress of keeping it to himself less pressing.

As implied, I sometimes sense that this kind of psychological and verbal intervention by a woman in a space has been reinforced by my presence as a man. This is not to say women do not notice aesthetic or spatial features in a physical space when they are on their own or with other women, but rather that my presence as a man seems to trigger a response (a need?) to take the role of 'the conscious one' when it comes to how a living, work or other shared space looks and is organised.

Once again this feels like contentious territory. Am I just describing the consequences of centuries of patriarchal oppression whereby men have been let off the hook where domestic ordering of living space is concerned? Or is this more about my sensitivity at having lived and worked in predominantly female environments during my life, thereby rendering me 'touchy' about not being able to easily find my place in them?

Well, I want to suggest that both of these speculations contain some truth, but also assert that something much deeper is happening which cannot be accounted for solely by patriarchy or my hang-ups about being a male amongst females. There are points here about *projection* and *power* which I will come back to, but there is also something about how the presence of the gendered other sometimes triggers patterned responses, which could be described in terms of contrasexual activation (in this case *thanimus* where the presence of a man may trigger an 'incomplete' reaction in a woman).

In turn, this also alludes to the importance of recognising the intersubjective nature of being human, where, our 'relations to others, not drives . . . [are] . . . the basic stuff of mental life' (Mitchell, 1988: 2). Inner process gets activated and developed via interaction with others. In the context of our discussion, the presence of the 'gendered other' constellates impulses to confirm our own differentiated identity, not least because of the many ways in which females and males are similar, and because of the possible fears of being drawn into contravening the sibling-based incest taboo.

So, the problem of otherness is 'solved' by deeply patterned responses by women to men, and men to women. As implied, the problem of 'the other' is more clear cut when we can locate 'otherness' in a physical or psychological space which is far away from us, such as in Kapuscinski's (2006) powerful critique of how the western world deals with people and cultures outside of our usual frame of reference. In Papadoupolos' (2002) terminology, this is the 'exotic other', which we can reassure ourselves is 'not us'. However, the 'familiar other' is more problematic. We can try to deny there are no strong connections and similarities between us and our siblings, or partners, but the moment we react irrationally to something they have said or done we know deep down they are holding something of us, and we something of them.

In respect to male–female relationships, we may need to find ways to distinguish ourselves from our partner in order to keep a sense of identity, even a kind of *sanity*, about our own integrity as an individual human being who finds themselves part of a close relational dyad. This in turn may evoke fears of being swallowed up, or lost, within it. So, conveying our gendered identity as opposite to the other attains a *protective* quality, in this case. This need for 'I' as a man or a woman to respond to the presence of 'you' as the 'other' gendered form of being, by emphasising my identification with a wider collective version of being a man, has roots which go deep into female and male territories.

The greater female tendency towards relational/completing as a style of being may show itself in a wish to want to 'make right' the living space if something seems out of place, and to be focused on what needs to be done *now* (rather than next week or next year). This tendency might predominantly be expressed, not in a competitive but in a completing way, a '*this is the way it needs to be*', style, which contextualises it within the relationship, as a necessary concomitant of it.

I want to stress again that these are predominating tendencies, not blanket ways of operating, based on a whole raft of factors: developmental, biological, socially constructed, plus an intersubjective response to the problems of familiarity and otherness. I think it is worth holding the possibility, however, that this need for completion in the moment *may* be what Jung (1953/1966) mistakenly decided was an inferior kind of *animus* rationalisation which could, supposedly, drive men nuts. What I am describing may still drive men nuts on occasion, because of the implied certitude of the position sometimes taken by a woman about what needs to be done in the house (say) in order to 'make things right *now*'.

However, the crucial distinction to Jung's position is when this becomes a more rigidified constellation of *thanimus* – it is *just* that and nothing to do with the intellectual capacity (and so on) of a woman. This is a difficult point to make, because of the link to Jung's highly problematic assertions about women, but one worth making because it shows up an edge (as do one or two points about men) between female and male territory which could do with being made more conscious.

In the *Beanstalk* story, Jack's role is to step out of the 'here and now' and recapture from the sky what is needed in order to enable his mother to 'make things right' on the ground. When he initially fails to do this, on returning home with the apparently useless beans, the suggested difficult edge between territories is constellated in mother's anger. When he later 'brings home the bacon' this provides a 'completion' for mother, and therefore for him. This is an uneasy dynamic – one which, I suggest, still informs 'gender electrics'.

Projection

There may be times when, in a compensatory way, women project their *thanimus* unconsciousness about 'sky' elements within them (which are more consciously prevalent in male territory as perfecting, future-bound, ultra-competitive etc.) onto a man and experience these as unhelpful and unrealistic. This then brings into play a need to focus on the 'completing now' and on immanent aspects of the situation they both find themselves in. This tendency would seem to find its biological apotheosis in becoming a mother: the whole impetus towards having a child – wanting to be a mother, experiencing pregnancy and giving birth – demands an obvious focus on the present moment, which is based on feelings, sensations and thoughts rooted in the body.

Pregnancy really brings into focus the differences in temporal and locational experiencing between men and women. While a man's experiencing of his partner's pregnancy may bring the *immanence* of relational reality closer to him, the unborn child is located outside of him and his immediate contact with her or him belongs in the future. For the woman, generally, she intimately experiences the baby *within* her as a living presence she has contact with in the 'now'.

Returning to the proposed *thanimus* projections onto men, there is a further possibility. A woman may get caught up in something pathological about the imbalance between a stifled 'completing' message from mother and a disproportionate 'perfecting' message from father (or, indeed, where this imbalance is constellated in the internalised version of a single parent who has been 'mother and father' to her at the same time). Here, it becomes very difficult to unconsciously unburden herself of her unwanted 'perfecting' tendencies.

As Woodman (1982) asserts, this situation can drive a woman towards obsessive or addictive behaviours, such as those associated with eating disorders or alcoholism. Here *thanimus* constellates in a rigidified attachment to perfecting oneself, for example in relation to the body: 'A woman addicted to perfection will view herself as a work of art, being so absolutely precious, may in one moment be destroyed' (Woodman, 1982: 52). Needless to say, a man's perfecting/solving tendencies can also lead him into addictive/compulsive patterns relating to the body, though the emphasis will not always be the same, especially if a man falls into the disembodied ways of relating to self described in Chapter 4.

Whether the psychological formulation of how each woman thus burdened with an addiction to perfection can be generalised to this degree (differences between the psychic influences on each individual woman being, of course, crucial) is open to question, but taken *predominantly* there is an important point here about how women may experience themselves and life when the unwanted projections about perfection cannot be healthily put onto men. *Thanimus* influences arising from a combination of a kind of invasive preponderance of the perfecting tendency from a demanding father and a faulty 'fusion' with mother at the start of life, which has left a woman never feeling quite 'right', promotes a move out of life, or indeed a state where she can 'never . . . enter it' (ibid.: 52).

The other concept to mention here is projective identification. This is where projection goes a step further than the more straightforward 'dumping' of aspects of ourselves onto another. Instead, whole versions of self get placed 'in' the other as a way of getting rid of aspects which cannot be borne (probably experienced as having been 'unacceptable' earlier in life). Here, the other feels as if they are *controlled* by the projective identification of the other. In the context of this discussion, a woman who unconsciously carries a real wound about whether or not she is unconditionally accepted by mother (or possibly father, or both) may projectively identify her own rejected potential to strive for perfection into a male partner.

She could do something similar with her children, friends or colleagues, but as partner, the man will be vulnerable to becoming a kind of 'object' which 'has to be perfect' for her. The proportionately healthy feeling a man may get that he needs to do his part to make things 'complete' for his female partner (though this can be problematic too) is superceded by something more manic and high-pressured. An example is a man I knew who said he was constantly on 'high alert' for any sign his partner was unhappy, and *uber*-responsive to any expression of material want by her. He seemed to feel she needed him to be 'the perfect husband', though this clearly had something to do with his pathology too (the boy in him needing to 'solve' things for his unsatisfied mother).

In a less pathological way, a 'solving–completing' mismatch can be a more common feature of male–female relationships. In relation to women's projections, some polarising can happen when a *thanimus* 'perfection' projection constellates, leaving her feeling incomplete (because he will not solve/perfect things) and the man gets pushed deeper, and in a more caricatured way, into male territory. The same can happen for a woman in female territory. A woman analysand I worked with described a situation which had developed in her marriage whereby her partner seemed to have 'completely given up' contributing his time or energy to help maintain the fabric and decor of the house, watching her go up ladders to paint the window frames in all sorts of weathers, for example. He seemed to have decided his perfecting notion of how things should be would never be 'completed' by her, so he had projected this unconscious 'incompleteness' onto her. There felt to be an air of something passive-aggressive, maybe even sadomasochistic, going on between them. He watched her struggle and suffer, while she got on with things and burned with anger, disappointment and an increasing focus on his 'imperfections'.

Here, although there are obviously a whole host of other individual and relational factors at work, her underlying *thanimus* projection of unconscious perfecting and his unconscious *thanima* projection about unconscious completing have crossed horribly. The more conscious aspect for the woman of needing to distinguish herself from his gendered otherness may now become a thorough *rejection* of it, and therefore of him (and vice versa).

So, inter-gender projection has both a compensatory *and* a separating/individuating purpose. As well as functioning to reveal the work of the contrasexual other and address its implications, there is a *deep-rooted need to experience the other as different*, so as to shore up the gendered identity of a woman or a man. I think this pressure has pertained for generations and formed a layer of psychic strata which often operates in an unconscious way to help frame male and female 'territories'.

One could label this influence 'patriarchal', though I think it *has* to be more complex than this, (i.e. the *matriarchal* is in the mix too). Either way, it has taken up a deeper residency in the western mind than a few generations of active deconstruction of it can undo. Patterns of projection between the genders, as well as being shaped in obvious ways by whatever mother or father complexes are at work in an individual, will be influenced by this more collective influence. In 'female territory', projection at an individual level onto men constellates more than a father (or brother?) complex; it is shaded subtly but influentially by the search for *completing*, as a consonant reaction to *perfecting*, distinguishing self as 'woman' not 'man', and protecting against taboo sexual energies and activities.

Power and authority

I have already touched on how women's power to act on the wider social, economic and political stage has historically been the target of some often systematic patriarchal strategies for emasculation. The backdrop to this story is well rehearsed but centuries of cultural and social oppression of a woman's freedom to define herself outside the home setting, or the mothering role, have left a residue requiring a truly revolutionary spirit to throw off these socially imposed bonds.

This has been a psychological as well as a social revolution, which has shifted self-perceptions and re-configured the organisation and distribution of work, home and wider social roles. The opening up of almost all dimensions of (most) western societies to women, particularly in the period since the Second World War, is not wholly dissimilar, as a socio-political equivalent, to the fall of the Berlin Wall in 1989, when the two sides of a country, West and East Germany, and then of a continent (Europe) were reunited.

This is a useful analogy for the talk of 'territories' in this book; outdated social structures were keeping a wall intact between male and female territories – so the ways in which women and men might be able to express themselves via historically fixed demarcations in role were prohibited. On the whole women could not go into 'male' territory, and vice versa. Then the wall fell and, like the Berlin Wall, once the first bricks were dislodged with a sledgehammer – like the first swipes of Jack's axe against the bean-stalk – there was no going back.

All territory would now be up for grabs for both men and women. We are living in the period after the dam burst, so our difficulty in seeing what distinctions there are between 'being a woman' and 'being a man' is not surprising, a problem for our *immanent* consciousness in the face of this *transcending* and, for now, all-consuming, development. Ann Snitow (1989) captures the spirit of the internal revolution for women, as they began to get hold of a real feeling of empowerment, when she quotes a woman who was talking at a meeting about her own moment of change: 'A. said she had felt, "Now I can be a woman; it's no longer so humiliating. I can stop fantasizing that secretly I am a man, as I used to, before I had children. Now I can value what was once my shame"' (Snitow, 1990: 9).

For some women at least, there has been an internal liberation to accompany the opening up of possibility 'out there'. The question this raises is how this shift has impacted on some of the patterned ways in which women's power and freedom can get emasculated. There remains a sense in which men sometimes still seek to control the behaviour and activity of women, where a man's overbearing (which also implies *fragile*) sense of his own dominance leads him to try to insist on curtailing what his partner can do or 'be'. His perfecting tendencies rigidify into the area of permission and demand of his partner an outdated 'submission'.

This is where 'perfecting' goes awry in its attempt to 'solve' rather than 'resolve' relational difficulties, and a man resorts to *dominance* as a form of patriarchal 'solution'. There is, of course, danger attached to this formula: where a woman steps outside what is 'permitted', say about who she can spend time with, then the threat, or even explosion, of aggression can result. This, and the tendency of some male-dominated institutions which continue to be tardy in letting women into their 'territories' (from the 'glass ceiling' of management pay scales to, in the UK, the Marylebone Cricket Club and to a degree the Houses of Parliament), seem to be the two main ways in which women continue to experience their potential being emasculated. These remaining parts of the wall between the traditional gender territories are maintained by men who retain a vested interest in these outdated, institutionalised, male strongholds (as opposed to the real, more deeply embedded male and female territories I am trying to map out).

There is a rather hollow quality about these attempts to emasculate women, though I am not meaning to downplay the very real and difficult consequences for women in their struggles to be treated equitably – respected for who they are rather than how they look – and find work which reflects their abilities and aspirations. Where retrograde, oppressive practices remain, they play into the hands of men who appropriate power in abusive ways on wider public and professional stages, as well through dark, hidden 'business' practices such as prostitution and human trafficking. There are also nasty and violent ways individual men may refer to their patriarchal inheritance to justify to themselves their acts of sexual or domestic abuse behind closed doors.

The patriarchal arguments, intellectual and ethical, have generally been lost; the old territorial walls have huge holes in them where they still straddle family, work and social spaces of westernised societies. Nevertheless, men still find subtle ways to emasculate women in the relationship context, by, for example, withdrawing from family responsibility or simply not communicating. A woman's predominating need for relational *completion*, apparently based on developmental, neurobiological – and possibly archetypal – factors can be insidiously undermined by men in such ways.

One could almost term such developments from the woman's point of view as the activation of a 'completion complex' where the external constellation of unfulfilling relationship mirrors a deeper feeling of lack and emasculation inside. As implied in the previous chapter, this may have its roots in an unsatisfactory relationship with father, when he did not supply the *erotic* foundations for 'completing' – and beneath *that* a relational incompleteness stemming from a faulty bonding with mother right at the start of life. Here, present-day emasculation of relational fulfilment with a man – and other experiences of emasculation in the workplace or elsewhere – become a reminder of deeper feelings of frustration whose roots may reach down to the underground streams connecting the present to Mum or Dad, or both.

Male territory: Perfecting individualism versus individuated relatedness

In contrast to women, I want to argue that men may predominantly experience a sense of being in the orbit of relationship (mother) rather than in the ground of it; relationships are experienced more tangentially, as something they are magnetically pulled towards or away from. In this sense I do not think it is just because of patriarchal conditioning that the originators of the *Beanstalk* story had a Jack (boy) rather than a Jill (girl) going up and down a beanstalk between earth and sky. This 'moving between' is a more predominantly male psychic feature. By this I am not saying men occupy liminal spaces any more than women may, but describing something about *movement*, a kind of 'coming and going' which is a form of male *deintegration–reintegration*.

Prospective tension predominantly at work in the male psyche relates first to a boy or a man needing to 'find' the path they 'should' be on in response to 'perfecting/transcending' influences which float somewhere in the spaces between unconscious, archetypal imprinting and a more conscious awareness of who they are and want to be. Second, as time passes and the perfecting, linear tendency of the male psyche becomes less dominant, often as a man adjusts his sense of priority to meet the presence of more immanent, completing elements in his life experience, the awareness of the significance of relatedness as potentially fulfilling (as well as inevitably *disruptive* of an exclusively 'male-perfecting' way of being) generates a competing pull. In archetypal imagery one could picture this as a constant 'moving between' open road and home. 'Perfecting' takes the boy or man down the road, but then potentially disconnects him from relatedness, while a 'completing' pull calls him back home.

Of course, all young people experience a version of this – a young woman needs to break free just as much as a young man does. The subtle distinction is in what has usually become embedded in male versus female territory: in the former case an attachment to linear movement ('through, forwards, away') compared with something more circular in female territory ('holding, staying, returning'). As I have emphasised, these territories are, in many ways, merging in the times in which we live, so these tendencies are shared more. However, there are underlying impulses which have been embedded over millennia and will not simply be 'wished away'.

Here, I want to revisit my terms in relation to what men 'do', driven by the legacy of an archetypal phallic imprint (fading, but still there) for 'perfecting/transcendence'. In response to the realities of life, relationship and family, rather than an ubiquitous attempt to 'perfect', the male territorial approach is to 'solve'. So, men may find themselves reaching out into the world around them in a way which usually recognises that the perfect solution does not exist (unless they are a localised version of a Hitler or a Stalin, where ultimate 'solutions' to social or national problems involve taking things to the ultimate political and military extreme – i.e. to find a pathological 'solution'). Predominantly, men may seek 'solutions' to challenges in wider society, the workplace or at home. As implied by this order, solutions at home may be avoided more than 'out there' in the community or workplace.

In relation to this, the tendency of male politicians to reach for solutions conveys to me a quality of something *linear*, which inevitably leads to a competitive atmosphere, as in 'who has the best solution' to whatever problem society faces at any particular moment. This is not necessarily 'wrong' but seems to reinforce the problem in our political culture of unrealistic optimism at the beginning of the upward trajectory towards finding a solution. There must be an answer 'up there' which can be 'brought home' to make things right, and this inevitably leads to feelings of bitter disappointment and disillusionment. This has led to a situation at present where many people want to throw all politicians out of the window, like a handful of useless beans. Where the limits to what can be solved are acknowledged at the outset – often easier to identify in a localised workplace or democratic decision-making setting – then this craving for a perfect solution at the end of a heroic quest can be better contained.

I propose, bearing in mind my suggestion that women may experience a kind of *completion complex* when a male partner's withdrawing behaviour reconstellates a deeper sense of lack or disharmony, men can be prone to being gripped by a 'solution complex', where their need to experience themselves as 'providing solutions' is not being fulfilled, and this refers back to a sense of not being able to 'solve' the oedipal problem – and 'make things right for mother', a man's first love.

On the political stage it appears there may be a collective 'solution complex' at work – the more a male politician or leader tries to solve problems of public policy, it seems, the more public dissatisfaction grows. The feeling of having 'solved' problems to the satisfaction of the electorate he is supposed to serve proves elusive. This may be as much to do with a public expectation (at least in the UK) of a perfected, transcending breed of politicians – a legacy of a patriarchal approach to politics and religion perhaps – as any perceived failings of MPs in the 'up in the sky' Houses of Parliament. This combination, and the remaining problem of gender imbalance in this institution, will remain until idealising projections towards politicians are further tempered, there are many more women in parliament, and male politicians stop trying to make things perfect for mother (the public).

In the case of 'home', men can participate in a healthy 'solving' dynamic which complements a more resolving/completing quality a woman brings to relationship. In general this dynamic seems to involve the woman looking to the man to supply, or reinforce, a sense of completion by 'solving' practical or romantic needs/problems of domestic life or preserving family stability by just 'being there'. A man may also seek a feeling of completion in the home *per se* but this, I suggest, is more ambiguous and may rely on how satisfying he finds it to provide what is needed to close the '*completing gestalt*' for the woman. This *gestalt* for the woman is a feeling based more in the present, whereas for a man the '*solving gestalt*' closes the discontinuity loop between present and future – and if he does not experience this sense of 'moving towards the future' within the relationship, then he may seek it elsewhere.

So, where there is a lingering feeling that things cannot be 'solved' – e.g. whatever he does it is 'not enough' – a man may give up or even lash out; the sometimes crude or destructive responses by some men to relationship or family breakdown reflects this dynamic. In the *Beanstalk* story, Jack apparently remains positive in the face of his father's death and his mother's despair. There *is* a place for naive optimism in the search for a 'solution', as long as the more transcending/perfecting end of this tendency can be pulled back down to earth by being grounded in a good-enough early attachment and a sustainable present relationship.

Time and space

Regarding 'time', alongside my comments above about the male need for feeling 'continuity' in close relationships, I have described the problematic ways some boys and men seem to get caught up in a *thanima* discontinuity (see Chapter 4), illustrating where *erosima* has got sidelined in a faulty early encounter with mother, hallmarked with deadness. So here I will make a couple of observations about *space* – or how male territory can literally be about staking, taking and defending it. Physical space can become an extension of self, and thus 'his land' may be experienced as something elemental to identity – at least in conventional, patriarchal readings of a man's relationship to his environment. From local arguments through to international wars, fighting to defend or acquire land has been experienced over many generations of men as a signifier of being male or of 'proving' maleness.

This predominance remains. Although, for example, more women are coming into national armed forces, they are still dominated by men – 9.4 per cent of members of the UK armed forces were reported to be women in 2008 (BBC News, 2008). And the literature on 'brain-sex' differences suggests male aggression, with its supposed preponderance towards overtly competitive expression (Moir and Jessel, 1991), seems to be more commonly directed towards associating 'territory' with combat. This can get translated in ways which have a social influence – as in the peer pressure evident in football hooliganism or gang culture generally.

I suggest that where *thanima* takes hold in the psyche of a man, space and the environment can become a problem: the disembodiment in not having a settled, continuous sense of self leads to awkwardness and disconnectedness with the immediate environment. A man explained to me that he only felt at ease with himself when out on the fells, walking. Home, work and social environments seemed to evoke feelings of alienation and depression much of the time. The temporal *thanima* discontinuity reflected in his difficulty in moving forwards in life was reflected in a relationship to the environment hallmarked by *dislocation*.

In male–female relationships this might take the form of alienation or awkwardness for the man in respect to the territory of home, and possibly generate a polarisation whereby the more female 'completing' tendency gets juxtaposed unhelpfully with this 'dislocated solving' (man thinking: 'it would solve things for me to be somewhere else').

Projection

I have suggested that women may be more likely to project their faulty, or hidden, perfecting tendencies onto men. Likewise, *thanima* projections of the 'incomplete' or faulty aspects of a man's relatedness and capacity for communication, which a man may throw out onto women as being 'too communicative/chatty', get compensated for by the man being the opposite: reticent and emotionally undemonstrative, or in Jung's classic formulation of negative *anima*, moody, resentful and over-sentimental (Jung, 1953/1966: para. 316).

The physical presence of a woman as 'gendered other' makes it more likely she will catch his projections around 'incompleteness', especially if his mother did not provide a 'good-enough' container for *erosima* to live and develop healthily. Where the early relationship with mother has not generated healthy *erosima* energies, then the man may launch unconsciously envious attacks on his partner because she apparently has the same power to evoke *erosima* in him – which he may feel he does not have – and this power becomes something the little boy in him would rather destroy than allow her to have for herself (or potentially others) even though this would deny him access to what he longs for and needs.

In male–female relationships, this moves things towards projective identification more than projection. A woman may feel as if she is being controlled into responding to her male partner as if she has no scope to be herself, separate and distinct. This becomes an experience of being split between being impelled towards fusion with him (as the little boy would have craved from his mother) and angry feelings of rejection (he would have experienced in response to the *thanima* disjunction between him and his mother). Sustained feelings of *incompletion* will remain as long as this split remains.

The potential impact of this powerful projective identification will be obvious – some kind of estrangement between a man and a woman based on his deep wound and her natural reaction to being controlled. Her *thanimus* difficulty with her dream of completeness being rendered imperfect will lock horns with his *thanima* rage and terror at the withholding power of mother, unless the nature of the container around their relationship allows for something different to happen.

Power and authority

Power is a hallmark of traditional male territory. This territory conventionally acted like a reflector of a man's sense of worth. This can no longer be taken, even partly, for granted. Holding down a high-profile professional position, or having social status in some other way, acted like mother's back to the little boy searching for affirmation and unconditional love from his first, all consuming object. Perhaps this is why sometimes men have become so invested in their professional lives – their jobs and achievements supply some sense of deep affirmation of self, something they may have once had (or not) from their adoring mother.

This may also say something about why men can experience their job as a kind of *phallus*, a sense of their own power – as leaders or achievers in the professional context they happen to work in, as well as potentially drawing erotic power through the glamour of their position.

Erosima is brought to life by the invigorating experience for a man of having his authority and his importance reflected in the respectful, even deferential, responses of other people towards him.

Here male power (and authority) is all about what is 'out there'. Andrew Samuels points out how rigidified the link between exclusively male 'territory' and leadership can be: 'There is hierarchical and heroic leadership based on male authority and a masculine approach to knowledge that assumes there is one objectively true social story' (Samuels, 2009: 4). The plurality of 'ways of leading' and using authority is both a breath of fresh air but also a deep challenge to the notion that men can feed their ego – and possibly their soul – by 'taking power'. This 'taking' implies a movement towards power which is acquisitive and proprietorial, something which will not sit easily with postmodern, post-feminist, sensibilities.

In this regard the traditional male version of authority and power has been thoroughly dislodged – or emasculated – by the 'fall of the wall' between traditional gendered territories. However, the hand of maleness still often reaches out towards the allure of external power as a signifier of power – vocational, professional positions which reflect some sense of authority – because this can be a way of recapturing the *erosima* feeling of mother's adoring, supporting, gaze. It is also a means of capturing a feeling in the present of holding the 'perfecting–solving' mantle which still lives in the male psyche even if the territory from which this particular beanstalk grows is flooded with the waters which have burst through the male–female wall. The beanstalk still manages to grow towards the light, towards the sky, a seemingly patterned movement upwards – however outmoded it can seem.

Outmoded perhaps, but there remains a sense that male territory *may* be able to connect with something archetypal that female territory does not provide for: the upward seeking of the impossible, like an old-fashioned male leader who goes to ridiculous lengths to 'prove' to the population he is heroically successful in every respect. The seeking of the heroic, impossible and perfect dimensions of life retains value, however, in maintaining connection with the 'heightened numinous' (metaphorically 'up in the sky' rather than the dark, dirty aspects of numinosity). This may facilitate imagining the future to help make 'good things' happen, and allow *erosima* to explore the extent and limitations of humanity's potential. Maybe here a visionary male politician does have something to offer, as long as he provides the vision from a grounded position which avoids *hubris*.

More than once I have worked clinically with men who feel as if they have lost *erosima* – finding themselves in relationships or life situations where they do not feel they have scope to explore themselves or aspects of their environment they might feel drawn towards. Of course this can happen for women, too, but the predominant difference, I would suggest, is in how this can get characterised, especially in mid or later life. These men tended to describe a *dead*, depressed version of *thanima*, where there is a sense of *nothing more* to do or look forward to, because their linear, perfecting/solving mode of movement through life has been mislaid, or experienced as emasculated, and they have not found the capacity to 'let go' and embrace a more balanced *erosima* capacity in response to the variable triumphs and sorrows of life.

Unknowingly, the flooding of conventional male territory with female 'waters' – itself a powerful metaphor for the oft suggested male fear of a watery inundation by the annihilating powers of the terrible mother (Ayers, 2003: 43) – may have swept a number of men off their feet, rendering them struggling to find *terra firma* without the traditional navigation aids of vocation and social status. Likewise, for some men, as I will consider further in the final chapter, though the only secure territory left is *home*, this can be experienced as predominantly *female* territory, based in the long-nurtured bond of mother and daughter. Where this is so, the sense of discontinuity and dislocation in the dimensions of time and space, as well as the generation of fearful or hostile projections, may get exacerbated and constellate together in a *home complex*, where the shared living space becomes a symbol of what, in a persecutory way, is 'other' to him.

If something equivalent happens for a woman, it is of course equally problematic – say where 'home' gets associated with abuse, neglect or low-level (but constant) unhappiness. I suggest that the predominating tendency in a woman may be more to want to 'put this right' by making a new home life for herself which meets her 'completing' needs in the present. A man may predominantly experience a need to find a different, even contradictory, 'solution', such as avoiding having to re-experience 'home' by isolating himself from relationships, or projecting his *relational* aspirations into an imagined future of 'a perfected relationship'.

Marriage as a psychological relationship

Jung's paper on this theme (1925/1954) provided some important observations about the dynamics inherent in long-term male–female relationships, some of which shed further light on the way projection may work between men and women. One of Jung's key ideas concerns the psychological presence of 'containment' in the marriage relationship. Rather than the marriage 'contract' between the man and the woman acting as the container, Jung argues that one person in the marriage tends to 'contain' the other, by providing a sense of containment by their very presence, while not necessarily feeling contained themselves. The distinction, as Jung puts it, is:

> The one who is contained feels himself to be living entirely within the confines of the marriage . . . outside the marriage there exist no essential obligations and no binding interests. The container on the other hand, who in accordance with his tendency to dissociation has an especial need to unify himself in undivided love for another, will be left far behind in this effort . . . by the simpler personality.
>
> (Jung, 1925/1954: 332–3)

An implication arising from this for his *anima–animus* formulation is that the partner who feels fully contained by the other is able to project their contrasexual image onto the other and explore and relate to it. On the other hand, the containing partner does not experience enough of a sense of their own containment to release themselves into such an equivalent fusion with the other person and therefore does not have the same projective relationship whereby they can 'see' and relate to their contrasexual image (whether *anima* or *animus*).

I think this remains a useful idea and highlights how there will always be a sense of imbalance between marriage (or long-term) partners in terms of how 'held' in the marriage and how much of the 'loving gaze' of the other each may feel – unless there is a kind of lowering of the threshold of individual consciousness around both of them which somehow keeps them swimming in a romantic *participation mystique* year after year. Normally a marriage's 'life' involves a subtle issue and flow in the experiencing of containment so there may be times when one partner contains the other before the container is subtly passed across to the other, and this continues back and forth.

A problem arises when one partner finds themselves fixed in the 'container' position. For Jung this *is* what happens, and that person has to grin and bear, at least for a while, being what the other person wants them to be without being able to be more or less themselves. Here, in a version of projective identification, they operate in ways which fulfil the felt and perceived notion of how their partner believes they 'should' function.

They are, in a sense, controlled by the marriage rather than helping to shape it in ways which reflect who they are. This, I suggest, is another way in which *thanima* and *thanimus* do their stuff in the male–female relationship; by not allowing us to see our positive contrasexual 'other' in our partner, and instead showing us only a version of our contrasexual other which highlights our weaker and less pleasant aspects. Rows and stand-offs in relationships tend to be the conflictual, rigidified manifestations of this.

This can be overcome if both partners follow the psychological dictum described here by Sandford (1980: 113): 'If our human relationships are to succeed we must be able to distinguish between the divine and the human partners in our lives.' Being gripped by the power of our contrasexual 'other' invokes a *thanima/thanimus* possession of the psyche, leading us to constantly compare our real partner with the idealised *anima* or *animus* figure. When this spell remains unbroken the rigidity of the container–contained dynamic gets exacerbated, possibly to a point where no container is left around the partnership as a whole.

I also suggested earlier how there is often a 'completing–perfecting' dynamic in male–female relationships, and predominantly this works with the woman holding the 'completing' and the man the 'perfecting' in how transactions between them operate. This is intimately linked with Jung's ideas on 'containment' *and* offers a parallel from Jungian psychology on self–ego relating. The 'completing' dynamic carries an implication of 'self', the prospective 'selfing' dynamic towards integration/individuation of the 'whole' psyche, while ego is about an active movement towards an 'end point' consciously envisaged – e.g. a targeted achievement. I am implying a feminine influence on the activity of the self, and a masculine one regarding ego – again a 'big' speculation, but worth pondering in terms of individuating in *relational* contexts.

Before exploring other ways of portraying the territorial relationship discussed, a further corollary of this line of thought refers back to Jung's 'container'. Containment by the man of the woman may have a different feel to the woman's containment of the man. In the former case it may be more a case of ego containing self – if one can imagine such a reversal of a basic Jungian notion (though Jung was of course comfortable with such an *enantiodromia* – *Answer to Job* [Jung, 1952/1969] springs to mind, where Job's ego consciousness has a healing effect on the uncontained vengefulness of Yahweh as 'self').

Here, a man provides both conscious and unconscious containment (as ego operates in between, and across, both domains) for the woman's 'selfing' search for completion. He acts as the screen on which she can see and engage with her *erosimus* perfecting ('masculine') strengths, which might enable the experience of 'completing' to be more available in the present. The woman contains by mirroring the place of self. The man then gets to see his *erosima* capacity for relational completion ('feminine'), which in turn supports his perfecting tendencies into getting channelled in healthy and satisfying ways.

Two models to describe the 'territorial deal'

I am suggesting the value of seeing ego/transcending/male–self/immanent/female as an axis which a relationship between a man and a woman moves along in all sorts of ways during its life (so a man may go into *completing* mode at times, and a woman *perfecting* ones) but which gravitates *predominantly* towards the base territory of *maleness* (men) or *femaleness* (women). This arrangement is portrayed in Figure 7.1.

Male	Shared	Female
Ego/transcending	———'On the beanstalk'———	Self/immanent
Perfecting	Shared ways of being.	Completing
Solving	Self as individual – unique.	Resolving
Future-as	Needs for personal space,	Present-as
– relational	satisfying relationships	– relational
	and general security, health	
	and fulfillment.	

Figure 7.1 Male, female and shared territory (1)

While this model illustrates where the predominating tendencies of male versus female may lie, and the woman's predominant '*completing gestalt*' is more like 'self' than the man's, it becomes problematic where it implies the female always takes the 'selfing' part in male–female relationships, when in reality it is quite possible for the man to 'contain' the thoughts and activity of a woman in the way the self–ego relation suggests. I want to propose instead that the 'self' aspect of heterosexual as well as other forms of relationship often gets projected into, or held by, the actual living space the two people share. So, it is *home* which symbolically provides this function, in which two egos try to function separately – and sometimes as *one*.

Put this way, one can see how challenging the enterprise of long-term relationship really is, as each partner will invest and project much into the *temenos* around the relationship, which in turn is given concrete form by the home which is shared. Bearing in mind my argument that female territory is more conventionally, neurobiologically and developmentally associated with mother, compared with the male territorial space, then the image of, and relation to, home for a woman will make it more firmly *female territory*. Again, I throw out my caveat of not wishing to imply that men cannot be territorial about domestic space or that women *need* to be identified with home more – I am simply suggesting that at this time and place in history, this is more or less the case. Figure 7.2 shows, *for better or worse* (to coin a phrase from the edgy 'there may be trouble ahead' flavour of the Church of England's wedding vows) how I suggest 'home as Self/ container' sits with female–male territorial relations:

Male ego	HOME	Female ego
Transcending/perfecting	Self	Immanent/completing
Solving		Resolving

Figure 7.2 Male and female territory (2)

As the diagram implies, female territory is (predominantly) closer to home (maybe 'in' it?). Male territory is more tangential and ambiguous. Two questions arising from this idea of home as 'Self' (the capital 'S' denotes its 'big' containing–directing quality) are: what might be the intrapsychic and interpersonal implications?, and, if there is a problematic gendered imbalance here, how might this be addressed?'

Midlife and male and female deintegration/ reintegration

Michael Fordham's model is valuable in describing how the archetypal nature of Jung's idea of an individuating 'self' can connect to the immanent ground of daily reality. Deintegration describes the initiation of this process, whereby an aspect of self – a 'deintegrate' (Fordham, 1985: 31) – allows itself to fall back from its integrated state in order to make contact with what is 'out there' (mother, breast, bottle etc.) for the infant and then take itself back (a reintegrate) into self, having been changed by the encounter.

For adult men and women, I propose, there is a similar process when it comes to the 'otherness' thrown up by gender. This does not just refer to a relationship to the contrasexual other within (*anima or animus*), which we project onto our partner and which needs to be withdrawn and 'reintegrated', but also to our need to contact and experience the *real* otherness of the other gender, and this need refers to the importance of gender to our sense of self.

In fact, it is as if our femaleness or maleness within a marriage or other long-term relationship is an *essential* component of our sense of ego integrity; two egos supposedly blended together within the 'self' of the relationship (or 'home' as I have suggested) needing to have some sense of individuality – not, as I have argued, just because of the historical, familial, fear of the incest taboo associated with sibling or peer relationships, but mainly because gender is usually the pivotal distinction between the two partners, and so this maintains some sense of individuality/separateness for each of them. The fear of loss of identity – with its roots in feeling 'lost' in the primary fusion with mother in infancy – is a key driver in the deintegration–reintegration dynamic in relationships, especially in the first half of life.

I suggest that where this dynamic does not get adequately reciprocated in a male–female partnership (when a man's predominating need to 'solve' challenges, in the relationship or home, or a woman's sense things are 'complete enough' within the partnership, are not well enough reintegrated), either partner can experience a kind of 'disintegration'. Either could become withdrawn or destructive in their behaviours towards each other as a reaction to these needs not being met.

In midlife, this need to accept the 'otherness of the gendered other', and thereby avoid falling into relational disintegration, becomes less pronounced, because a sense of identity less bounded to gender has usually been established and can be relied upon by the man or woman not to be subsumed by relationship, family or social pressure.

In any heterosexual relationship, there will be ways in which this need to *deintegrate* towards the other, and then *reintegrate* the experience of difference, may become patterned in male and female ways. These ways refer back to the predominating tendencies described earlier. So, for example, some men (some younger ones in particular) may deintegrate in an overtly 'male' way towards his partner – a 'masculine' look, tone of voice, or way of standing which provides him with an experience of *being different to her*, and conveys this difference to her.

This may also extend to how he talks about women in a generalised way, emphasising – exaggerating perhaps – the mysterious 'otherness' of the other gender, e.g. 'she's having a girly talk on the phone again', 'shopping is a girl thing' (notice with this, and the examples I give from women about 'boys', how these asides regress the gendered other). What he *really* experiences as different about the woman is then reintegrated in a rather confused way, via this pronounced need to maintain the gendered support for his sense of separate identity from her, so there is a risk both the full picture of her difference as well as the shared commonality between them gets clouded, or even filtered out in some cases.

Or, in a less overt way, he might not feel such a defensive need to convey his 'difference' but instead deintegrate more subtly by offering his 'solving' tendency to his partner – sometimes by simply being present as the 'solution' to her need to be listened to, for example. This offers the sense of gendered differentiated identity he seeks without making a display of it to her (or himself).

Likewise, a woman may find herself conveying an overt sense of 'being different' to her partner by deintegrating towards him in her most overt 'female territorial' way, choosing momentary identifications with a caricatured feminine through how she touches or looks at him, or by talking about him as part of a collective male way of operating ('boys will be boys', 'football is a boy's thing' etc.).

The stronger connection I have proposed between female territory and home may come out in the way a woman's spoken attention is given to how home is organised. Or, she may also simply connect with a feeling of completeness within the relationship or family, as she reintegrates what of him is experienced as different to her in order to remind herself of her pivotal – but at all costs *different* to him – role in the family.

Paradox and the need to feel different

There is a paradox here – each needs the presence of the gendered other to remind themselves of their own separate ego identity so as not to be swamped by the intimate presence of both their very *sameness* (as another human) and any threatening aspects of their *otherness*. As implied, the need to deintegrate/reintegrate in this gendered way may tend to be more pronounced in younger people. Alongside Jung's emphasis on a natural process of change in midlife (Jung, 1960/1969a), the gender 'problem' may become less problematic after midlife, where there is often a greater ease with *contrasexual* ways of expressing oneself, including greater variations in expressing one's sexuality.

So, the *completing feminine* (which I would picture as a function of *erosima*) in a man at midlife (whenever this arises, from around forty onwards) demands its place. As John Beebe puts it, there is an alchemical recipe whereby 'Luna . . . [is] . . . the developed feminine principle, . . . [and] . . . men have the special task in midlife of making sure Luna is well enough integrated' (Beebe, 1988: xvi). A contradistinctive (but similar in emphasis) movement in women regarding versions of the masculine – which may include looking for new *solutions* to life questions – can also present itself.

I will argue in the concluding chapter that it may be possible for men to integrate contrasexual elements earlier in life but that 'the problem of home' – i.e. the unhelpful ways in which home acts as a container, or as a representation of 'Self' – can block this from happening smoothly. I will also argue, in the context of the well-established feminist arguments already explored (mainly in Chapter 2), that women's capacity to get hold of healthy, active 'masculine' (*erosimus*) ways of being can likewise get curtailed by 'the problem of home' when a woman's sense of self gets overly identified with home/mother.

The trends in life trajectories of women and men suggested in this chapter are in some ways paralleled. But, to reiterate the point, it only takes the smallest of differences between 'I' and 'Thou' to create a fork in the road which can then take each of 'us' in quite separate and distinctive directions. The man then walks on the male *cirrocumulus* clouds, and the woman on the *altocumulus* ones, as thunder rumbles in the *cumulonimbus* clouds in the distance – even when, to all appearances, they are walking together, looking at the same horizon.

Chapter 8

Bringing the giants down from the sky: Men, women, relationships and the problem of home

> The beanstalk came down with an almighty crash, and the giant fell to his end, making the earth shudder for miles around. The sky kingdom was never seen again, but Jack and his mother lived happily ever after, Jack having recovered his father's riches at last.

> Conscious femininity and conscious masculinity will never be acceptable to patriarchy. If we become sufficiently conscious, however . . . we do not have to be sacrificed.
>
> (Woodman, 1990: 110)

We inhabit living spaces (home, work, school, local and wider communities – real and virtual) where it is not so easy to pick up an axe and get rid of the problem of gender. Instead, our consciousness about gender identity, similarity, difference, reality *and* illusion presses in on us, like the sky – or the giants up there – falling on our heads, thinning the air and stifling our freedom to 'be'. Likewise, when we hold a magnifying glass up to what gender *is*, the meanings scatter in all sorts of directions.

The elusive and irritating nature of gender even gets *under* our skin, like the scene in the film *The Mummy* (Sommers, 1999) where scarab beetles crawl under the skin of one or two unfortunate characters, racing around their bodies before finding their vital organs and killing them. While the gender problematic does not usually have such deadly consequences directly, it can kill relationships and render us confused, conflicted and disempowered when there are *thanima/thanimus* presentations. We can also think of it as a *trickster*: 'gender' can change shape, or disappear, in the blink of an eye, then reappear in a totally different guise.

This is one of the problems of gender as *reality* versus *illusion*. The growing body of research into differences between female and male brains, for example, speaks to us of a constitutional, 'brain-sex' set of differences which appear to have significant implications for our understanding of differences between 'being a woman' and 'being a man'. By itself, this often does not work in translation. Suggesting, for example, that a more relational way of being in women is largely a consequence of their brain-formation can tie human experiencing into a straitjacket of scientifically defined parameters, obscuring the whole phenomenological story. Nevertheless, as I continue to stake out possibilities of what 'male' and 'female' territories might look like, these neurobiological influences do have an important part to play, in my view, once we unhitch them from fixed meanings and place them alongside the postmodern, feminist and depth psychological positions.

The anomalous differences in the way some brain researchers read 'gender' as against the more fluid, deconstructing modes of thinking arising from arts, philosophy and socio-political perspectives, help explain why there can be a strong temptation to chop the beanstalk down – thereby killing the problem of gender difference and allowing the 'sky kingdom of gender' to float away from consciousness, and leave us in peace.

It can feel safer to say that gender is only skin deep, but this denies the ubiquity of its influence, and the way it reaches so much deeper into the unconscious issue and flow of the archetypal masculine and feminine. Above this, layers of gender identity constructed, or half constructed, in our early relations with mother and father, then through social influences, mediate between what may inhabit our inner world (or 'up in the sky') and our experiencing of the present moment.

I suggest that gender is a problem in the era in which we live partly because of a tendency in the culture to wish it away as an unreconstructed, out-of-date, 'modern' fallacy we can now gaze at deconstructively through our postmodern glasses. Taking into account the many patterned ways men can predominantly perceive and behave on the one hand (e.g. 'housework as a lower *transcending* priority') and women on the other ('housework as a higher *immanent* priority'), there is, to say the least, a lot of slippage back into modern ways of doing things, however unconsciously patterned, rather than 'consciously choosing', this may be.

This movement back and forth on the beanstalk between postmodern and modern ways of being a man or a woman is paralleled by the question of where the presence (or problem) of gender in our social and political discourses is to be 'found'. As Andrew Samuels puts it: 'The very idea of gender also has a hidden bridge-building function: it sits on a threshold half-way between the inner and outer worlds and thus is already half way out into the world of politics' (Samuels, 2001: 35–6).

Alongside emphasising how current the question of gender is, this observation allows for the possibility that there are layers to being a man, or being a woman, which we do not understand properly and this problem may be having a bigger impact on wider political and social questions than we realise. When trying to address 'big' problems involving public policy, ranging from childcare through to criminal behaviour, we may either resort to outdated 'modern' ideas about what men and women 'do' in society (e.g. women look after young children, men do not) or go wholly 'postmodern' and say there are *no* gender certainties (e.g. there is no gendered pattern to criminal behaviour). We try to *solve and resolve* problems in areas such as this through a cross-gendered consensus – which is quite right at one level, but at another means that we assume our consensus renders gender difference as a less than significant factor in how we have reached it.

What, for example, would we find if we drew up proposals from a socio-economically, cross culturally, representative group of Britain's women on the best ways to deal with, say, criminal behaviour, and set them alongside proposals from a similarly representative group of men? Would any clear distinctions in view which arose not be relevant in informing what the final 'look' of a policy, or a piece of legislation, would be?

I am not suggesting this is how we should make public policy *but* where policy in areas like family law, childcare and education, for example, are being reviewed and drawn up, it might have more of a place. The predominantly male territory of the UK parliament – at 19.7 per cent, the percentage of women members is only slightly above the worldwide average of 18.3 per cent (IPU, 2009) – means women's legislative preoccupations generally rely a good deal on men fully 'knowing' what these are, and being able to act on them – an unsatisfactory arrangement to say the least, assuming one gender can represent the other's needs on often crucial matters. Taking gender-specific views on certain issues may also help men to better see what women generally want – and vice versa – countering the problems of *collective thanima/thanimus* and the difficulties of 'seeing' into the other's (male or female) territory.

I propose that there is another dimension to this 'not seeing' which takes us back *home*. By 'home' I mean all the associations to, and experiences of, 'home', but in particular the one(s) we grew up in, plus all the fantasises we may have had about what 'home' could mean for us in the idealised present and future. As John Hill argues, 'home' is a crucial motif for us, something we carry around with us as a signifier of our crucial attachments (Hill, 2006). I want to argue how 'home' – or the way it is experienced and symbolised within heterosexual and familial dyads – plays a powerful part in making it hard to 'see' into the *genuine* territory of the gendered 'other'.

The centripetal force of significance, and the problem of home

I floated the possibility in the previous chapter that our concepts of 'home' act symbolically as the container for our associations, projections and aspirations about male–female partnership. In the *Beanstalk* story, Jack's task is to solve the problem of a home bereft of father and resources, while mother's wish is for a re-completing *gestalt* to restore her home. 'Home', as container for what relationship and family is about for each person living within it, can influence in important if subtle ways the rationale for why we are in a partnership.

Differences between men and women about what home is 'for' can lie at the heart of the problematic dimensions of heterosexual relationships. These spill over into patterns of separation between men and women, and between fathers and their children. When ex-cohabiting fathers were interviewed (in Bradshaw *et al.*, 1998: 84) 38 per cent had not seen their children in the past month. The problems fathers experience in maintaining contact with their children have spawned campaigning movements in the UK (Langford, 2008).

In order to lay the ground for my argument about what 'home' might 'do' to the male–female dynamic, I refer to a psychological trend in how we generally invest in symbols as we oscillate between modern and postmodern ways of thinking and experiencing. I have written elsewhere (Goss, 2008a) about the possibility that the psychic (and possibly *numinous*) energy the westernised woman or man used to invest in religious, political and other social signs and symbols has become more dispersed into the *frame*, or container around them (like being in an art gallery and realising the frame of a picture holds more interest and significance than the picture we had originally come to see).

An example would be the Christian cross: as people have become generally less invested in the ascribed meaning of the cross as handed down by the Church, the energy invested has been dispersed centripetally into the invisible 'frame around it'. In the case of the cross this leaves some kind of diamond shape – a border which has formed around the empty space left in the middle by the faded cross. So, the energy remains but is no longer attached to the sign or symbol which once held the power to attract the collective gaze. Instead it hangs around the edge of the space, with its 'electric charge' occasionally shooting across it like lightning in an empty sky, challenging us to make something of this 'live emptiness' for ourselves.

In this way, I propose, the 'modern' ascription of female = feminine and male = masculine, as exemplified by the image of the 'happy ever after' married couple – the *archetypal eternal couple* as a symbol of traditional love, fidelity and stability – is fading and deconstructing. This process is given extra momentum by the legacy of feminism, as well as our overdue recognition of the equal validity of same-sex relationships and transgendered sexuality, alongside the conventional heterosexual model. The figure below shows the relational energy as now 'in the frame' around the edge of the empty space where dispersed 'archetypal couple' semiotic-symbolic energies intermingle and wrestle.

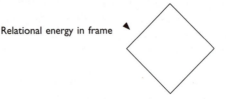

Figure 8.1 The heterosexual, post-patriarchal, relational diamond

In this context, the archetypal constellating power of male–female sexuality and relating has been looking for somewhere to base itself, out of an emerging consciousness that it is 'not alone' in the universe of gender and sexuality. So, this power, I suggest, is dispersing into the outline around the traditional, exclusive, dyadic symbol of the man–woman/mother–father, couple; in alchemical language the energy is dispersing from the *conuinctio* happening inside the *vas*, into the *vas* itself. So really this outline around couple energies needs to home-shaped – as home is the obvious container for our investment in romantic and familial love.

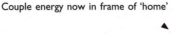

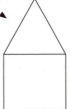

Figure 8.2 The dispersal of 'archetypal heterosexual marriage' energies to 'home'

When marriages and other heterosexual relationships break down, the priority has to be to provide a stable home life for any children involved. 'Home' – either as the house they are in, or the new living arrangement which might arise from staying with either Mum or Dad (and seeing the other regularly or otherwise) – becomes the replacement container for love, fear, hope and whatever other feelings and aspirations are around for the child. For a man or a woman, likewise, the loss of relationship gets contained through 'falling back' onto the presence of home in some form – whether the house/flat/home they remain in while the other leaves, or a new (physical) home environment they move into by themselves or maybe with children and/or a new partner. These spaces can come to act as representations of previous associations of home, or hopes for the future about home and family. In turn these can help contain the hurt and disorientation of the present, or conversely, serve as a painful reminder of what has been lost.

A further historical, and archetypal, dimension here is the way 'home' has always carried such a deep imprint on what it means to be human. Without a home our sense of self has no anchor. While at times in life this can feel liberating, generally we need somewhere to 'go back to' when things do not go to plan, our resources are low or we just want the relief of the familiar and the known. In this regard, home is invested with great significance for all of us, and will pull on our thoughts and feelings even more where early experiences of it have been deeply damaging.

So, 'home' is where the heart is, however ambivalent, angry or broken we might feel about it. I will consider if there are any 'predominant' gender differences in how men and women perceive and feel about 'home'. My intuition, based on my own life and professional experience, is of a *predominating* difference (always bearing in mind individual variation). The unspoken *semiotic* of the feminine is strongly invested and symbolised in 'home' in powerful ways. Meanwhile, 'the male *symbolic*' has its way of expressing the significance of 'home'. Men invest their own indescribable, pre-verbal feelings and instinctual drives in this container for the parental dyad and family.

In describing 'home' as a symbol, the 'dispersal' of symbolic energy from the feminine–masculine 'marriage' dyad which I propose is happening would appear simply to involve a replacement of one symbol by another. However, the outline of 'home' continues to evolve as a *frame* for the space in which the archetypal male–female/mother–father dyads continue to evolve. This space is becoming more of an 'empty space' of the 'less definable'. Here there is *more semiotic than symbolic*, and a powerful charge of 'gender electrics'.

On the other hand, 'home', as a 'stand alone' symbol, is also seeking out a frame of reference which can hold the many layers of semiotic as well as symbolic energies which are reverberating towards and through it because of the dispersal of symbolic energy from the image of 'the married couple'. These energies may well simply be *too much*, or *too big* (in other words, 'giant energies') for the 'home' to contain, as both feminine and masculine forces need more than just 'home' to express themselves. So, what this emerging frame around the symbol of home may look like is not clear. It is something which is currently seeking form – 'a work in progress', or a form taking shape between earth and sky – though I have one intuited image to offer which refers back to our post-Christian era: the 'diamond' shape left by the 'gone cross', a shape which refers to the need for us to work on the *ground* of our being to bring out new *ways* of being – the diamond in the dirt.

I am not suggesting that marriage as a form of institutionalising heterosexual romantic love and fidelity, as well as family, is 'dead' or even 'dying'; there is a deep archetypal significance to the vow of commitment between a man and a woman, approved by society, which then acts as a robust container for the establishment of a stable family environment. What I *am* suggesting is shifting is our consciousness of other ways of doing things, and the lessening of the religious sanctifying power over the institution of marriage. This means it is now *what lies behind* marriage and long-term male–female relationships – i.e. the idea of 'home' – which holds the archetypal power previously concentrated in the patriarchal version of marriage.

The problem this throws up (as hinted at in the previous chapter), which I believe has a profound impact on the long-term viability of many heterosexual relationships, is the possibility of there being a significant imbalance in the proximity of female territory towards home compared with male territory. In other words, 'home' may be defined more by *female* than male territory. If this *is* so then in classic Jungian language there may be a one-sidedness to the relationship between woman–home compared with man–home which helps explain in a compensatory way why, for example in the UK, there has been so much marital break-up and familial unhappiness. The container in which male–female relationships function does not, in general, evenly 'contain' both protagonists in the marital/partnership drama.

This one-sidedness – where female territorial points of reference have become woven into the fabric of 'home' to a fuller degree than those arising from male territory – has three roots: the developmental significance of the mother–daughter–home triangulation; the implications for gendered relations arising from *brain-sex* research; and the legacy of hundreds of years of patriarchal oppression of women which has now conversely shifted power into the woman/mother–home relation in a way men are hard pushed to compete with. The way the language of mother–daughter was repressed by patriarchy, generating semiotic, 'pre-symbolic', forms of the hard-to-articulate pre-verbal has, I suggest, written this pre-linguistic hidden language into the walls, ceilings and floors of our 'homes'.

In this regard it is worth remembering that we live in two homes anyway. First, the one we are conscious of, in the present moment, in which we share, battle, enjoy, and negotiate the space with our partners and our children. Secondly, there is the 'home' we carry around inside us, which is a repository of early, pre-verbal experiencing and communication, as well as other unconscious influences from later experiences of family life where we have imbibed ways of 'being in a family or relationship'.

These get transmitted from the family heritage of each of our sets of parents and the wider culture; not to mention what messages we may pick up from the physical spaces of the homes we have lived in and those who have shaped them before we lived there (these factors subtly impact on how we organise the space and live together in it). There is a bigger version of 'home' we carry around in us, arising from the archetypal imprint of our need for a home and the formative experience of it in early life, which enlarges and deepens as we grow up and experience more ways of being 'at home'. Finally, it carries a teleological aspect of the home we may aspire to 'live in forever'.

This is another way in which the *Beanstalk* story works psychologically – the *little* rickety house in which Jack lives with his mother representing the destruction, the dilapidation, of a dream of home which would have been complete emotionally, and well resourced, had his father not been murdered. It is a corrupted and lost version of the home up in the sky – the giant's castle – and so the bigger version of home 'up there' becomes a fantasised, compensatory version of what has been snatched away from Jack and his mother, charged with their grief and rage in the shape of the murderous giant. This could also be seen as a mythological version of how we experience 'home' as we pass through childhood, experiencing it as a 'giant space' where we, as little versions of our parents (or other primary carers), are offered a template for what we can have when we are 'giant like them'.

In the story the castle in the sky seems to be more the possession of the giant (as he won it by killing Jack's father) and the giant's wife is subservient to his needs, at least when he is around. This *big* house, the castle, has the blood of father in the walls, a murderous 'unspoken', as opposed to the female semiotic. There is an implication that the masculine-infused home can only be thus when built on the 'blood of an Englishman'.

The polarisation between the impoverished, helpless, feminine home on the ground and the enriched, menacing one in the sky throws into relief 'the problem of home'. The archetypal masculine has wrenched the feminine 'home' from the very ground it is based on through a definitively distracting and relocating battle with itself – the 'giant' father killing the real one. This drastic manoeuvre, I suggest, is a way men may try to outwit being 'in mother's house' (both their real mother's house as well as shared space with a woman partner). Historically, going to war, for example, may have afforded a sense of going off into territory which was 'male' and which, via the most tragic of means, meant men could unconsciously change the *status quo* either in their own home (by putting themselves at peril) or in the home of somebody they injure or kill.

This may sound a perverse, extreme suggestion but it is there in the fabric of the story; Jack is only able to change the balance of power by going away from mother's home and up into a very dangerous space where he comes within a whisker of becoming the giant's breakfast. The anxiety Jack creates for his mother would have been excruciating – not knowing if he would return from the 'battlefield' up in the sky, like partners, mothers and sisters waiting for news of their husbands, sons or boyfriends, down through countless years of bloody wars. The uncertainty about their return moved the balance of power away from home and even when men returned, this male territory could be maintained through the threat of some other distant or local conflict arising.

This principle may still apply to men setting up working practices which involve them 'going away from home' – whether the long-distance voyages of discovery or empire building by explorers or soldiers in the past, or a businessman jetting around the world to generate trade in the present – in order, unconsciously, to keep a sense of the locus of power being not solely in the physical home space. This implies not only a male unease with 'being at home' but, behind this, a 'fear' of the feminine, as something which could overwhelm, like the image of 'flooded male territory' I described in the previous chapter. As Samuels puts it: 'What scares men is *women*' (Samuels, 2001: 37).

So, the historical manifestations of patriarchal behaviour and aspirations (i.e. aspects of the *primitive* and *ancient* and, particularly, *modern* periods of archetypal–personal gender eras I alluded to in Chapter 6) may in part have been a reaction to men feeling caught in female territory – in a claustrophobic sense – in the home. This leads to pronounced forms of collective male activity and symbolisation about defining themselves *away* from home.

Where men may, historically, have found a sense of identity through *home* – alongside their role to provide fathering, particularly in an initiatory sense for their sons – was in the physical construction of a house or equivalent shelter for their wives and the family. This 'building of the nest' is still a way some more traditional partnerships register the contribution of the man to the family. He can be working ridiculous hours, as long he funds home and family (i.e. a traditional 'breadwinner' model). This is obviously now only one of a number of models for 'sustaining the nest' (or paying the bills) – including women doing the same thing while the male partner stays at home with the children.

The house that Jack built

Another *Jack* – who pops up in a well-known rhyme – conveys the sense, in ancient and modern times at least, that *home* predominantly accrued meaning in male territory through not only having been built by the man (or men) but also by its connection to the wider community:

> This is the farmer who sowed the corn,
> That kept the cock that crowed in the morn,
> That waked the priest all shaven and shorn,
> That married the man all tattered and torn,
> That kissed the maiden all forlorn,
> That milked the cow with the crumpled horn,
> That tossed the dog, That worried the cat, That killed the rat, That ate the malt
> That lay in the house that Jack built.
>
> (in Opie and Opie, 1951/1997: 229–32)

There seems a wish here to connect 'home', as physically built by a man, with the community which surrounds it. Everything 'out there', from the farmer's crop to a marital drama and then the pecking order of animals, leads back to this version of *home*, and the poem has a certain 'all's-right-with-the-world' quality about it. I suggest this is where 'home' can often work for men, as providing a sense for father and husband/male partner of his home acting as a 'solution' to what is 'out there', as well as within it.

So, women (predominantly) may experience their home as an *erosimus* version of *relational completion*, reflecting how the unspoken semiotic potential – as manifested in children, other family members and the living space – is set up (recognising that they have needs for completion and achievement in professional and other spheres too). Men, meanwhile, may experience their home as predominantly a symbol of their capacity to *produce, resource and solve the puzzle of* the connection between the longed for, *erosima*, nurturing feminine/mother 'at home', with the more prospective and transcending question of their place in the wider world. Where home does not fulfil this function well enough, there may be an experience of a split: a *thanima* fracture between these two spheres of need.

A fascinating example of a man's struggle to locate himself in relation to home is in the American hospital drama *House* (Shore and Jacobs, 2007–present). As his name implies, the lead character, and 'house' surgeon, seems to be identified with a version of male territory which leaves him struggling with an attempt to locate himself (find 'home') successfully and comfortably in the world. His personal life is in a state of flux and work supplies him with his sense of belonging. The huge popularity of this series seems a testament to our fascination with the uncertain 'place' of men. House is powerful but confused, ruthless but vulnerable, attractive but unpredictable – all dichotomies which refer to an ambivalent presence of 'man-in-the-world' and his relation to 'home'. In *The Sopranos* (Chase, 1999–2007) the 'main man', Tony Soprano, moves between the world of the gangster 'mafioso' and his family home via the therapy couch. This is his way of locating himself between spaces of brutal macho renumeration and empowerment, and the 'home' where his marriage and family reside. 'Home' is in inverted commas as it is not clear where he feels he most belongs.

While many men may wrestle with this tension, women have been confronted for a long time with a different one. Historically, many women have been downtrodden by an emasculating denial of access to a life 'out there' (let alone the overt levers of power in society). They may well have compensated for this by consolidating their identity in the home – through keeping it ticking over, doing almost all domestic tasks, and via mothering. So while female territory was experienced as a movement *inwards*, towards home, male territory took the opposite direction, *away* from home – a movement reflecting an awareness that this was a route into social and economic power for men, with all the expansive consequences, such as the aggrandising of the masculine and the oppressive implications for women arising from this. I suggest that the reality and symbol of the *road* is 'male territory' – the route away from home, towards whatever separate reality a man may envisage for himself.

In compensation for the oppression described above, female territory moved further back into 'home', where the unspoken centrality of love and care for family fell into the background of the grand patriarchal picture, like the giant's wife quietly and skilfully holding things together in the castle while her husband roamed the sky kingdom doing his monstrous work. In this respect *home* represents a more powerful symbolic – or maybe *semiotic* – identificatory space in female territory. Though for many women 'getting away' from home and onto the road (and for some men staying identified with home rather than embracing the road) is central to their life journey, I propose an underlying, gendered locational identification, which suggests itself as *road* and *home* as predominant symbolic spaces for male and female territory respectively – and I will come back to this.

In terms of female territory, what interests me is the question of what happened to the power invested in the home space – however unconsciously – by centuries of hard domestic *female* graft, familial love and care, and the semiotic, unspoken psychic female *materia*, woven into the fabric of it. This was complemented by the – at times wilful, at other times unconsciously patterned – turning away from this territory by men, reinforced by strong political, social and religious messages about their role 'out there' from religious, military and other institutions.

The accumulation of female territorial investment in home has left a truly powerful legacy, something male territory struggles to relate to at times, let alone compete with. It is something males are born into and have to find their way through, as an induction into *otherness*: first there is engagement with mother and then, as awareness of the home environment emerges, it is experienced principally as an extension of her. Later, father and other figures emerge from the 'background', but a layer of unconscious experiencing is established as a fundamental equation of 'home equals mother', on which other layers such as 'sometimes father equals home', get built.

So, within the 'frame' of home, something of deep, feminine, power is at work. Drawing on Jung and Kristeva, Adams (in Adams and Duncan, 2003: 60) captures the mystery of this well:

> How do we represent primary maternal communication, or – as she [Kristeva] puts it – maternal *jouissance*? It could be argued that Jung, by framing the "magical power of the female" as archetypal, has in fact anticipated the nature of Kristeva's pre-occupation with this irrepresentable element.

Here the legacy of the unexpressable, pre-oedipal semiotic becomes not merely an undefinable presence in the home (and elsewhere) but also a phantom-like presence for male territory, a foreign country which cannot be seen – or a strange cloud formation, the wisps of which slip through the fingers if one tries to grasp it.

A developmental origin of relationship to 'home' applies to girls, too, but I suggest – because of the relational bonding which is a hallmark of the pre-oedipal stage for the daughter–mother relationship – the experiential schedule of contact (first mother, then home as 'ground', then the emergence of other figures from the ground, in particular father) is experienced mainly as an induction into *sameness*. This is double-edged for the girl: she has entered a space where she can 'belong' for a lifetime, but on the other hand this may have an overly deterministic, even claustrophobic, quality, hallmarked by submissiveness.

This is not to say the masculine is absent from the child's experience of home; rather, it tends to be experienced nearer the surface of home life, like a top layer of paint readily available to view, because describing what men 'do' has been easier, at least until recently. This argument suggests itself on the basis of two premises – one is that man's role in the home is 'simpler' (less multi-tasked and emotionally layered), and the other refers to the relationship of gender to language. This argument, already described in Chapter 2, concerns the supposed 'absence' of the genuinely feminine in our patriarchally derived language system.

After Lacan, (1966/1977), Irigary's proposition to this effect complements Kristeva's idea of the *semiotic*; the genuine depths of experiencing by woman, mother, girl cannot be properly captured and expressed by the symbolic language which arises from the paternal and patriarchal 'male'. This is in apparent contrast to male experiencing, which can be seen and described in representative ways, symbolised through the spoken and written language we all use – in dream images in the individual psyche, which we 'interpret' within the conventions of this language, or as a collective symbol in the shared imagistic treasure trove of patriarchally driven culture.

This argument about how the symbolic language of the Father unfolds and makes itself available, to the exclusion of the language of the gendered other, is further supported if we really *do* know more or less how maleness and/or the masculine operates in the home. This presumably would be characterised as the father presence which has conventionally moved in and out of the space – providing for family, building and mending things, and offering loving guidance to his children – and as the speaker of the language of the outer world. Sons and brothers would then learn to emulate these functions.

I want to consider this alongside my proposition about home as predominantly 'female territory'. I argue that female and mother territory, in how it imprints on home, goes deeper than male/father – in the sense of its embedded presence as maintaining the living space and principal provider of nurturing. This is less easy to see as so much about it goes unspoken, and – conventionally at least – is taken for granted. However, this gives it tremendous power in the heterosexual parental home because, unspoken, it acts as the nexus for home life.

So while the male 'wallpaper' is on display and can be described in terms of where the father 'steps in' to family life, the female elements in the 'wall' behind cannot be seen so clearly, other than vaguely through the 'male wallpaper', and often in an over-simplified way. It is, though, the essential fabric of the building, the *semiotic* lifeblood of the *temenos*. This is the other dimension of the argument which suggests we cannot 'know' properly what being female is because the language we use to think, talk and write about it is the symbolic one, the language of the father, leaving our attempts to describe it doomed to fail.

This is broadly true – the *semiotic* by its nature is not representable in a conventional way by the language of the *Symbolic Order*. However, if Jung's premise (1928/1969) that by making something conscious we can engage with it (and *give it a name*) is applied, then perhaps the 'empty space' left by the centripetal movement of the energy dispersing from 'the eternal couple' archetype image at the centre of the 'home-shaped' frame may begin to reveal the unspoken language of the pre-oedipal, the maternal and the feminine.

This development may well be supported by the growing body of theoretical and clinical work focused on this very area. Our attempts to understand what may go on in the earliest phases of life, within the maternal *claustrum* (Meltzer, 1992), and what the experiences of being female, a mother, or a child of either gender within the sphere of the maternal may be like can help us find authentic forms of expression, without being warped by the predominantly paternal language we inherit.

There is also a question of whether the language of 'being a man', and a man's articulation of predominant masculinity, as well as his articulation of the feminine within him, is 'fully known'. This *cannot* be the case if we agree that the patriarchal arrangements regarding masculine and feminine representation, as well as the less well known (or even *unknown*) aspects around transcendence–immanence and perfecting–completing polarities, have yet to be properly seen. This has been a key theme of this book – what we do *not* know about being male and female, and how outdated versions we are currently renegotiating act as a *thanima–thanimus* block to being able to properly 'see'. In this respect men cannot have a full vocabulary within the 'Symbolic Order' to express what they experience.

So many times in my practice, and in my communications with men outside the consulting room, I have encountered aspects of 'male territory' which seem inexpressible, or at least difficult and awkward to express. An apparent given in the culture is that men have trouble expressing their feelings. While this is another glaring generalisation, made sometimes by women about men, or by men about themselves, and while many men and boys are becoming more conscious of their feelings and capacity to express them in our increasingly emotionally literate world, the grain of truth in this assertion remains.

The combination of factors here is formidable: the patriarchal socialisation of boys into acting out their part in the world (rather than nurturing self and other closer to home); 'brain-sex' limbic differences to the female brain (less connection across the cerebral hemispheres, and so to feeling and the language of it); *and* the setting up of *erosima* as counterpoint to, and pursuer of, mother/female lover. Together, these render the articulation of feeling by men less than straightforward.

'Being a man' can mean at times schooling yourself into self-expression. However, once you put the work in – by which I mean not forcing feeling out, but pulling back from the 'solve/perfect/defend' position to let your guard down and listen to self, *and*, if necessary, practising the expression of how you feel in-the-moment (being 'congruent', in humanistic therapeutic language [Tolan, 2003]) – then what has been wired into the brain, or made unavailable by the early split away from mother (in a relational sense) in early life can be countered, to a degree at least.

For some men this can be managed via the use of healthy *erosima* aggressive energy to convey a masculine liveliness, humour and potency while noticing the need to restrain the expression of anger where this might, in a manifestation of *thanima*, damage relations in an unhelpful way. For others, finding a gentle but assertive clarity of purpose and expression has the same value, i.e. sometimes having to check against how inhibiting *thanima* messages may block or break up connection with the capacity to congruently express feelings. Men fighting this tendency can seem to be in a struggle with *thanima* before our eyes, e.g. say in not getting hold of a feeling until sometime after a difficult exchange, wishing they had expressed it sooner, and returning to express their anger or disappointment later (when the other person may have almost forgotten about it).

This latter difficulty can equally apply to women, particularly where they have been given strong messages about 'keeping feelings to yourself' for the supposed good of the family/others. Blocks to expressing feelings may be something learned in the intimate space of relational bonding shared with mother, where a message about sacrificing personal need in order to fulfil their future role as mother is conveyed and thoroughly imbibed. So, a woman may have less trouble initially accessing a feeling of, say, protest, but the inner *thanimus* censor may come swiftly along to remind her forcefully not to say anything but to smile, or nod circumspectly, and be compliant.

These forms of negative *anima* or *animus* have, as I have argued, more than one root, but the psychosexual and brain-sex developmental influences appear to have been unconsciously reinforced through the patriarchal structures of gendered socialisation. Through the work we do on ourselves, in therapy and outside of it, on our own and with partners and others, we can counter (though not banish) the oppressive aspects of these influences. This is a big individuation task, but one could say that this is where our struggles with gender are a kind of *gift* as they help us become aware of where we find it hard to express ourselves, and simply 'be'; the presence of the opposite gender can constellate this difficulty and therefore confront us with our need to do something about it.

But, back to the main arena in which this struggle takes place – *home* and arguments between women and men. When one doesn't hear or see the other as they try to express their unhappiness or anger, there is not only a clash of languages going on in patriarchal terms – i.e. between the symbolic (overt male) and the semiotic (hidden female) – but also, I would argue, between two 'unspoken' languages. In the home, there is the non-symbolised expression of the disallowed feminine, curtailed by the sub-suming of the girl into the 'law of the Father', *and* there is the pre-verbal, deep but unexpressable, feeling of the little boy and his profound experience of struggle with the *erosima/thanima* bond with his mother and his erotic closeness to her *otherness*.

On the one hand there is the woman's (*thanimus*) oppressed and disallowed language of being, which reflects what she has felt unable to express in a contiguous way from early life up to the 'now' of adult womanhood, and the *erosimus* demands she overcomes in order to move further into life. On the other there is the man's sense of something being inexpressable, a legacy of when he was cradled in the arms of mother. There may be something risky and fearful associated with this, the risk in engaging in conflict with his current partner being related to the fear of losing her love – a *thanima* voice which speaks of the terror of being emotionally abandoned by his mother, putting *erosima* on the line.

So, there is little that is simple about the underlying influences at work in the home. One could say that where a male–female partnership, and the family it maintains, is functioning well, where the 'gender electrics' are flowing around the circuit smoothly enough, then it is the most obvious things which women and men in a partnership do differently which may most clearly represent their 'togetherness'. So, for example, when the woman is pregnant and needing to pace herself in relation to this, then the man may pick up the bulk of the care of the other children, or be more active in ensuring the house is running well. To an observer, there is an impression of *complementarity*.

However, when a partnership, or family, is under strain, the 'territorial differences' show up the cracks in relationships. This is where the *semiotics*, the unspoken language of maternity and womanhood, can come seeping out of the woodwork. Beneath the complaints made by a new mother that her partner is not pulling his weight with the night feeds, or does not seem to know what he is doing in managing the needs of the other children, there is a presence of something consciously unfamiliar for the man, and which the woman may struggle to put into words: the unarticulated, pre-oedipal language of the feminine, and of mother–child reverie. Here, the sense of being in 'other territory' becomes strong for the man.

This is one of the themes arising from this discussion on 'home'. I want to play further with the idea that whereas traditional male territory – 'the world out there' and in particular the workplace – has been significantly opened up to women, home largely remains more female than male territory within the dynamics of heterosexual relationships, despite a shift towards greater involvement by fathers and male partners in domestic and childcare activity.

This is a consequence of both the division of labour under patriarchy, which created a *matriarchal* stamp on the home through the oppressive loading of domestic responsibilities onto women, as well as a consonant disallowing of the language of pre-oedipal experiencing, which generally gets absorbed into the 'walls' of home and comes out into the living space at key times, such as when early mother–child stuff is re-constellated (childbirth etc.).

A combination of female territory recognising that historically home was often the only place a woman could securely find some source, however covert, of power and identity – as well as the unconsciousness of patriarchal male territory enabling this seat of female power to embed itself so strongly – has lead to imbalance in the home. This is absolutely *not* because men do not have power in the home – which would be a ridiculous assertion, not to mention a cause of offence against all those women and girls who have suffered at the hands of abusive or tyrannical men – but because female territorial power is less conscious and more deeply embedded in the 'fabric of home', and is unconsciously passed on from mother to daughter in ways it is *not* to sons.

However, the possibility of family and home becoming a genuinely shared relational space is becoming stronger as men become more conscious of self in relation to others, and take more responsibility in the domestic and childcare arrangements in the home, and women require more of them in this regard and relinquish assumptions about 'who should care' or 'manage the home'.

Predominantly female territory: Semiotic conditioner in the washing machine

If domestic tasks and organisation of the shared living space which is home for heterosexual couples – how it looks, is furnished, and is kept clean and tidy, and what routines are established for managing this – tends to be the preserve of female more than male territory, then where does this leave relationships between men and women? Why does it seem that the domestic space remains such a source of discord, dissatisfaction and divorce?

I am going to start from a basic set of assertions:

1   Men have been pushed by feminism into relinquishing their exclusive hold on previously dominant patriarchal territory, i.e. formal positions of authority in the home and the workplace, as well as a deal of freedom to roam in the local and wider communities rather than attend to home.

2   Men have rightly had demands made on them (as well as making them on themselves) to become more involved in family and domestic life.

3   Women had their needs for personal, professional and creative expression oppressed to varying degrees over the years of patriarchal domination, and were expected to submit themselves to performing largely domestic roles.

4   Now women have gained a significant but uneven and incomplete degree of freedom and opportunity in the workplace as well as equality in the home (usually).

5   Women in heterosexual relationships *predominantly* continue to hold the key to the running of a household and the way a home environment is organised and looks.

6   Men's remaining power 'out there' in the world has a shaky, surface feel to it, while women's burgeoning power is more deeply rooted, based more firmly on 'home' ground.

There are crude, generalised, assertions which must be taken with a pinch of salt as well as a reflexive check on how *you* as a male or a female reader feel about them. Nonetheless, the question here is whether the apparent difficulty some men may still have with rolling up their sleeves and scrubbing the bath one more time, or opening their arms for the twentieth time in a day to scoop up their young child, is because men are still growing up socialised into being 'men who do not have to do' domestically, *or* whether there is something happening in *female* territory which is blocking the establishment of a secure base for male territory in the home.

I do not *know* the answer to this question, but on the basis of many conversations and clinical experiences with men in heterosexual relationships, it does feel at the least to be a relevant question to ask. My sense is that some men in long-term relationships find themselves referring back to wife/partner as the anchor of home life but often seem puzzled as to why this should automatically be so.

One man I worked with clinically saw his wife as 'having the strength to hold the household together – and the power to chuck me out.' His take on domestic politics was coloured by his own stuff, of course – a mother complex based on his experiences as a child and a rather timid, introverted fear of conflict – but all the same he was describing an intuition about where the power can lie in the home that I have heard a number of times from men, as if some kind of *thanima* fear of the indefinable semiotic influence of the feminine in his home was the powerbroker in the domestic space. I do not think it is an adequate response to suggest that this reflects more of a 'masculine' deficit in a man than anything tricky he may be intuiting about the semiotic female territory in the home; this would imply that somehow the 'male symbolic' can strong-arm its way psychologically to put the 'female semiotic' in its place. It surely is not a question of which is 'bigger and stronger', but which may have the *deeper*, more embedded authority within the base of home.

The 'symbolic' (male) may be fearful of the 'semiotic' (female) in the home for all sorts of archetypal and developmental reasons relating to mother, but this situation is not helped where men remain the ones who only 'come in and out' of domestic duty. Both men and women have a responsibility to address this problem. Men need to be proactive (and there is evidence they are steadily becoming more so) in taking on domestic duties as *erosima* tasks, moving themselves into the life of home more fully. Women may need to be less predominantly territorial about domestic responsibilities, and about specific areas of the home which they may have been brought up by their mother to regard as 'theirs' – e.g. the kitchen – and about assuming they hold the key role in defining how rooms and spaces 'look'.

The female tendency, based on the 'brain-sex' literature (Moir and Jessel, 1991), to automatically notice what is 'right' or 'wrong' in the *immanent* spaces around them and revisit the details – and the contrariwise predominant tendency in men to focus elsewhere and accept lower standards (whatever this means) – appears to set up potential conflicts which may or may not be familiar to readers.

Nonetheless, here is an opportunity to allow the male symbolic to have its say alongside the female semiotic. James Park (1995: 5) observed: 'All boys confront the same problem: how to feel strong in the presence of an all-powerful and demanding mother.' In the adult, domestic sphere some men can be caught full-on with a lingering feeling that their partner is always demanding things of him – and the most worked-through mother complex in even the most 'sorted', individuated man can still constellate in feeling he is 'on the spot', having to prove he can hold his own in embedded female territory, rather than being relaxed and confident.

In this respect, this is an area, in the collective sense, where there is work for women to do as well as men. Men were not conscious of the outdated and oppressive way they clung to the levers of patriarchal power in wider society. *They did not need to be aware of it as on the whole they benefited from this arrangement.* Likewise, perhaps there is some way to go before women become fully conscious of how much power they hold in the home – having predominantly been passed the self-appointed power of mother to manage home and family, sometimes letting their male partner into their territory only so far as they choose.

Angela Phillips got hold of this problem within the wider context of how 'the trouble with boys' can get replicated in fractured fathering patterns, when she wrote: 'The hard thing for both men and women to cope with is the realization that both sides need to give something up in order to make something new' (Phillips, 1993: 254). While factoring in how some women may have legitimate concerns about sharing parenting with men who have been unreliable or even brutal, she goes on to assert that: 'If men were as closely connected to their children as women are, far fewer boys would grow up without a real sense of what it means to be a whole human being' (ibid.). This is in part a plea, from a woman *to* women, to help facilitate the opening up of the longstanding female territory of *home*.

Saying we want someone to take more of the load in our 'territory' is one thing; genuinely giving them the space to do so is another. This is not to say that this is an ubiquitous phenomenon by any means – there are many couples whose territorial demarcations at home are usually flexible, inter-changeable and supportive. I am describing here the workings of a post-modern (in my 'gendered–historical' terminology) male–female relationship. I would still argue, though, that the ancient and modern versions of territorial workings around and in 'home' will show through in ways which can be either helpful (e.g. during pregnancy) or unhelpful (e.g. when a rigid division of roles re-constellates when either a woman or a man has been working away from home, creating a battle over 'territory' on that person's return).

A man told me how his girlfriend, when they were setting up home, had told him the 'correct order' in which his clothes should be stored in a chest of drawers – underwear in the top drawer, T-shirts and tops in the middle and 'bottoms' (trousers etc.) in the lower drawer. This is the way her mother had told her, so this was the way it 'is'. He felt a mix of bemuse-ment and irritation at this – the woman assumes this is right and that her male partner will accept this. This seems an example of where home 'rules' are defined by handed-down 'laws' of female territory, and by references to male territory as not as *au fait* with them (e.g. the way men's supposed 'difficulty' in finding something in the fridge or a drawer can get pejora-tively characterised as 'man looking'). This eerily echoes patriarchal presumptions about there being a 'right way' of ordering politics, society and gender relations, away from home as well as in it, and in which women supposedly were naturally 'inferior' in their contribution.

Another example of what seems a peculiar state of affairs between female and male territory in the home is portrayed in a humorous way by Lucy Mangan (2009). She describes the instructions she gives to her partner before leaving him for a few days. She takes him around the house, reminding him there is a flush on the toilet, and confesses to the reader she has hidden all the clean towels so he will not wastefully use a new one each day. He appears to be wholly ignorant – or maybe wilfully avoidant – of basic facts about the running of the home. She feels she needs to point out: 'This is the kitchen. There's bread in the bread bin – that's the bread bin – milk in the fridge – that's the fridge' (ibid.), and so on, like it's a foreign country to the man.

Although this is a funny caricature, it suggests that some heterosexual relationships, or at least some women's expectations of them, are based on the premise that their male partners are simply so unattuned to established 'female territory' in the home that they cannot or will not manage the most basic domestic tasks. I have had a number of experiences of hearing women describing their sense of what men know about, or do, in the home in this way. While some men may be this unrelated to – or lazy and presumptive about – domestic responsibilities, it raises a question about why they are so cut off from the reality of the environment they are in. Here, socialisation into such a state *must* relate to what women – mothers and partners – do and have done at least as much as to the still pervasive patriarchal influence on the upbringings of boys and young men. I suggest that there may be a component of a *thanimus* investment in defending female territory, and even, on occasion, satisfaction or pleasure in ridiculing the 'incompetence' and avoidance of domestic responsibility by the man.

An example of this appears in a television advertisement for an oven cleaner in which a man's ignorance and incompetence about domestic tasks is ridiculed with the strapline: 'so easy even a man can clean it' and by images of a man struggling to clean an oven. A total of 673 complaints were made against this advertisement on the basis of sex discrimination but these were not upheld by the United Kingdom Advertising Standards Agency (2009).

I notice in myself a retreat into male territory in response to this – feelings of discomfort and annoyance at the patronising (it seems to me) characterisation of the man as incompetent and ignorant about cleaning an oven, something a woman is supposedly thoroughly *au fait* with. This may be a 'humorous' jibe about a man's lack of domestic *nous*, but I detect something aggressive here, too – perhaps a resentment about how much women have to do around the house generally?

However, this example reflects what Clare (2001) suggests is a curious imbalance in how it seems to be 'okay' within our culture to ridicule men in ways women are not. Lovable but dumb fathers – like Homer in *The Simpsons* (Groening, 1989–present) – are an example. The advert above also seems to suggest a link between the *semiotic* and the power of *thanimus* responses to close down the possibility of shifting the territorial status quo in how domestic tasks are shared out in the heterosexual home context. Taking the washing machine as another symbol of *female* territory, meta- phorically, the woman feels the invisible presence of the *semiotic* con- ditioner which whirls around inside it with the clothes, water and washing liquid. Unconsciously, I suggest, this influences how she responds to the man's lack of awareness and may mean he is more likely to feel emasculated, provoking a *thanima* reaction, such as withdrawal and/or hostility.

Likewise, I want to stress that men are as capable of being dogmatic about how things in a home 'should be', and of being critical of their partner, as women might be. A man may 'see' solutions to problems around living space and how it is organised which in a rigid *thanima* way he expects his partner to fall into line with. Men can struggle to dis-identify from this where they have learned, or adopted, a patriarchal notion of the home they share as *really* theirs (a negative *'House that Jack built'*). However, the *predominant* sense of 'ownership' of how the shared living space is *organised* and *looks* tends to lie in female territory, which has been primed by a woman's maternal relationship, and which then gets replicated in how living spaces and routines 'should' be organised.

As I have illustrated, at its less helpful this might include a learned presumption that men will be incompetent and/or careless about domestic activity. Where this occurs, I suggest it is a version of *thanimus* which places a less than fully conscious kind of judgement on the man, and may be an area where there is scope for some women to look at their assumptions about home, men and the shared domestic space. I notice my anxiety about generalising on this, and on 'what women may think or feel', but none-theless this feels important for freeing up the domestic arena for the symbolic and semiotic to intermingle healthily.

Childbirth, and mother and father

While there is a consonant point to be made in terms of how parenting is shared, especially in the earliest stages of an infant's life, it is important to start this section with a recognition of how often it is men – or rather the figure of *father* – who can be the problem in terms of being able to offer a child a stable home with both parents being available. I am not asserting that the latter is always the best equation – there have been long-running debates on the impact on children of having one parent as their main carer and much clearly depends on the individuals and the context. However, the lack of father for son *or* daughter is a loss – and where the two-parent partnership breaks down, it is predominantly the father who the children lose.

Men who are not ready to be fathers, or who struggle with the domestic grind, or who treat their partners in a way which implies it is *mother* who should do all the parenting – there are many ways for a father to blow his chance to be 'a real Dad'. If he does, and because home/family is still more predominantly 'female territory', it can be very hard for an 'errant' father to find his way back into home – as he has broken the unspoken condition which kept him there: to be 'the good father and partner'.

The unreadiness to be a Dad has been relatively unexplored, perhaps because there can be an overtone of moral weakness or 'unmanliness' about any man who is perceived as having 'let down' his partner or children. More recently, the phenomenon of 'unready fathers' has begun to open up via 'confessional' literature which highlights how challenging the experience of becoming a father can be for some men. In his book describing his experience of becoming a father, Michael Lewis writes of

> this persistent and disturbing gap between what I was meant to feel and what I actually felt. I expected to feel overcome with joy, while instead I often felt only puzzled. I was expected to feel worried when I often felt indifferent. I was expected to feel fascinated when I actually felt bored.
>
> (Lewis, 2009: 14)

He also reported feelings of hate for his interminably crying child, who took up constant attention and effort for seemingly no reward.

As there is no definitive 'solution' available for the presence of an inevitably demanding infant, this can be experienced as a huge block to attaining future goals, and something may well fracture in a man's capacity to stay with the business of raising a child. Lewis goes on to interpret this experience in a wider socio-political context. He argues that men have been 'fleeced . . . [into becoming] . . . really just a second-string mother' (ibid.: 43–4). However, the profound malaise – a kind of *male* postnatal depression – transformed slowly into equally profound, and adoring, love for his daughter.

A developmental explanation for this kind of reaction by a father to the birth of his child (and/or his partner's pregnancy) could relate to how utterly overwhelming a little boy might experience the beginning of his own life to be, including how overwhelmed by mother's presence he may have felt; or it could be to do with how unavailable or disconnected they may have experienced *their* father as being while they grew up. There is also the teleological explanation I have alluded to – a man feeling truncated from his future (so important to 'male territory') by the 'in-your-face' *immanence* of sleepless nights and wet nappies.

However we may speculate about influences or 'causes', the consequences as described by Lewis are real enough and – however temporarily – the 'completion' for a woman in having a child can sometimes be experienced by the new father as a threat to his capacity to solve, transcend and connect with his own present and future. This area would benefit from extensive research, as it suggests that complexes arising after childbirth, including 'sensing' a barrier to their sense of future self, can set up a reactive pattern in new fathers which may cloud the potential of their relationship with the mother, and the child.

This may be a difficult area to open up because it suggests a father who is not only non-heroic in his difficulty in supplying stability and self-sacrifice, but a *rejecting* father – and this shatters the idealised version of 'father' we may all carry at an archetypal level. Nevertheless, there is a reality to the presence of the 'unready father' or the 'depressed new father' and we owe it to ourselves and our children to get a fuller understanding of what happens in this shady area of male territory, so as to identify what interventions might address the needs of all affected by this malaise.

Feelings of being trapped or even emasculated by assuming the role of father do seem to assail some men to varying degrees. So, how they are helped to prepare for fatherhood – including how they make choices about when to become fathers (admittedly, not an exact science) – and then how they deal with the *immanent* presence of their new son or daughter, could make all the difference to whether they stay in the home and are able to genuinely support their partner.

On occasion this problem can turn the *container* of home into a *cage*, and the unspoken semiotics of the pre-oedipal maternal *jouissance* embedded in the fabric of home promotes a feeling of a territorial *fait accompli*. This sad, difficult equation, where *thanima* infects what could be a joyful and invigorating life experience by exposing a man in his unconsciousness to a more smothering version of home and family, could be countered by a more conscious dialogue within our culture about how childbirth can affect men as well as women. This would make the preparation for reproduction less weighted towards *female* territory, and locate it more fully in the shared space between male and female spheres.

There are clear indications that men are becoming more committed and enthusiastic about this happening. For example, between 1975 and 1997 British fathers' care of infants and young children rose from fifteen minutes to two hours (i.e. 800 per cent) on the average working day (Fisher, McCulloch and Gershuny, 1999) and it seems the majority of women, consciously at least, want this, too (ONS, 2005). This broadly supports the view from research that children with heavily involved fathers tend towards fewer behaviour difficulties, greater levels of empathy and capacity for friendship and higher self-esteem (Bartlett, 2000). The embedded mysteries of maternal pre-oedipal semiotics may be what sometimes creates *thanima/thanimus* blocks to fathers being more involved in a child's early life. Without trying to overturn the archetypal force of a mother's elemental bond with her child, it should still be possible to loosen the powerful predominance of mother over father in influencing the first stages of a child's life, offering her or him the riches of both in this most formative period of life.

The problematic male diamond: Disembodiment, violence, abuse and learning difficulty

I want to sketch an unhappy *thanima* diamond which characterises more difficult aspects of male territory and reflects the predominant aspects of male experiencing and activity itemised above. This is set out next to an *erosima*, life-enhancing version of the 'male diamond' below. It is worth noting the *erosima* or *thanima* versions of 'road' in each of these. Where 'road' gets problematic is in how it can generate a *thanima* locational split in the male psyche ('do I belong at home or on the road?'), in a painfully unresolvable way – like being torn unbearably between mother and father (re-constellated by the present partnership and family) – rather than there being an ease of movement between 'home and away'.

Another dimension of this *thanima* split can be a (largely unconscious) attempt to achieve a satisfactory relationship to 'home' through a senti-mental romanticism (referring back to an early *erosima* union with mother, before it was ruptured) which can be shattered without too much difficulty by the usual strife which goes with partnerships. Then the man, psychologically or literally, retreats to the 'road'. The figure below, as with the following female version (see p. 222), shows the 'empty space' in the diamond where symbolic and semiotic energies intermingle and wrestle with each other.

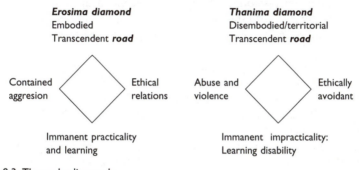

Erosima diamond
Embodied
Transcendent **road**

Contained aggresion

Ethical relations

Immanent practicality and learning

Thanima diamond
Disembodied/territorial
Transcendent **road**

Abuse and violence

Ethically avoidant

Immanent impracticality:
Learning disability

Figure 8.3 The male diamonds

At the apex of men's *thanima* diamond ('up in the sky') is a tendency to be less *embodied* than their female counterparts. Here, I am thinking of the well documented lesser consciousness found in male territory about health and illness – in particular a traditional unwillingness to go to the doctor if unusually troubling symptoms arise, or indeed in just monitoring overall health. Studies suggest, for example, that while women between sixteen and forty-four average five visits to their GP a year, the average for men in the same age range is three visits a year (ONS, 2005).

Life expectancy figures show a consistent gender divide, with women on average having a distinctly longer life span than men – on average in developed countries men die seven years younger than women (Stanistreet, Bambra and Scott-Samuel, 2005) – and although this has physiological as well as psychosocial roots to it, physical health is not always prioritised. This is not to downplay the ways in which women can also be highly vulnerable to serious risks to their health which are specific to them – such as breast and cervical cancers. I am focusing more here on a tendency for one gender (males) to overlook potentially serious health problems.

Some of this distinction seems to be related to social influence. Research by Alan White (2008) demonstrates that men predominantly are not as tuned in to 'having their bits prodded' in the same way women may be, through for example cervical smears. It is possible that the way women's health problems may predominantly get identified and therefore caught earlier relates back to the greater rootedness of the female/semiotic in the underlying patterns of family life than the male/symbolic. The male symbolic dislocation between identification with *home* and *road* is reflected in a dichotomy between identifying 'with my body' as against the workings *of* it; i.e. what it can do (as a means to an end).

If a man's body appears to not be working properly in some way (too many visits to the toilet, say, or intermittent chest pains) then a man may not regard this as relevant information as long as he can still do the physical and mental activities he has always done to achieve, solve or defend what matters to him. The greater preponderance of testosterone in the 'brain-sex' dimension of his being may feed this, so a tendency to drive himself towards a goal or solution can override the more worrying information he is receiving from his body.

This apparent tendency in male territory to not take care of one's physical well-being as much as in female territory has been made more conscious in recent years. The avid attention to fitness in some men, or to preserving a 'look' (e.g. 'metrosexuals'), is testament to the shifts in body awareness in men. However, it remains an embedded problem of the transcending quality of male territory that men may take risks with what is close to home in order to grasp what they feel driven to have or prove away from it.

The left-hand median point of this problematic male diamond is shaded in darkness by male *violence* and *abuse*. In terms of violence, the spectre of a disembodied loss of control, which feeds and reflects an apparent inability or unwillingness to constrain behaviour, can lead some men into a predominantly greater tendency to act violently. Out of a total of 734 homicides in the United Kingdom during 2006–7, 547 were down to males and 187 to females – and 44 per cent of women killed were killed by current or ex-partners (male) compared with 5 per cent of men killed by women partners (Home Office, 2008).

These figures baldly illustrate the 'problem of home' in gender relations. The container of the male–female relationship – whether a symbolic sense of being at 'home' in the relationship, or the actual physical home in which dramas and routines get played out – cannot always prevent acts of awful violence and destructiveness from happening, predominantly by some men against their female partners. Here the problem of a man's relationship to feeling and body, as against his ethical and human responsibility towards the safety and well-being of those around him, can lead to a somatisation of his anger, which explodes towards the gendered other. Whatever degree of disembodied unrelatedness is present, or apparent 'brain-sex' preponderance towards snapping in reaction to feeling is provoked, cannot begin to justify these deadly male expressions of rage.

When the violent gender electrics of the thunderclouds descend on a home, the outcome of the storm cannot be predicted. But if there is enough consciousness of this danger, and sufficient *erosima* presence of the sustaining need for intimacy and relationship, those men who linger in the far reaches of potentially violent male territory can pull back and find other ways to express their anger. Brownhill *et al.* (2005) suggest a link between this and the tendency to avoid looking at health problems discussed above.

They propose an 'upward trajectory of the masculine enactment of emotional distress', which goes from initial inner avoiding and numbing, through attempts to escape the distress, then turning internalised aggression outwards. Once this stage is reached anything can happen, from self-harm and suicide to violent acts against others, including their partners and children. This is a most useful way of thinking about male violence as it suggests its roots lie in a *thanima* tendency to split oneself away from distress and eventually find oneself throwing it outwards aggressively in what is certainly an unrelated way (as compared with the predominantly relational female strategies for dealing with distress).

So, without meaning to oversimplify what is another complex area of gendered expression, it does seem as if *thanima* internalisation – avoidance and deadening of difficult feelings – can act as the source of apparently contrary explosions of rage and violence against self or others. There is clearly scope for working with such influences and experiencing in men, as many professionals do to such good effect.

Projects such as STOP – Start Treating Others Positively – based in Leeds, aim to reduce abusive behaviour in the home and enable men to notice potentially destructive patterns before they create tragic consequences (Steen, 2008). These approaches, centred on preventing a cycle of domestic abuse from becoming established, illustrate the need for male territory to continue to become more reflexive about what unpleasant and dangerous behaviours and attitudes can emanate from it. This also applies to child sexual abuse – and in the language fostered in this book, this problem could be characterised as a manifestation of a *thanima* tendency to turn the potentially healthy erotic into an abusive tool for gratification. This involves thoroughly transgressing the boundaries around the relational bond with a child, instead of taking the opportunity to experience the *erosima* joys (and challenges) of the potential inherent in this bond. There is a parallel with the patterns men may get into with violence in so far as, referring to Brownhill *et al.*'s schema, inner avoiding and numbing provides a *thanima* strategy for ignoring the relational consequences of their actions (such as the deep psychological scarring of the child they sexually abuse). While one can speculate as to what developmental influences may make this more possible – such as faulty *erosima* patterns in the early relationship to mother (and father) – there does seem to be more capacity in men to be able to disconnect from a proper consideration of the consequences of their actions in the moment of deciding to act abusively.

From a 'brain-sex' point of view this *may* link to the way the male brain appears less 'joined-up' in its capacity to draw on relational, intellectual and overtly physiological (e.g. sexual) functions, but this does not satisfactorily explain the choices abusing men make. Women abuse, too, and in both cases there is an array of possible factors at work. The principle of working with self-awareness about potentially becoming abusive applies, again, in the face of *thanima* or *thanimus* 'not seeing'.

The right-hand median point of the diamond is surrounded by a thin mist through which the potentially grounded personal and ethical qualities of male territory cannot be seen properly and are instead distorted by the wisps of cloud lying in front of them. This is where tendencies in male territory to avoid responsibility, especially in relation to children, partnership and home, get generated. This kind of avoidance of ethical responsibility is implied by Noddings (2003: Ch. 1) as a reflection of how 'caring' has broadly come to be seen as a female domain and is historically an undeniable feature of how some men have responded to becoming partners and fathers. When one looks at the *Beanstalk* story as a tale of a young man (Jack) breaking into another's (the giant's) territory, stealing his valuables and then killing him, one can see why men and ethics do not always make good bedfellows. Jack's actions are all justified by the crime committed against his father – a *justified* or *unjustified* act of vengeance?

This problem could be described as a concomitant of patriarchal ways of thinking about the role of men – they are not, in this frame of reference, 'supposed' to care other than in a paternalistic way, where providing for the family and home acts as an apparently equivalent (at least) contribution to the family. In other words, the man shows a kind of care through *not* being there – no wonder things have got so muddled for men in relation to their presence and role in the home. The lazy thinking associated with this model contributes to the impression of male territory as a place which is more about opting 'out' than 'in'.

Another way in which this ethical 'lack' presents itself lies outside the home but harks back to a search for territorial meaning which one might associate more with 'ancient' or early 'modern' ways of operating as a man. I am thinking here of the more tribal behaviour which can hallmark gang cultures, particularly in the large cities of the western world. While these may have a function of providing a sense of identity and protective belonging, they can also generate antisocial behaviour and even murderous violence, where a sense of ethical responsibility for the impact of these behaviours gets lost.

Young women can also get caught up in such activity alongside young men, but these behaviours do seem to belong predominantly in male territory. Another version of this, in some western European countries in particular, is football hooliganism. In the UK, through systematic policing strategies as well as the power of peer pressure, this has declined significantly in recent years, but there is still the odd outburst of frightening violent and 'tribal' behaviour between opposing supporters in and around a match. After one such outburst, Terence Blacker (2009) wrote of the 'joyful' look on the faces of the men engaged in the fighting, racist chanting and territorial battles. Here, men are literally 'getting off' on being part of a male battle for territory which 'helps transcend the dullness of their lives' (ibid.).

Violence provides an experience of the 'male transcendent'. It does this with a loss of mindfulness about the consequences for self and others. This seems to reflect a dark side of male territory which is constellated by a capacity to 'switch off' ethical responsibility for consequences while carrying out illegal, violent or abusive acts. Financial scams, war crimes and a whole range of abusive behaviours, from trafficking women for prostitution through to paedophilia, get carried out because of this capacity, which may have more of a 'brain-sex' root in male behaviour, linked to the less well connected sites of neurological influence in the male brain. This does not, as with other behaviours described, explain away or justify actions or attitudes which are allowed to 'float free' from their ethical implications. Personal responsibility, as a principle reinforced by healthy social influence, is missing in these situations. Like Jack in versions of the *Beanstalk* story where his indolent and spoilt behaviour is described as bringing him and his mother to the verge of rack and ruin, these men need to be confronted with the implications of allowing drives for material wealth, sexual gratification or violent territorial triumphalism to supercede their ethical awareness, and they need to make reparation for this.

Located at the base of this unhealthy male diamond are learning difficulties, a manifestation of male vulnerability, impracticality and psychological dependency. As mentioned, there is a general predominance of around 2:1 between males as compared with females with learning difficulties – and here I include the full range of learning difficulty, from dyslexia and dyspraxia, through severe and profound and multiple learning difficulties, to various conditions on the autistic spectrum, including Aspergers syndrome.

The possibilities around why this male predominance exists are many, ranging from the apparent fragility of the 'Y' chromosome through to whether some presentations of learning difficulties in males are influenced by the ways in which boys may develop their capacity to articulate understanding and feelings compared with girls. This, for example, may create blocks for them in facing, or telling others about, what they are struggling with. It is also valuable to consider the affective vulnerability of infant boys to the vagaries of the *erosima–thanima* conflict around attachment to mother, and whether where *erosima* loses out dramatically in this struggle, cognitive and communicative capacities in the nascent male brain's formation may be impacted upon.

It is beyond the scope of this book to explore these areas in detail, but from the overarching archetypal–historical perspective developed, the placing of learning difficulties at the base of the 'problematic' male diamond throws into relief the place of 'failure' in the male psyche. Learning difficulties provide a tough but, I believe, helpful counterweight to the problem of transcendence for the male psyche, keeping male territory 'on the ground' as it struggles to realise that some problems or challenges simply are not solvable. All learning difficulties, in my experience, can be worked with and ameliorated to some degree; but usually they remain in some form, whatever heroic efforts are made to 'overcome' them. This brings male territory face to face with something more immanent, and therefore helpful in a compensatory way to the predominant male tendency to try to 'transcend' or 'solve' at all costs.

The female unhealthy diamond: Home territory, (s)mothering, perfectionism and abuse

Female territory also has its unhealthier aspects. If one thinks in terms of a juxtaposed female diamond set alongside the male version, it may well have too much feminine–immanent energy at its base in the same way the male one has too much masculine–transcendent energy at its apex. This can generate assumptions about how 'home' should be, where the woman may presume to 'know best' when it comes to the routines of family and the organisation of the living space. Although this may well have deep archetypal, historical and developmental roots, where it operates in rigidly *thanimus* ways, it circumscribes what can be shared in terms of ownership with male partners regarding home and family. As with the 'male' diamonds, semiotic and symbolic energy wrestle and intermingle in the 'empty space' in the middle.

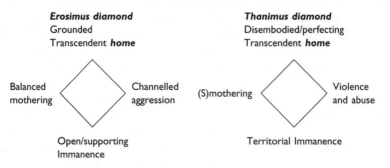

Figure 8.4 The female diamonds

At the apex of the diamond I propose that a split relation to parents, particularly to father, can result in a striving for perfection which could be an inherent part of an eating disorder, for example, with its striving for a 'perfect' body shape and weight (Woodman, 1982). This is a version of female transcendence where the feminine takes the form of *puella* reaching for the skies, to try to transcend the breakdown of immanent potential for relational completeness. The faulty relation to father implies this 'reaching up' carries an identification with him in order to recover a fuller link to him; the unrelated perfecting tendency in female territory meets the disembodied, 'unconscious-of-health-problems' found in the male 'sky'. This problem can then become a giant threatening to destroy the lives of people on the ground. On the left-hand side of the unhealthy female diamond is a version of *thanimus* which can manifest itself in a kind of mothering which may become smothering, and this can impact on the gendered other. It relates to energies 'floating up' from the preponderance of semiotic, pre-oedipal feminine energy, which is found at the base of the diamond and which may sometimes become smothering or deadening in close relationships with partners or children.

My experiences in the overwhelmingly female environments of special schools, where the children and young people were often very needy, sometimes brought this to life. Although most of the time a balance was struck between protective care and educational challenge, there was at times a sense of a collective female need to 'mother' taking precedence, with children who sometimes could not feed, dress or toilet themselves. Though a measure of maternal function was needed here, it sometimes felt as if *thanimus* constrained the individuating *erosima/erosimus* energies available to both male *and* female pupils.

The right-hand side of the diamond refers to themes of violence and abuse. Here, though less pronounced than in male territory, the potential for girls and women to be violent or abusive remains nevertheless. There is evidence to suggest this may be becoming more prevalent as females become less inhibited by patriarchal injunctions to be good, submissive partners to men (Kirsta, 1994: Ch. 3). Women can hurt, kill and sexually abuse others but, referring to the developing 'brain-sex' research suggesting the female brain may be more fully 'wired' to stay 'in relation' to the other whom they may have some murderous or abusive instincts towards, they seem less likely to split off their human and ethical connection to them.

There is also a link to the developmental schema offered. Mother and daughter remake home – a *temenos* contract between them – which means female territory becomes more oriented towards completing the familial/home nexus, and *keeping* it complete. So, the draw a woman may have towards, say, sexually abusing her child, would be countered by a *semiotic* pool of instincts and feelings subtly influencing her not to disrupt the relational situation in such a profoundly damaging way. However, recent cases of abuse by female nursery workers indicate some women still grossly misuse their power under the cloak of 'caring' (*Daily Mirror*, 2009).

The base of the diamond, which points directly away from the sky and into the earth, is the fundamentally *immanent* influence from the pre-oedipal feminine alluded to – or rather the potentially problematic aspects of this. My metaphor of a 'semiotic conditioner' in the washing machine illustrated how the unspoken maternal–feminine is just 'there' in the bubbly liquid which washes the 'clothes' of our relationships (i.e., how we present ourselves to, and see, each other). The *semiotic* is likewise 'always there' in other established domestic areas, like the oven cleaner in the cooker, or the air freshener in the toilet.

To restate, this line of thinking is *not* saying men never put bleach down the toilet or iron their clothes – they do, and increasingly men in hetero-sexual relationships in the west *are* taking a fuller part in domestic routines such as cleaning (*USA Today*, 2002) – although there is some way to go before it can be confidently asserted that men are pulling their weight in the domestic sphere in the great majority of households in the UK. Women are still doing twice as much housework as men (ONS, 2002).

While women may not overtly 'ban' men from domestic tasks, men have complained to me of feeling they are not genuinely included in areas of domestic life. One sometimes has to take these grumbles with a pinch of salt, but behind bemused comments such as 'the kitchen is her inner sanctum', men may sometimes be excluded or marginalised from embedded female territory handed from mother to daughter. This seems to sometimes involve an unspoken assumption that men are not 'capable' of performing some tasks. This can get reinforced by the initially cack-handed and uncertain way men, who were not 'inducted' into female territory as their partner was, may approach them. Or a man may feel he has only been let in 'so far' to female territory and it is in the woman's gift to decide what he does in it.

The oven cleaner advert referred to reasserts the boundaries of this territory. It also has a hint of mother–son rather than partner–partner interaction. The man is regarded more as a 'boy', who is not grown up enough to cope with adult tasks. Other examples of this phenomenon are publications on 'training your husband' (e.g. McCann, 2008) or articles (e.g. Midgeley, 2006) which 'humorously' ridicule men's reliability, domestic capacity and maturity. These kinds of 'lighthearted' disparagements of what a man is capable of in domestic and other spheres are only likely to activate *thanima* responses in men. While some will shrug it off as 'gender wars' ribaldry, others who may have had a less satisfactory installation of *erosima* in the bonding with mother may experience this as reconstellating earlier *thanima* humiliations, and feel provoked into hostility or withdrawal.

I wonder whether Jung himself experienced any of these feelings in relation to his home life. Though he seemed to revel in being a *paterfamilias*, he often withdrew to his study in Kussnacht or his Bollingen retreat on Lake

Zurich, and the tone of his writing on negative *animus* conveys more than a hint of *thanima* discomfort about his place in domestic life. Jung's intuitions, which he expressed so crudely and pejoratively, may have contained a germ of truth about this 'home-based' power of the feminine/semiotic/pre-oedipal, which *sometimes* lapses into 'irrationally', disparaging a man's capacity in relation to it. While the leaps of flawed logic which took him into stereotyping women as 'irrational/quick to judge/unable to look beyond family or home, hang in the male 'air' as horrible misapprehensions, the underlying sense in a man of how it feels to be on the receiving end of a female defence of her domestic 'territory' might relate to Jung's intuitions in ways *not* so easily discounted.

This possible territoriality about the home space may include the reproducing, nurturing, 'preserve' of pregnancy and infancy, feeding the difficulties some men have with early fatherhood. Thankfully the days when the mother-in-law (a figure who as the butt of a lot of inappropriate jokes nevertheless may carry a kind of *thanima* quality for some men) might become more of a partner to the mother during pregnancy and childbirth than her male spouse seem to have faded.

However, men may still feel 'left out' – not just because of the obvious factor of a new, ubiquitous presence in the home who is getting the bulk of his lover's attention. In the run up to the birth, for example, there can be a sense that this is 'female territory' which 'she' has been long prepared for while he has to learn about it, and adapt to it. When this process of learning is more of a shared journey these difficulties do not have to intrude particularly – but where there is a *thanimus–thanima* 'not seeing' between the man and the woman, something more problematic can develop. Here, the *immanence* of the 'home space' of the mother–daughter dyad may turn the base of the diamond more sharply into the ground, away from the view, or purchase, of the man.

Gendered territories – antagonistic or therapeutic?

The *thanima* and *thanimus* diamonds portray the malaises which can afflict being a man or a woman, and how each suffers these vagaries in the other. These shadowy aspects of gender can – as in Jung's formula for working with *shadow* – help us address these malaises, e.g. by noticing and withdrawing what gets projected onto the gendered other. Male–female relationships can act as a kind of therapeutic space in which one reflects back (in however weary or angry a way) the experiencing of the impact of a particular presentation of the other's *thanima* or *thanimus* attitudes or behaviours. By placing each of the two *thanatos*-infused 'diamonds' against the *eros* versions of the other gender, there are some equations within the male–female dyad which may enable one gender to 'be the therapist' of the other. Here I am drawing on Andrew Samuels' ideas about how political and social groupings can shed light on what is lacking or problematic in the other (Samuels, 2006).

To take a feature of the *male thanima diamond*, a possible tendency towards a lack of ethical responsibility in respect to a man's relationships may be thrown into relief by an opposite focus on these very responsibilities by his female partner. Though this happens the other way around, there seems to be a historical predominance towards stronger relational ethics in women. Likewise, possibly over-weening maternal characteristics can be thrown into relief by *erosima* ethical interventions by men who have a capacity to 'free up' potential in a child. Again, this does not only happen one way, but speaks to a predominant 'territorial' tendency. In such ways, the intersubjective space generated in relationships can generate 'gender electrics' which promote self-awareness and healthy change.

Implications for education

I want to make some observations about how 'the problem of home' may get replicated in educational settings. The unspoken 'semiotic' which lives in the fabric of home can also be found in dominant form in some educational, health and social care settings. My main interest here is in schooling, which is so critical to a child's sense of identity. This relates to my experiences as a teacher and manager in special schools for children and young people with learning difficulties. In such contexts women overwhelmingly outnumber men on staff teams – 93 per cent of support staff and 82 per cent of teachers in schools surveyed (Goss, 2003: 88) – in contradistinction to the preponderance of boys and young men who present at the severe, and profound and multiple, end of the learning difficulties spectrum. This staff gender imbalance is echoed in mainstream primary schools in the UK, where only one in eight teachers is male (Clarke, 2009) and early years provision presents an even more dramatic disparity – only 2 per cent of staff are male (Ward, 2009). In the context of the points I have made about female territory and home, one could say schools for younger children and those with significant learning difficulties are predominantly *female* territory. So what might the implications of this be?

In my research on special schools (Goss, 2003) there was a consensus that the lack of male staff did have an impact in terms of the personal, social and emotional development of the predominantly male population, both in terms of the curriculum (ibid.: 89–90) but also for the overall ethos of such schools. This included the help needed with 'toileting' and the impact on the dignity of, say, a young man of sixteen being 'changed' by a female member of staff, and also the perceived need for male social role models, especially where (not uncommonly) there was no father at home.

In these and the other settings alluded to – primary and early years settings – the unspoken mothering, mother–daughter, semiotic prevalence pertains, so that boys experience a sense of 'otherness' in the air. Their unconscious *erosima–thanima* struggle will bring in a dimension which pulls them in two directions – *towards* 'mother' and *'away'* from her. This could impact on behaviours and attitudes towards being taught mainly/only by 'mother figures': from compliance to get their approval to resistance and reaction to constellated attachment difficulties, unmoderated by the presence of father/male teachers.

Just as important for girls, dimensions of the mother–daughter compact might re-constellate around female authority figures (e.g. in a wish to 'be like' or maybe 'different to') and carers who dominate the learning landscape. Again this may impact on behaviour and attitudes in class ('I will/ will not do my best for mother'). The scarcity of male figures in these settings is just as unhelpful for girls as for boys. It conveys a message about the limited importance of there being men present – a *thanimus* 'removing' of father/men from view which could reinforce a sense of the fundamental primacy of female territory when it comes to parent–child relations. What is more, when a girl grows up her attitude towards relations with men may well be predicated even more strongly on a 'mother knows best' attitude to domestic life so, that when she establishes 'home territory' with a man, she assumes she hold the balance of power in it.

Many girls go through nursery and primary (and sometimes secondary) schooling with barely *any* male input. It is not that men offer any particular skill set that women do not; rather, the absence of men in the classroom simply perpetuates absent fathering, and overlooks how different, for a child, the presence of a man *feels* compared with the presence of a woman. This is not an argument about a lack of male teachers affecting educational achievement (or, hence, unfounded assertions about the capability of women teachers in certain subject areas). There is no clear correlation between this and the gender imbalance (Francis and Skelton, 2005). It is rather about having a balanced *presence* between male and female teachers.

If the *status quo* does not seem a problem, I invite you to imagine how it would seem if this situation were inverted, and men dominated early years and primary education, with very few women offering versions of 'mother'. Would this be okay?

I suggest that this area has become such embedded 'female territory' that we have lost sight of the harm this situation may be doing to the child's balanced sense of mother–father, and how this gets replicated in adult heterosexual relations. This replication of 'the problem of home' in schools and nurseries needs to be addressed not just at the level of the representation of women and men in them, but in terms of facing a historical trend for men to be either 'on top of'/transcending schools (as headteachers, for example, so more remote from day-to-day contact with pupils) or not there at all, a most unhelpful patriarchal legacy. As things stand these settings are a dimension of female territory which perpetuates gender rigidities 'at home'.

Gender electrics: Beanstalk, magic beans and the diamond

To conclude, I want to make some generalised comments about where the discussions in this book might leave us in terms of our understanding of the nature of gender, its interplay with socio-historical influences, and the never ending archetypal interplay of feminine and masculine. I will refer back to Jack's story, and to my idea of the 'empty space' within the diamond-shaped 'frame' left by the faded Christian cross (signifying the fading of patriarchal ways of thinking and being). As argued, powerful psychic energies relating to the interplay of masculine–feminine and female–male continue to hover around its frame. This is where the centripetal energy spinning out from the partly deconstructing 'eternal couple' of husband–wife marriage now resides, though it also has a living residue in the 'empty space'.

In this space the hidden dynamics of feminine–masculine and male–female territories continue to wrestle with one another, charged with the erotic, relational and aggressive energies which are the unpredictable features of 'gender electrics'. On occasion, 'magic beans' become available, generated by the momentum of accumulated shifts in ways of gendered being and attitudes. I suggest that we may be in the midst of such a shift at present, crossing between 'modern' and 'postmodern' ways of 'being female' or 'being male' and how we relate to the gendered other.

On the one hand, the challenge here concerns the problem of individual and collective *thanima–thanimus* attitudes, which can make it difficult to acknowledge that we only partially understand – or simply do not know – how to satisfactorily describe differences between being a man compared with being a woman. Where we intuit differences, we do not always have sufficient language to describe these without *thanima–thanimus* defensiveness or hostility being en-'gendered'. I expect some of my use of language in describing female and male ways of being will have jarred with you as the reader because, I suggest, it is impossible to get it 'right'. However, it is too easy to either rely on an outdated formula of patriarchal stereotyping *or* say 'there is no difference', as a way of avoiding this problem.

On the other hand, as I hope this book has highlighted, there is *so much* potential in this area in terms of understanding and working through implications of what arises from trying to consider together psychosexual and developmental, 'brain-sex' neurological, and socio-historical themes on gender. The 'magic beans' of looking at gender from as many angles as possible, while drawing on our own subjective responses to these ideas, allows for the kind of momentum that can build strength, in lieu of a greater freeing up of awareness and being, in relation to gendered *self*, and gendered *other*.

This is happening in a context where there are some powerful influences at work, opening up possibilities of better understanding what belongs to women, to men and to both. There is a general intermingling happening in terms of globalisation, with its exposure to differing cultural ways of operating in male–female relationships. Then there is the deconstructing of 'gender' as a descriptor of 'norms' and the ways in which differing ways of expressing sexuality throw into relief the traditional tendency to ascribe certain attributes and relational qualities to men and to women.

New technologies and relationships

Another interesting factor is the internet. As Civin (2000: 19) puts it, we may be witnessing 'a "slippage" in the meaning of *relatedness* and *relationship*', in the sense of connections with others getting mediated by technology which brings us into relational contact with a range of other people, often from around the world, who we often would never have had any kind of relationship with. On the other hand 'these relationships may serve to facilitate that individual's paranoid withdrawal from personal engagement' (ibid.).

So, while having a profile on Facebook or uploading a video on YouTube may compensate for the disappointments and complexities of 'real' relationships and enable someone to reveal aspects of themselves otherwise not seen, it can be a way of avoiding having to deal with living, interpersonal relationships. Having said this, the popularity of internet dating websites could be taken to imply there is a *genuine* relational function for the internet – people can get to meet 'real' partners through it, not just virtual ones.

The problem Civin highlights is how persecutory anxiety about others' views of us can encourage us to go into cyberspace to gain more control over how we relate to others and how they might perceive us, so filtering out the risk of being disliked, judged or rejected. In Kleinian language, the internet might serve as a way of driving us back into the paranoid-schizoid position (Klein, 1946), where we can hold onto our regressive attempts to keep the uncomfortable messiness of real relationships at bay by convincing ourselves relationships with others will go well if we stay online. The challenges associated with maintaining the depressive position – dealing with others in a real, 'warts and all', way – is avoided.

Engendering 'gender'

In the context of this danger, and of how overwhelming the diversity of human 'being' is, I want to 'talk up' (to the sky?) one last time the value of Jack's story for making sense of where we find ourselves in our individual and collective humanity, particularly in respect to the vexed question of 'gender'.

In concluding this book, I feel the value of the term 'gender', in how it tries to capture 'what it is like' being male or being female and also offers meanings in *both* variable *and* fixed ways, remains strong. Like any archetypal polarity worth its salt, 'maleness' and 'femaleness' work both as highly differentiated 'territories' as well as thoroughly intermingled or even interchangeable ones. The more *collectively* gendered ways of being present themselves, the stronger (usually) the sense of differentiation from the gendered 'other'. Individually the opposite often pertains.

The dramas of our lives illustrate the struggle between masculine and feminine energies to help us arrive at a more individuated sense of self, plunging us into episodes which appear to confound this possibility but which actually offer us a route towards fuller integration. Jack's story is a case in point. He has unresolved parental complexes and is caught by *thanima* as 'disappointing/inadequate son', unable to take his father's place and rectify his relational problem with mother.

The archetypal masculine helps him by providing magic beans via the *senex* old man. The archetypal feminine then generates the beanstalk via mother's anger, by 'throwing the masculine out of the window'. This idea is important, as it signifies the longstanding presence of the anger located in women against the unrelatedness of men in patriarchal societies, which reached a tipping point via a feminist-inspired declaration that women would no longer put up with this status quo. The problem for men was that this seemed to push them up into the sky, so that they were floating in a space between masculinist over-identification and a 'new man' identification with the feminine. Archetypally speaking one could say men were 'sent away from home' by women to find a solution (via the 'beanstalk') to the problem of gender relations.

The beanstalk enables Jack to reconnect with father – though this is via a titanic struggle with the Giant. Like the ship of that name, this can be taken to infer the problem of male inflation and hubris – '"This ship will never sink", the owner proclaimed, before it did.' (Butler, 1998). Thankfully, this one-sided *modern* attitude is now passing from centre stage. Instead, the 'solution' suggested in the *Beanstalk* story involves reclaiming 'father's treasure' through the death of the 'overblown masculine' (the Giant) and a settlement with *thanimus* (the disarming of the more judgemental, angry aspects of Mother). Or, in real terms, fathers finding their place in the home through claiming, and taking responsibility for, what is theirs; mothers giving them the space to do so; and children receiving a more balanced template of the two (with individual variations to this template respected by all).

A counterbalancing attitude men might adopt towards the problem of an overbearingly transcendent approach to archetypal and personal gendered imbalance can be found in detective fiction. Rowland (2010) usefully points out how although on the surface male detective figures such as Sherlock

Holmes can appear to personify a strongly masculine approach to solving crime and restoring the ethical balance, they cannot achieve this without the relational qualities brought by their sidekicks, such as Watson.

As Rowland argues, the evolution of the male hero-detective conveys a growing self-awareness and relatedness (as aspects which could come to be shared with 'female territory') alongside the sharp intellect and problem-solving skills associated with more traditional 'male territory'. The further examples Rowland provides, such as the struggles detectives Dalziel and Pascoe (Hill, 1996) have in dealing with their relationship, and their internal struggles, illustrate how the 'detective grail' is able to combine 'the justice-delivering properties of a masculine knight, with the relational compassion of the feminine detective' (Rowland, 2010: 24).

From my reading of how male–female and feminine–masculine may be intermingling *and* waiting to be seen in their differentiated forms more clearly, this is where the beanstalk, with its opening up, and connecting between, the 'sky' of the masculine and the 'ground' of the feminine has such a crucial part to play. It suggests that there is an *organic*, natural tendency in the human psyche to try to make living connections between the two 'spheres'. Being a man and being a woman can operate within this space, a 'third area' where movement between female and male territory has an archetypal as well as a cultural and individual impetus.

However, as I have reiterated, this gets held back by our difficulty in 'seeing' what may be genuinely distinct between these territories. When Jack comes back down the beanstalk with the treasure and kills the Giant, the temptation to 'live happily ever after' is understandable but the closing off of the archetypal realm is neither desirable nor possible – as the children's story *Where Giants Hide* (Kelly and Collins, 2009) so neatly portrays. At the story's end, a girl who has decided giants, witches, trolls and fairies are not real is portrayed as being carried, unbeknownst to her, on a giant's shoulder. These archetypal presences 'carry us' through life and challenge us to acknowledge their continuing deep influence, whatever our day-to-day reality is throwing at us.

The emerging diamond of gender electrics

I cannot pretend to know what the emerging 'diamond' which may result from millennia of familial, peer and sexual relations between men and women may look like. This process does not have an 'end point' but is a work in progress, a development from what went before. All the shifting currents in gender relations, at archetypal (feminine–masculine) and per-sonal (male–female) levels touched on in this book remind us over and again how extraordinarily complex the relationship between bodily sex, brain development, early relationship with mother and father, sexuality, and social influence are – meaning any version of what gender 'is' we come up with is necessarily fluid and opaque. Yet, the *thanima–thanimus* alliance seems to want to hide its realities from us, preferring us to lazily stereotype the essentialist behaviours of our partners or, conversely, assert all differences between women and men are not really relevant to where we are at the start of the twenty-first century.

I close this book convinced gender is 'still there': I encounter it every day (whether it is socially constructed or not). I recently picked my daughter up from a dance lesson and waited outside in a school corridor with a group of around eight mothers. Four conversations were going on at once. This, plus an echo in the corridor, generated a surreal effect from the cacophony of female voices. I felt surrounded by the presence of feminine/maternal/pre-oedipal energies, and it felt thoroughly 'other' (though familiar) to me. It was a powerful moment – collective 'female territory' constellating an experience of gendered difference.

On another occasion I sat with my son watching a local men's cricket match. The echoing green lent masculine atmosphere to the shouts of 'go, run', 'out' and 'let's squeeze 'em!' bouncing between earth and sky. Here, a traditional 'male' activity – patriarchal *par excellence* some might say – provided a strong presence of the Symbolic Order at play – phallic, competitive, but nonetheless graceful, with a homoerotic tinge.

Both cases throw into relief the individualised deconstruction of gender roles and attitudes in the postmodern world as against the collective constellation and transmission of generalised differences between male and female territory. One of the areas this may have a particularly sharp impact on is parenting, where we try to find our own ways of being a mother or a father while still under the eye of encultured as well as possibly archetypal influences. The demands of parenting, or what Tim Dowling (2009) has neatly described as 'low-level heroics, all day long', require a couple (where two parents are available) who mostly work together. In the current fluid state of gender relations the miracle is how couples manage to keep their *thanima* or *thanimus* presumptions about the other at bay to achieve this. To conclude, I want to refer back to the notion of a *diamond in the dirt* – the evolution of gender relations as a lengthy, dirty process but one out of which a more integrated/balanced version of relating may be emerging – via the interface between *eros* and *thanatos* versions of the male and female 'diamonds'.

The beanstalk climbed by Jack represents the archetypal presence of this bridging process, asking of each of us a willingness to travel up and down it, between earth and sky, home and road, across the empty space of gender relations, between the archetypal eternal couple and the deconstructed versions of gendered being. The process never ends, but the rewards can be felt by each of us in the present if we trust in the enduring presence of the magic beans of relatedness, self-awareness and the prizing of difference and similarity. Then we can move between the other, *transcending* country of archetypal feminine and masculine, and the immediacy and *immanence* of our close relationships, in ways which slowly nourish the diamond of satisfying and balanced heterosexual relations.

If thou wouldst complete the diamond body with no outflowing
Diligently heat the roots of consciousness and life
Kindle light in that blessed country ever close at hand,
And there hidden, let thy true self always dwell.

(*The Hui Ming Ching*, quoted in Jung, 1929/1968: 77)

Bibliography

Adams, T. (2003). Jung, Kristeva and the maternal realm. In T. Adams & A. Duncan (eds.), *The Feminine Case: Jung, Aesthetics and Creative Process* (Ch. 3). London: Karnac.

Advertising Standards Agency (2009, July). Adjudication on Ovenpride Advertisment. Retreived from http://www.asa.org.uk/asa/adjudications/public

À Kempis, T. & Shirley-Price, L. (1952). *The Imitation of Christ*. London: Penguin Classics.

Allen, R. E. (ed.) (1991). *The Concise Oxford English Dictionary*. London: BCA.

Anderson, R. (1999). Response to Richard Kradin's 'Generosity: A psychological and interpersonal factor of therapeutic relevance' and his 'Reply to Ann Casement'. *Journal of Analytical Psychology, 44*(2), 221–36; 245–8.

Arlow, J. (1961). Ego psychology and the study of mythology. *Journal of the American Psychoanalytic Association*, IX, 371–93.

Astor, J. (1995). *Michael Fordham: Innovations in Analytical Psychology*. London: Routledge.

Ayers, M. (2003). *Mother-Infant Attachment and Psychoanalysis: The Eyes of Shame*. Hove: Brunner-Routledge.

Balint, M. (1968). *The Basic Fault*. London: Tavistock.

Bandura, A. (1977). *Social Learning Theory*. Englewood Cliffs, NJ: Prentice Hall.

Baring, A. & Cashford, J. (1991). *The Myth of the Goddess: Evolution of an Image*. London: Arkana.

Baron-Cohen, S. (2004). *The Essential Difference* (Ch. 6, Ch. 10). London: Penguin.

Bartlett, D. (2000). *The Role of Fathers in Child Development: Challenges and Opportunities*. London: Department of Health.

Baum, F. (1900/1993). *The Wizard of Oz*. New York, NY: Tom Doherty LLC.

BBC News (2008, June 19). Women in the British armed forces. London: BBC News.

Beebe, J. (ed.) (1988). *C. G. Jung: Aspects of the Masculine*. London: Ark.

Benjamin, J. (1988). *The Bonds of Love: Psychoanalysis, Feminism, and the Problem of Domination*. New York, NY: Pantheon.

Bett, H. (1950). English Legends. In J. Westwood & J. Simpson (2005), *The Lore of the Land* (p. 97). London: Penguin.

Blacker, T. (2009, August 28): Bring on the hooligan cup. *The Independent*, p. 35.

Bly, R. (1990). *Iron John: A Book About Men*. New York: Addison-Wesley.

Bohm, D. (1981). *Wholeness and the Implicate Order*. London: Routledge & Kegan Paul.

Bovensiepen, G. (2000). The search for the father: The adolescent boy's obtrusive identification with the inner father. *Journal of Jungian Theory and Practice, 2*(1), 5–21.

Bowlby, J. (1969). *Attachment*. London: Hogarth Press.

Bradshaw, J., Stimson, C., Skinner, C. & Williams, J. (1998). *Absent Fathers*. London: Routledge.

Branney, P. & White, A. (2008). Big boys don't cry: Depression and men. *Advances in Psychiatric Treatment, 14*, 256–62.

Brizendine, L. (2007). *The Female Brain* (pp. 23–32). London: Bantam.

Brownhill, S., Wilhem, A. & Barclay, S. (2005). The big build: Depression in men. *Australian and New Zealand Journal of Psychiatry, 39*, 321–331.

Buber, M. (1923/2004). *I and Thou*. London: Continuum.

Butler, D. A. (1998). *Unsinkable: The Full Story of the RMS Titanic*. Mechanicsburg, PA: Stackpole.

Butler, J. (1990). *Gender Trouble*. London: Routledge.

Carlson, N. (1990). *Psychology: The Science of Behaviour*. Boston, MA: Allyn.

Casement, A. (1995). *Rites of Passage* (unpublished teaching materials).

Chaffin, M., Hanson, R., Saunders, B. E., Nichols, T., Barnett, D., Zeanah, C., Miller-Perrin, C. (2006). Report of the APSAC task force on attachment therapy, reactive attachment disorder, and attachment problems. *Child Maltreatment, 11*(1), 76–89.

Chase, D. (producer) (1999–2007). *The Sopranos*. Los Angeles, CA: HBO.

Chase, R. (1971). *The Jack Tales: Folk Tales from the Southern Appalachians* (Ch. 1). New York: Houghton Mifflin.

Chasseguet-Smirgel, J. (1986). *Sexuality and Mind*. New York, NY: New York University Press.

Chodorow, N. (1978). *The Reproduction of Mothering: Psychoanalysis and the Sociology of Gender*. Berkeley and Los Angeles, CA: University of California Press.

Chodorow, N. (2001). Family structure and feminine personality. In D. Juschka, *Feminism in the Study of Religion: A Reader* (pp. 81–105). London: Continuum.

Civin, M. (2000). *Male, Female, E-mail: The Struggle for Relatedness in a Paranoid Society*. New York, NY: Other Press.

Cixous, H. (1975). *Le Rire de la Meduse*. Paris: L'Arc (pp. 39–54). K. Cohen and P. Cohen, Trans. (1976) in E. Marks and I. de Courtivron (eds.) (1981) *New French Feminisms*. Brighton: Harvester Press.

Clare, A. (2001). *On Men: Masculinity in Crisis*. London: Arrow Books.

Clarke, L. (2009, July 23). Primary schools launch drive to recruit more male staff as only one in eight teachers is male. *Daily Mail*, p. 3.

Colman, W. (2006). Aspects of anima and animus in Oedipal development. *Journal of Analytical Psychology, 41*(1), 37–57.

Connell, R. (2002). *Gender*. Cambridge: Polity.

Daily Mirror (2009, June 10). Nursery worker charged with seven sexual offences related to children. *Daily Mirror*, p. 1.

De Beauvoir, S. (1973). *The Second Sex* (E. M. Parshley, trans.). New York, NY: Vintage.

Dell'Orto, S. (2003). D. W. Winnicott and the transitional object in infancy. *Pediatric Medicine Chirurgic, 25*(2), 106–12.

Dickens, C. (1843). A Christmas Carol. In C. Dickens (1994), *Christmas Books*. London: Penguin Books.

Dowling, T. (2009, June 13). 'He's thinking about the poor fish stuck in the pipework. So am I.' *Guardian*, p. 5.

Eichenbaum, L. & Orbach, S. (1982). *Outside In Inside Out*. Harmondsworth: Penguin Books.

Eigen, M. (2004). *Psychic Deadness*. London: Karnac.

Erikson, E. (1950). *Childhood and Society*. New York, NY: Norton.

Everitt, M. (2007, December 15). I am a giant. *Guardian Weekend*, p. 15.

Falzeder, E. (ed.) (2002). *The Complete Correspondence of Sigmund Freud and Karl Abraham 1907–1925* (Complete Edition). London: Karnac.

Fisher, K., McCulloch, A. & Gershuny, J. (1999). British Fathers and Children: A Report for Channel 4's *Dispatches*. Technical report, Colchester: University of Essex, Institute of Social and Economic Research.

Fordham, M. (1957). *New Developments in Analytical Psychology*. London: Routledge & Kegan Paul.

Fordham, M. (1985). Integration–deintegration in infancy. In *Explorations into the Self* (Ch. 3). London: Academic Press.

Fordham, M. (1985a). *Explorations into the Self* (pp. 34–40). London, Academic Press.

Foucault, M. (1992). *The Use of Pleasure. The History of Sexuality Volume Two*. (R. Hurley, trans.). Harmondsworth: Penguin.

Francis, B. & Skelton, C. (2005). *Reassessing Gender and Achievement* (Ch. 1). London: Routledge.

Frankel, R. (1998). *The Adolescent Psyche*. London: Brunner-Routledge.

Freud, S. (1917/1957). The Taboo of Virginity. In *On Sexuality*, Penguin Freud Library, Volume 7 (pp. 278–279). London: Penguin.

Freud, S. (1920/1991). Three essays on the theory of sexuality. In *On Sexuality*. London: Penguin Freud Library, Vol 7.

Freud, S. (1924). The Passing of the Oedipus Complex. *International Journal of Psycho-Analysis, 5*, 419–24.

Freud, S. (1938). Splitting of the Ego in the Defensive Process. *Standard Edition, Vol. 23*. Hogarth Press: London, 1964.

Frosh, S. (1994). *Sexual Difference: Masculinity and Psychoanalysis*. London: Routledge.

Gilligan, C. (1993). *In a Different Voice* (Ch. 1). Cambridge, MA: Harvard University Press.

Gordon, R. (1993). *Bridges*. London: Karnac.

Goss, P. (2003). The gender mix among staff in schools for pupils who have severe and profound and multiple learning difficulties. *British Journal of Special Education, 30*(2), 87–92.

Goss, P. (2006). Discontinuities in the male psyche: Waiting, deadness and disembodiment. Archetypal and clinical approaches. *Journal of Analytical Psychology, 51*(5), 681–99.

Goss, P. (2008). Envisaging animus: An angry face in the consulting room. In L.

Huskinson (ed.), *Dreaming the Myth Onwards: New Directions in Jungian Therapy and Thought* (Ch. 12). London: Routledge.

Goss, P. (2008a, June). *Nigredo of the Symbol*. Unpublished paper presented at the International Association of Jungian Studies conference, Zurich.

Goya, F. (c. 1809–12). The Colossus (Prado Gallery, Madrid). In M. Howard (2002), *History and Techniques of the Great Masters: Goya* (pp. 44–7). London: Quantum.

Graves, R. (1955/1992). *The Greek Myths: Complete Edition*. London: Penguin.

Gray, M. (1992). *Men are from Mars, Women are from Venus*. London: Harper Collins.

Green, A. (1986). *On Private Madness*. London: Karnac.

Groening, M. (1989–present). *The Simpsons*. Los Angeles, CA: Fox Network.

Guttman, H. (2006). Sexual issues in the transference and countertransference between female therapist and male patient. In J. Schaverien (ed.), *Gender, Countertransference and the Erotic Transference* (Ch. 12, pp. 213–22). Hove: Routledge.

Halliwell, J. (1849). *Popular Rhymes and Nursery Tales of England*. In J. Westwood & J. Simpson (2005), *The Lore of the Land* (p. 111). London: Penguin.

Hauke, C. (2000). *Jung and the Postmodern*. London: Routledge.

Hawkins, P. & Shohet, R. (2000). *Supervision in the Helping Professions*. Buckingham: Open University Press.

Haynes, J. (2007). *Who Is It That Can Tell Me Who I Am? The Journal of a Psychotherapist*. London: Cromwell.

Heidegger, M. (1962). *Being and Time* (J. Macquarrie & E. Robinson, trans.). London: SCM Press.

Hill, G. (1992). *Masculine and Feminine: The Natural Flow of Opposites in the Psyche*. Boston, MA: Shambhala.

Hill, J. (2006). At home in the world. *Journal of Analytical Psychology, 41*(4), 575–98.

Hill, R. (1996). *The Wood Beyond*. New York, NY: Random House.

Hillman, J. (1975). *Re-visioning Psychology*. New York, NY: Harper and Row.

Hillman, J. (1979). *Anima*. New York: Spring.

Hillman, J. (1979a). *Puer Papers*. Dallas, TX: Spring Publications.

Hillman, J. (1990). *The Essential James Hillman: A Blue Fire*. London: Routledge.

Home Office (2008). *British Crime Survey*. London: Home Office.

Honda, I. (dir.) & Kayama, S. (1954). *Godzilla*. Tokyo: Toho Film.

Horney, K. (1967). *Feminine Psychology*. New York: Norton.

Huskinson, L. (2002). The Self as violent Other: The problem of defining the self. *Journal of Analytical Psychology, 47*(3), 437–58.

Inter-Parliamentary Union (2009). *Women in National Parliaments*. Geneva: Inter-Parliamentary Union.

Irigaray, L. (1977/1985). *This Sex Which is Not One*. Ithaca, NY: Cornell University Press.

Jacobs, M. (2006). *The Presenting Past*. Maidenhead: Open University Press.

Jacoby, M. (1985). *Individuation and Narcissism*. London: Routledge.

Jung, C. G. *The Collected Works*, 20 Vols, Trans., R. F. C. Hull, H. Read, M. Fordham, and G. Adler (eds.). London: Routledge & Kegan Paul, unless otherwise stated.

Jung, C. G. (1911/1968). *Symbols of Transformation*, CW5.

Jung, C. G. (1912/1952). The Battle for Deliverance from the Mother. In *Symbols of Transformation*, CW5.

Jung, C. G. (1916/1969). The Transcendent Function. In *The Structure and Dynamics of the Psyche*, CW8, pp. 131–93.

Jung, C. G. (1918/1970). The Role of the Unconscious. In *Civilization in Transition*, CW10.

Jung, C.G. (1921/1971). *Psychological Types*, CW6.

Jung, C. G. (1925/1954). Marriage as a Psychological Relationship. In *The Development of Personality* (paras 324–345), CW17.

Jung, C. G. (1928/1969). On Psychic Energy. In T*he Structure and Dynamics of the Psyche*, CW8.

Jung, C. G. (1929/1968). Commentary on *The Secret of the Golden Flower*. In *Alchemical Studies*, CW13.

Jung, C. G. (1933). The Stages of Life. In *Modern Man in Search of a Soul* (Ch. 5). London: Routledge & Kegan Paul.

Jung, C. G. (1934/1969). A Review of the Complex Theory. In *The Structure and Dynamics of the Psyche*, CW8.

Jung, C. G. (1936/1954). Concerning the Archetypes, with Special Reference to the Anima Concept. In *The Archetypes and the Collective Unconscious*, CW9i.

Jung, C. G. (1936/1968). Individual Dream Symbolism in Relation to Alchemy. In *Psychology and Alchemy*, CW12.

Jung, C. G. (1938/1968). Psychological Aspects of the Mother Archetype. In *The Archetypes and the Collective Unconscious*, CW9i.

Jung, C. G. (1938/1969). Psychology and Religion (The Terry Lectures). In *Psychology and Religion: West and East*, CW11.

Jung, C. G. (1940/1968). The Psychology of the Child Archetype. In *The Archetypes and the Collective Unconscious*, CW9i.

Jung, C. G. (1948/1968). Concerning the archetypes with special reference to the anima concept. In *The Archetypes and the Collective Unconscious*, CW9i.

Jung, C. G. (1951). *Aion*, CW9ii.

Jung, C. G. (1951/1968). The Syzygy: Anima and Animus. In *Aion*, CW9ii.

Jung, C. G. (1951/1968a). The Self. In *Aion*, CW9ii.

Jung, C. G. (1951/1968b). The Structure and Dynamics of the Self. In *Aion*, CW9ii.

Jung, C. G. (1952/1969): Answer to Job. In *Psychology and Religion: West and East*, CW11.

Jung, C. G. (1953/1966). Anima and Animus. In *Two Essays on Analytical Psychology*, CW7.

Jung, C. G. (1954) *The Development of Personality*, CW17.

Jung, C. G. (1954/1966). *The Practice of Psychotherapy*, CW16.

Jung, C. G. (1954/1966a). The Psychology of the Transference. In *The Practice of Psychotherapy*, CW16.

Jung, C. G. (1954/1968). On The Psychology of the Trickster-Figure. In *The Archetypes and the Collective Unconscious*, CW9i.

Jung, C. G. (1958/1969). A Psychological Approach to the Trinity. In *Psychology and Religion: West and East*, CW11.

Jung, C. G. (1960/1969). *The Structure and Dynamics of the Psyche*, CW8.

Jung, C. G. (1960/1969a). The Stages of Life. In *The Structure and Dynamics of the Psyche*, CW8.

Jung, C. G. (1963). The Conjunction. In *Mysterium Coniunctionis*, CW14.

Jung, C. G. (1964). The Spiritual Problem of Modern Man. In *Civilisation in Transition*, CW10.

Jung, C. G. (2009). Liber Secundus in *The Red Book: Liber Novus*, S. Shamdasani (ed.). New York: W. W. Norton & Co.

Juran, N. (dir.) (1962). *Jack the Giant Killer*. California: Edward Small Productions/ Samuel Goldwyn Studios.

Kahn, C. (1979). *The Art and Thought of Heraclitus*. Cambridge: Cambridge University Press.

Kopuscinski, R. (2006). *The Other*. London: Verso.

Kavaler-Adler, S. (2006). Lesbian homoerotic transference in dialectic with developmental mourning: On the way to symbolism from the protosymbolic. In J. Schaverien (ed.), *Gender, Countertransference and the Erotic Transference* (Ch. 9). London: Routledge.

Kelly, M. & Collins, R. (2009). *Where Giants Hide*. London: Hodder Children's Books.

Killgore, W., Oki, M. & Yurgelun-Todd, D. (2001). Sex-specific developmental changes in amygdala responses to affective faces. *NeuroReport, 12*, 427–33.

Kirsta, A. (1994). *Deadlier Than the Male: Violence and Aggression in Women*. London: HarperCollins.

Klein, M. (1928/1975). Early stages of the Oedipus complex. In *Love, Guilt and Reparation and Other Works 1921–45*. London: Hogarth.

Klein, M. (1945). The Oedipus Complex in the Light of Early Anxieties. *International Journal of Psycho-Analysis, 26*, 11–33.

Klein, M. (1946). Notes on some schizoid mechanisms. In *The Writings of Melanie Klein, Vol 3* (pp. 1–24). New York, NY: Free Press.

Klein, M. (1952). Some Theoretical Conclusions Regarding The Emotional Life of the Infant. In M. Klein (1988), *Envy and Gratitude and Other Works 1946–1963* (Chapter 5). London: Virago Press.

Klein, M. (1957). Envy and Gratitude. In *The Writings of Melanie Klein, Vol. 3* (pp. 176–235). London: Virago Press, 1997.

Klein, M. (1988). *Envy and Gratitude and Other Works*. London: Virago.

Klein, M. (1937). Love, Guilt and Reparation. In M. Klein & J. Riviere (1964), *Love, Hate, and Reparation* (pp. 57–112). New York: Norton.

Kohlberg, L. (1966). A cognitive-developmental analysis of children's sex-role concepts and attitudes. In E. Maccoby (ed.), *The Development of Sex Differences*. Palo Alto, CA: Stanford University Press.

Kohon, G. (ed.) (1999). *The Dead Mother: The Work of André Green*. London: Routledge.

Kristeva, J. (1980). *Desire in Language: A Semiotic Approach to Literature and Art*. New York: Columbia University Press.

Kristeva, J. (2004). Some observations on female sexuality. In I. Matthis (ed.), *Dialogues on Sexuality, Gender and Psychoanalysis* (Ch. 3). London: Karnac.

Kulish, N. (1986). Gender and transference: The screen of the phallic mother. *International Review of Psycho-Analysis, 13*, 393–404.

Lacan, J. (1912). The mirror stage as formative of the function of the I as revealed in psychoanalytical experience. In J. Lacan (1966), *Ecrits* (A. Sheridan-Smith, trans.). London: Tavistock.

Lacan, J. (1957). Les formations de l'inconscient (Seminars, 1956–7). *Bulletin de Psychologie*, 1956–7.

Lacan, J. (1966/1977). *Écrits*. New York, NY: Norton.

Lacan, J. (1966/1977a). Some reflections on the Ego. In *Écrits*. New York, NY: Norton.

Langford, N. (2008). *The Official Fathers 4 Justice Handbook: A Survival Guide to the CSA and Family Courts*. Retreived from: http://www.fathers4justice.org

Leather, E. (1912). *The Folk-lore of Herefordshire*. In J. Westwood & J. Simpson (2005), *The Lore of the Land* (p. 324). London: Penguin.

Lemaire, A. (1977). *Jacques Lacan*. London: Routledge.

Levinas, E. (2000). Quoted in Psychotherapy as the Practice of Ethics. In F. Palmer Barnes & L. Murdin (2001), *Values and Ethics in the Practice of Psychotherapy and Counselling* (pp. 23–31). Buckingham: Open University Press.

Levinson, D. & Levinson, J. (1996). *The Seasons of a Woman's Life* (Ch. 3). New York: Ballantine.

Levinson, D., Darrow, C. N., Klein, E. B., Levinson, M. H. & McKee, B. (1978). *The Seasons of a Man's Life*. New York, NY: Ballantine.

Lewis, M. (2009). *Home Game: An Accidental Guide to Fatherhood*. London: Norton.

McCann, M. (2008). *Husband-ry 101: How to Train Your Husband to be the Spouse You've Always Wanted Him to Be*. NewYork, NY: Global Business Café.

McGuire, W. (ed.) (1980). *C. G. Jung Speaking*. London: Picador.

McKenzie, S. (2006). Queering gender: anima/animus and the paradigm of emergence. *Journal of Analytical Psychology*, *51*(3), 401–21.

McTaggart, J. (1964). *A Commentary on Hegel's Logic*. New York, NY: Russell & Russell.

Maguire, M. (1995). *Men, Women, Passion and Power: Gender Issues in Psychotherapy*. London: Routledge.

Main, S. (2008). *Childhood Re-imagined: Images and Narratives of Development in Analytical Psychology*. London: Routledge.

Male, D. B. (1996). Who goes to SLD schools? *Journal of Applied Research in Intellectual Disabilities*, *9*, 307–23.

Mangan, L. (2009, August 8). Lessons in love and the subtle art of toilet cleaning. *Guardian Weekend*, p. 62.

Marshak, M. (1998). The intersubjective nature of analysis. In I. Alistair & C. Hauke (eds.), *Contemporary Jungian Analysis: Post-Jungian Perspectives from the Society for Analytical Psychology*. London: Routledge.

Martin-Vallas, F. (2005). Towards a theory of the integration of the Other in representation. *Journal of Analytical Psychology*, *50*(3), 285–93.

Mathers, D. (2001). *An Introduction to Meaning and Purpose in Analytical Psychology*. London: Routledge.

Maurer, F. & Smith, C. (2005). *Community/Public Health Nursing Practice: Health for Families and Populations*. Philadelphia, PA: Elsevier.

Meltzer, D. (1992). *The Claustrum: An Investigation of Claustrophobic Phenomena*. Worcester: Roland Harris Education Trust.

Midgeley, C. (2006, August 9). Lobal Warfare. *The Times T2*, pp. 1, 4–5.

Mind (2007). *Statistics 7: Treatments and Services for People with Mental Health Problems Factsheet*. London: Mind.

Mitchell, S. (1988). *Relational Concepts in Psychoanalysis: An Integration* (Ch. 7). Cambridge, MA: Harvard University Press.

Mitchell, J. (2004). The difference between gender and sexual difference. In I. Mathis, *Dialogues on Sexuality, Gender and Psychoanalysis* (Ch. 5). London: Karnac.

Moir, A. (2009). *Male and female: Equal but different*. Unpublished course notes, MindFields College, East Sussex.

Moir, A. & Jessel, D. (1991). *Brain Sex: The Real Difference Between Men and Women*. London: Mandarin.

Monick, E. (1987). *Phallos: Sacred Image of the Masculine*. Toronto: Inner City Books.

Moore, T. (ed.) (1990). *The Essential James Hillman: A Blue Fire*. London: Routledge.

Murray, J. (1901). *Handbook for Travellers in Northamptonshire and Rutland* (2nd edn.). In J. Westwood & J. Simpson (2005), *The Lore of the Land* (p. 539). London: Penguin.

Neumann, E. (1955). *The Great Mother: An Analysis of the Archetype*. New York, NY: Pantheon.

Noddings, N. (2003). *Caring: A Feminine Approach to Ethics and Moral Education*. Berkeley, CA: University of California Press.

Office for National Statistics (2002). *EOC Analysis of Labour Force Survey*. London: Office for National Statistics.

Office for National Statistics (2005). *Social Focus on Women and Men*. London: Office for National Statistics.

Office for National Statistics (2007). *Mortality Statistics Series DH2, No. 30 & No. 32*. London: Office for National Statistics.

Office for National Statistics (2009). *Divorce Statistics Series Trends 133*. London: Office for National Statistics.

Ogden, T. (1994). The analytic third: Working with intersubjective clinical facts. *International Journal of Psycho-Analysis, 75*, 3–19.

Ogden, T. (1995). Analysing forms of aliveness and deadness of the transference/countertransference. *International Journal of Psycho-Analysis, 76*, 695–709.

Opie, I. & Opie, P. (1951/1997). The House that Jack Built. In *The Oxford Dictionary of Nursery Rhymes*. Oxford: Oxford University Press.

Orbach, S. & Eichenbaum, L. (1994). *Between Women: Love, Envy and Competition in Women's Friendships*. London: Arrow.

Papadoupolos, R. (2002). The other other: When the exotic other subjugates the familiar other. *Journal of Analytical Psychology, 47*(2), 163–88.

Park, J. (1995). *Sons, Mothers and Other Lovers*. London: Abacus.

Perls, F. (1969). *Gestalt Therapy Verbatim*. Lafayette, CA: Real People.

Phillips, A. (1993). *The Trouble with Boys: Parenting the Men of the Future*. London: Pandora.

Phillips, A. (2007, December 1). In Your Dreams. *Guardian Review*, p. 4.

Piaget, J. (1955). *The Child's Construction of Reality*. London: Routledge & Kegan Paul.

Pope Osbourne, M. (2005). *Kate and the Beanstalk*. New York: Aladdin.

Pretor-Pinney, G. (2006). *The Cloudspotter's Guide*. London: Sceptre.

Rank, O. (1993). *The Trauma of Birth*. Toronto: Dover Publications.

Rogers, C. (1961). *A Way of Being*. London: PCCS Books.

Rowland, S. (2002). *Jung: A Feminist Revision*. Cambridge: Polity.

Rowland, S. (2005). Culture: Ethics, synchronicity and the goddess. In *Jung as a Writer* (Ch. 7). Hove: Routledge.

Rowland, S. (2007). *Wild Writing: Jung and the Goddess of Nature*. Unpublished paper presented at the Nature and Human Nature conference, Pacifica Graduate Institute, California, 2–4 April 2007.

Rowland, S. (2010). The Wasteland and the Grail Knight: Myth and Cultural Criticism in Detective Fiction. In *Clues: A Journal of Detection*, (in press).

Rowland, S. (in press). Anima, gender, feminism. In C. Weldon & K. Bulkeley (eds.), *Teaching Jung*. Oxford: Oxford University Press.

Rycroft, C. (1995). *A Critical Dictionary of Psychoanalysis*. London: Penguin.

Samuels, A. (1985). *Jung and the Post-Jungians*. London: Routledge.

Samuels, A. (ed.) (1985). *The Father: Contemporary Jungian Perspectives*. London: Free Association Books.

Samuels, A. (1989). *The Plural Psyche*. Hove: Routledge.

Samuels, A. (2001). *Politics on the Couch*. London: Karnac.

Samuels, A. (2006, October 2). Islam and western self-disgust. *Guardian*, p. 18.

Samuels, A. (2009). Transforming aggressive conflict. *International Journal of Applied Psychoanalytic Studies, 6*(4): 283–99. doi: 10.1002/aps.200

Samuels, A., Shorter, B. & Plaut, F. (1986). *A Critical Dictionary of Jungian Analysis*. London: Routledge.

Sandford, J. (1980). *The Invisible Partners: How the Male and Female in Each of Us Affects Our Relationships*. New Jersey: Paulist Press.

Sandler, J. & Sandler, A. (1998). *Internal Objects Revisited*. London: Karnac.

Sarup, M. (1992). *Jacques Lacan*. New York: Harvester.

Schaverien, J. (2006). *Gender, Countertransference and the Erotic Transference*. London: Routledge.

Schaverien, J. (ed.) (2006a). Men who leave too soon. In *Gender, Countertransference and the Erotic Transference* (Ch. 1). Hove: Routledge.

Schwartz-Salant, N. (1982). *Narcissism and Character Transformation*. Toronto: Inner City Books.

Scott, J. (2005). *Electra after Freud: Myth and Culture*. New York, NY: Cornell.

Segal, H. (1979). *Melanie Klein*. London: Karnac.

Segal, R. (1992). *The Gnostic Jung*. London: Routledge.

Sharp, D. (1991). *Jung Lexicon: A Primer of Terms and Concepts*. Toronto: Inner City Books.

Shore, D. & Jacobs, K. (producers) (2007–present) *House*. Los Angeles, CA: Fox Network.

Smith, A. (1998). *Julia Kristeva: Speaking the Unspeakable*. London: Pluto Press.

Snitow, A. (1990). A gender diary. In M. Hirsch & E. Keller (eds.), *Conflicts in Feminism*. New York, NY: Routledge.

Solomon, H. (2007). *The Self in Transformation*. London: Karnac.

Sommers, S. (dir.) (1999). *The Mummy*. Los Angeles, CA: Universal Studios.

Stanistreet, D., Bambra, C. & Scott-Samuel, A. (2005). Is patriarchy the source of men's higher mortality? *Journal of Epidemiology and Community Health, 59,* 873–6.

Starr, D. (creator) (1998). *Sex and the City.* New York, NY: HBO.

Steen, M. (2008, October 8). *Start Treating Others Positively (STOP Study).* Presentation to the University of Central Lancashire Men's Health Conference, Preston.

Steinberg, W. (1993). *Masculinity: Identity, Conflict and Transformation* (Ch. 1). Boston, MA: Shambhala.

Stoller, R. (1968). *Sex and Gender: On the Development of Masculinity and Femininity.* London: Hogarth Press.

Stoller, R. (1975). *Perversion.* New York, NY: Pantheon.

Swift, E. (1954). *Folk Tales of the East Midlands.* In J. Westwood & J. Simpson (2005), *The Lore of the Land* (p. 581). London: Penguin.

Tacey, D. (1997). *Remaking Men: Jung, Spirituality and Social Change.* London: Routledge.

Tatham, P. (1992). *The Making of Maleness.* London: Karnac.

Thorne, B. (1993). *Gender Play: Girls and Boys in School.* New Brunswick: Rutgers University Press.

Tolan, J. (2003). *Skills in Person-Centred Counselling and Psychotherapy.* London: Sage.

Tustin, F. (1990). *The Protective Shell in Children and Adults.* London: Karnac.

United Nations (2005). *The Millennium Development Goals Report.* New York, NY: United Nations.

USA Today (2002, December). Men doing more; women doing less – Housework. *USA Today* (Society for the Advancement of Education), p. 1.

van Gennep, A. (1960). *The Rites of Passage* (Ch. 6). London: Routledge.

Ward, H. (2009, January 23). Extra pay needed to coax more men into early years. *Times Educational Supplement,* p. 4.

Westwood, J. & Simpson, J. (2005). *The Lore of the Land.* London: Penguin.

White, A. (2008). *The Bradford & Airedale Health of Men Initiative: A Study of its Effectiveness in Engaging With Men.* Research paper. Leeds: Centre for Men's Health.

Whitehead, T. (2009, June 9). Number of 'ladette women' fined for drunk and disorderly behaviour rises by a third. *Daily Telegraph,* p. 3.

Wilkinson, M. (2001). *Coming into Mind – The Mind-Brain Relationship: A Jungian Clinical Perspective.* Hove: Routledge.

Williams, S. (2006). Women in search of women: Clinical issues that underlie a woman's search for a female therapist. In J. Schaverien (ed.), *Gender, Counter-transference and the Erotic Transference* (Ch. 8). London: Routledge.

Winnicott, D. W. (1958). Primary Maternal Preoccupation. In D. W. Winnicott, *Collected Papers: Through Paediatrics to Psycho-Analysis* (pp. 300–305). London: Tavistock.

Winnicott, D. W. (1960). The theory of the parent-child relationship. *International Journal of Psycho-analysis, 41,* 585–95.

Winnicott, D. W. (1960a). Ego distortion in terms of true and false self. In D. W. Winnicott (1965), *The Maturational Processes and the Facilitating Environment* (Ch. 12). London: Karnac.

Winnicott, D. W. (1962). Ego integration in child development. In D. W. Winnicott

(1990), *The Maturational Processes and the Facilitating Environment*. London: Karnac.

Winnicott, D. W. (1963). From dependence towards independence in the development of the Individual. In D. W. Winnicott (1990), *The Maturational Processes and the Facilitating Environment*. London: Karnac.

Wolf, N. (1991). *The Beauty Myth: How Images of Beauty Are Used Against Women*. London: Vintage.

Woodman, M. (1982). *Addiction to Perfection: The Still Unravished Bride*. Toronto: Inner City Books.

Woodman, M. (1990). *The Ravaged Bridegroom: Masculinity in Women*. Toronto: Inner City Books.

Young-Eisendrath, P. (1997). *Gender and Desire: Uncursing Pandora*. College Station, TX: Texas A&M University Press.

Young-Eisendrath, P. (1998). Contrasexuality and the dialectic of desire. In A. Casement (ed.), *Post-Jungians Today* (Ch. 12). London: Routledge.

Young-Eisendrath, P. (2004). *Subject to Change: Jung, Gender and Subjectivity in Psychoanalysis*. Hove: Brunner-Routledge.

Young-Eisendrath, P. (2009). Empty rowboats. In D. Mathers, M. E. Miller & O. Ando (eds.), *Self and No-Self: Continuing the Dialogue Between Buddhism and Psychotherapy* (Ch. 10). London: Routledge.

Zipes, J. (ed.) (1991). *Spells of Enchantment: The Wondrous Tales of Western Culture*. New York: Viking.

Zukerman, M. (1994). *Behavioural Expressions and Biosocial Bases of Sensation Seeking*. Cambridge: Cambridge University Press.

Index

abandonment 127; terror of 208
Abraham, K. 76
absent fathering 2, 43, 197
abuse: *thanima* and the problematic
male diamond 217(Fig.), 218–22;
thanimus and the female unhealthy
diamond 223–4
Adams, T. 25, 204
adolescence 147–69 *see also* puberty;
the adolescent brain 162–8; boys
vs girls: the race up the beanstalk
160–2; collective 168; mapping
contrasexual influence from
puberty to adulthood 168,
169(Tbl.); and a psychological
history of archetypal and personal
gender 152–60; and the
relationship between masculine/
feminine and male/female 148–52
aggression/aggressiveness 24, 73, 86,
113; adolescent 163; aggressive
energies 138, 142, 144, 207;
aggressive fantasies 84, 140; double
bind of aggression 139–40; male
sexuality and 70; and oppression
139–44; passive aggression 103, 128;
rage and 103; repressed 141–2;
socialisation and 163; trickster-like
expression of aggression 129–30;
women and aggression 129–30,
139–44
amygdala 164, 166
anal stage 61, 69, 76, 82
analysts: countertransference *see*
countertransference; men working
with women analysts 111–13;
women working with women
analysts 134–9; working as a man

with female antipathy towards male
territory 126–9
'analytic third' 56
androcentric social system 41
anima: Colman 86–7; ego integration
and 83–4; experiencing 50–1; fairy
as positive *anima* figure 26; negative,
deadened see *thanima*; and the
oedipal struggle 88–90; positive,
alive see *erosima*; projected 58
anima/animus relationship *see also*
contrasexuality: experiencing *anima*
and *animus* 50–1; inter-gender and
interpsychic gender experiencing
model 53–4; Jung 1, 30–1, 46–7,
188; and the mother–son dyad 15;
and the trickster 46–7; yoked 51, 86,
88–9
animus: Colman 86–7; as 'culprit' in the
western collective 159; ego
integration and 83–4; experiencing
50–1; Jung 50, 121–3, 176; negative
see *thanimus*; and the oedipal
struggle 86–7, 88–90; positive, alive
see *erosimus*; and the pre-pubescent
moment 75; projected 58;
relationship with *anima* see *anima/
animus* relationship; shared level of
122, 131
archetypes 9, 16; *anima/animus* dyad
see *anima/animus* relationship; the
archetypal feminine 30, 148–9,
153, 155, 157, 195, 230; archetypal
feminine and masculine forces 12,
16–17; archetypal gender *see* the
feminine; the masculine;
archetypal good father 17;
archetypal intuitions 63; the